Asien- und Afrika-Studien der Humboldt-Universität zu Berlin

Band 59

2023

Harrassowitz Verlag · Wiesbaden

When the West meets the East

Early Western Accounts
of the Languages of the Sinosphere
and their Impact on the History
of Chinese Linguistics

Edited by
Barbara Meisterernst

2023
Harrassowitz Verlag · Wiesbaden

Bibliografische Information der Deutschen Nationalbibliothek
Die Deutsche Nationalbibliothek verzeichnet diese Publikation in der Deutschen
Nationalbibliografie; detaillierte bibliografische Daten sind im Internet
über https://dnb.de abrufbar.

Bibliographic information published by the Deutsche Nationalbibliothek
The Deutsche Nationalbibliothek lists this publication in the Deutsche
Nationalbibliografie; detailed bibliographic data are available in the internet
at https://dnb.de.

Informationen zum Verlagsprogramm finden Sie unter
https://www.harrassowitz-verlag.de

ISSN 0948-9789   eISSN 2750-1388
ISBN 978-3-447-12065-4   eISBN 978-3-447-39431-4

Table of Contents

Part Two: Chinese linguistic traditions

Part Three: Early Western Accounts of the Chinese language and Chinese linguistics

Part Four: Early West-East contacts on the Silk Road and their impact on linguistic studies

Introduction

'When the West met the East':
Early Western Accounts of the Languages of the Sinosphere
and their Impact on the History of Chinese Linguistics

Brief Introduction to the volume

This volume was inspired by the conference *'When the West met the East': Early Western Accounts of the Languages of the Sinosphere and their Impact on the History of Chinese Linguistics*, held at National Tsing Hua University, Taiwan, 2018, September 10-11. Some of the articles in the volume are revised versions of papers presented at this conference.

The volume approaches the topic of Western encounters with the Chinese languages from a unique angle, because it does not exclusively focus on either Western or Chinese linguistics on the one hand, or on history or linguistics on the other. Instead, it provides a bridge between West and East, linguistics and history. Furthermore, the selection of articles emphasizes the special influence Taiwanese linguistic studies have on the history of linguistic studies of East Asian languages; the chapters in the first part of the volume are entirely devoted to the topic of Sinitic and Austronesian languages in or related to Taiwan. Many of the early grammatical works that have survived on languages of the Sinosphere are closely connected to the history of Taiwan and the Taiwanese languages; accordingly, this connection constitutes a central topic of this volume. Additionally, the collection of articles demonstrates the great influence, the encounter with Sinitic languages had on linguistic studies and on the development of new linguistic concepts in the West. Thus, this book provides a window into cultural and linguistic relations from a different perspective, transcending a Eurocentric view, and probing the motives of the missionary and colonial activities in the East.

All articles of the volume are devoted to the analysis and historical assessment of the early linguistic data particularly obtained from the first missionary grammars and other original sources. The articles of the first part focus on Taiwanese Southern Min or Hokkien in Spanish transcriptions; i.e., they discuss the circumstances and the value of the early Hokkien manuscript lexicography, and compare the collection and analysis of linguistic data by early missionaries with today's fieldwork approaches. Additionally, they include original sources of and discussions on indigenous Austronesian languages in Taiwan and the cultural characteristics of their speakers. The latter are particularly valuable for diachronic research on the Austronesian language family, because the Taiwanese languages constitute the oldest branches of Austronesian. In the remaining parts, the volume provides analyses of Chinese grammatical and philological studies and their influence on both Western and Eastern linguistics. Several early grammars in China and in the West are at issue in this part of the volume. The last article by Yutaka Yoshida contributes an entirely different perspective in including the earliest contacts between West and East on the Ancient Silk Roads and the relevance of the Silk Road manuscripts written in alphabetic scripts in languages unrelated to Chinese for Chinese historical linguistics. Thus the volume assembles representative research from most relevant aspects of East-West encounters spanning from the Silk Roads in the West to the study of indigenous Taiwanese languages in the East, and it reveals the relevance these studies have for the establishment of linguistic traditions and concepts in the West and in the East.

Ample evidence for the increasing international interest in the topic of the history of East-West contacts in linguistic research has been provided by several recent international conferences on related topics and by numerous publications in the field.

In the following, the respective articles in the volume will be introduced briefly. In chapter 1, "In Search for the Dialectal Variants of Hokkien Based on the Early Bilingual Hokkien-Spanish Dictionary", Chinfa Lien analyzes subdialectal variations of Hokkien. His research is based on a Spanish-Hokkien-Sinitic bilingual dictionary, a seventeenth century manuscript dubbed Libro Tomo 215 (LT215), in the historical setting when the Hokkiense diaspora encountered the Spaniards in Luzon during the heyday of the Spanish maritime era. Lien uses two kinds of linguistic evidence in order to pin down the subdialectal variation: (1) phonological patterns of finals, and (2) the use of functional words. In a careful examination of phonological patterning of finals and key functional words coupled with the knowledge of the present-day distribution of dialectal elements he identifies the dialect represented in LT215 as a Zhangzhou variety. As a concomitant benefit, Lien points out that the Hokkien diaspora's strategy of learning seventeenth century Spanish based on Chinese characters for the spelling of Spanish words helps in mapping out the early modern Spanish consonantal values. Thus he shows the value, these studies have not only for historical Sinitic linguistics, but also for the study of the history of Romance.

In chapter 2, "Language contact, wishful thinking or bad fieldwork? How to make sense of consistent language documentation in missionary sources", Henning Klöter introduces some of the earliest missionary sources documenting the Hokkien variety spoken by Chinese settlers in Manila during the 17th century. By looking at the contents and explanatory devices found in these sources, Klöter examines the purpose behind the compilation of these grammars and dictionaries asking whether they were analytical treatises, teaching manuals or field notes or a bit of everything? He points out that some data in the sources display a remarkably high degree of consistency in contrast to the variability in modern dialects, e.g., for the transcription of the second person singular pronoun. He takes this consistency as a starting point for discussing the reliability of the missionary compilers' linguistic description, wondering whether the sources consistently describe the language as it was spoken, or whether the missionary compilers 'manipulated' their data and, if this were true, what would be the reason for this manipulation. Klöter emphasizes the importance of this question for document-based research on Sinitic language history. As fieldworkers, missionaries would qualify as witnesses of language use, and a high degree of 'objectivity' would be expected. However, there is solid evidence that missionaries played an active role as contributors to language change.

In chapter 3, "West meets East: The influence of Dutch clergymen in 17th century Taiwan", Alexander Adelaar discusses the impact the missionary activities of the Dutch clergymen sought to make on the Siraya, a local Formosan population, through a combination of medical aid, education and religious instruction. Adelaar provides a brief historical overview of the Dutch in Formosa (1627-1661) before concentrating on the Protestant clergymen who came in the wake of the Dutch East India Company. The Dutch clergymen left a large corpus of material for two languages, Siraya and Favorlang, as a by-product of their missionary activities. The two languages belong to separate branches of Austronesian and differ considerably from one another. Siraya is represented in two dialects, the Gospel dialect and the Utrecht Manuscript dialect. Apart from a few odd developments it is typologically not unlike many other Austronesian languages and as such its appearance and structure has much in common with Philippine languages. The clergymen's collection of linguistic data would become invaluable for a better understanding of the history of that part of the island. The scholarly achievements of the missionaries include the 'Discourse', a detailed ethnographic description written in 1628 by Georgius Candidius, and various texts and vocabularies. The linguistic materials signal the challenges the clergymen must have encountered while learning these languages and trying to use them in their religious teachings. They not only had to master the linguistic structures of these languages but also had to learn how they reflected a rather different conceptualisation of the world. Finally, they had to figure out how they could adapt these languages in order to represent concepts and values that were typical of 17th century European culture as well as of the biblical world at the time of Christ. The chapter provides examples of some neologisms and linguistic circumscriptions used by the clergymen to that effect on the one hand, and valuable background information on the problematic cultural and linguistic relations between the indigenous Taiwanese and the missionary attempts of the colonizing powers on the other.

In chapter 4, "The 18th century Siraya – songs from "A Tour of Duty on the Raft in the Taiwan Sea", Izumi Ochiai and Chao-Kai Shih provide another, entirely different, contribution to the research on the Siraya language, one of the languages also at issue in chapter 3. The paper presents the results of a preliminary decipherment of the words to Siraya songs recorded in the 18th century. At that time, Taiwan, excluding the mountainous areas where non-Sinicized aboriginal people lived, was under the rule of the Qing dynasty. According to the present stage of research, the songs discussed in this paper are from the oldest document of Siraya songs. They were compiled as appendices in "Barbarian Customs Under Six Heads" (*Fan-su Liu-K'ao* 番俗六考), which is included as a chapter in the book "A Tour on Duty on the Raft in the Taiwan Sea" (*Taihai Shichalu* 臺海使槎錄), published in 1722. Later, "Barbarian Customs Under Six Heads" were cited in the "Reedited Gazetteer of Taiwan Prefecture" (*Xuxiu Taiwan Fuzhi* 續修臺灣府志), to which Florenz (1898) and Sato (1936) referred, when they transliterated and analyzed Siraya songs and other Formosan songs. Since the language is extinct and due to numerous additional difficulties, there have been limited attempts to decipher Siraya songs recorded in the early 18th century. One of the problems is that the songs were transcribed in Chinese characters using Southern-Min pronunciation and that the Chinese transcription has neither word boundaries nor word-by-word glossing; i.e., they were transcribed with the means of a typologically entirely different language. Although there exist Chinese translations by phrase or by clause of the songs, these translations were rather free; additionally, there is no large-scale Siraya dictionary. Progress was made in overcoming these difficulties by identifying Siraya words from Chinese characters. The present paper shows these results alongside the relevant grammatical observations.

In chapter 5, "Bazin, Edkins and Bi Huazhen's *Yǎnxù cǎotáng bǐjì* (Notes on the abundant heritage of the thatched cottage)", Alain Peyraube and Xiao Lin discuss the first grammatical book in Chinese, written around 1840, half a century earlier than the *Mǎ shì wén tōng*. The *Mǎ shì wén tōng* (*Basic principles for writing clearly and coherently from Mister Ma*) by Ma Jianzhong 马建忠 (1844 -1900), published 1898, was generally accepted as the first grammar of Chinese written by a Chinese scholar. Although relying heavily on Chinese tradition, this grammar is clearly designed like a Western grammar; what the author has in mind are obviously grammars on Indo-European languages written by European scholars. Peyraube (1998, 1999, 2001a) has concluded that, among all the grammars that Ma Jianzhong could have had at his disposal, it is likely that the *Grammaire de Port-Royal* by Arnauld (1612-1694) and Lancelot (1615-1695) had the most influence on him. Additionally, some European grammars of the Chinese language - compiled by missionaries or sinologists – could also have served as a model for the *Mǎ shì wén tōng*, for instance, the *Notitiae Linguae Sinicae* by Prémare (1831). The grammar by Gabelentz (1881), briefly discussed in chapter 8, was obviously not among the models of the *Mǎ shì wén tōng*. However, Joseph Edkins' mentioned Bi Huazhen's 毕华珍 *Yǎnxù cǎotáng bǐjì* 衍绪草堂笔记 (*Notes on the abundant heritage of the thatched cottage*), which is supposed to be the first grammatical book before the *Mǎ shì wén tōng*. Chapter 5 mainly analyzes the characteristics of these *Notes on the abundant heritage of the thatched cottage,* in order to check whether they, instead of the *Mǎ shì wén tōng*, can really be considered as the first systematic grammar. The authors conclude that Bi Huazhen's *Notes on the abundant heritage of the thatched cottage* is certainly much more developed in its grammatical analyses than the previous works, from the point of view of the classification of parts of speech within the traditional division between 'full words' and 'empty words'. It is also an original treatise in that it contains purely syntactic analyses, with detailed accounts of the sentence structure and its various components. However, the authors conclude that these analyses are far from being clear and consistent and that the *Mǎ shì wén tōng* is undoubtedly much more advanced in this respect. Its grammatical analyses are more systematic, more consistent, and undoubtedly closer to Western grammatical treatises than those of the *Notes on the abundant heritage of the thatched cottage.*

In Chapter 6 "Cultural Interaction Studies and Linguistic Research", Keiichi Uchida introduces "Cultural Interaction Studies" as an entirely new field of study to be pursued. The author proposes that the fundamental concepts of Cultural Interaction Studies take the complex of East Asian culture as a whole, and carry out comprehensive and systematic analyses on its inherent processes of cultural development, transmission, contact, and transformation. Uchida claims that in the past, when conducting research on cultural interaction, individual analyses and investigations from the particular perspective of scientific fields such as linguistics, thought, ethnography, religion, literature, and history served as the basis for research on, e.g., cultural interaction between China and Japan; the two countries were seen as basic units. According to the author, this method is not able to yield the complete picture of cultural interaction. Therefore, the concept of "Cultural Interaction Studies" which he advocates for in his chapter, aims to change the former practice to take the country, the nation, as well as the individual scientific fields as basic units, and to replace this practice with a more holistic view. The article takes the perspective of linguistics (Chinese linguistics) as a point of departure and analyzes as well as examines the relation between the "periphery" and the "center". Furthermore, the author explores the possibility and effectiveness of the "approaching the center from the core" approach for Chinese linguistic research by analyzing the connection between concepts such as "individual" and "general", "special", and "universal".

In chapter 7 "Transposing Linguistic Categories and Terminology: Interactions between Western and Chinese Linguistics", Mariarosaria Gianninoto discusses the way in which Western missionaries integrated Chinese linguistic traditions into their grammars and primers. Since the 17th century, Western missionaries wrote grammars and primers of the Chinese languages as didactic tools for Western learners. Teaching Chinese languages to Westerners required adapting categories and methodologies that had been devised for Western languages. Although the Western model was predominant in the grammars and primers written by missionaries, diplomats, and academics in the 17th, 18th, and 19th centuries, which used Western categories and terminologies to describe the features of the different varieties of Chinese, these works also integrated aspects of the Chinese linguistic tradition by borrowing native categories and methodologies, thereby amalgamating Western and Chinese concepts. Gianninoto focusses in her chapter on the classifications of parts of speech and the analysis of empty words, considered as two representative examples of the merging of Chinese and Western elements in the development of Chinese grammar studies. In her study, the author concentrates on three particular works: two grammars of Chinese, the *Notitia linguae sinicae* ([1728] 1831) by J. H. M. de Prémare, and the *Syntaxe nouvelle de la langue chinoise* (1869) by S. Julien (with particular attention to the *Traité chinois des particules et des principaux termes de grammaire*); and a grammar of Latin translated in Chinese, the *Làdīng wénzì* 辣丁文字 (1859). In her analysis, she underlines the impact of these works on the history of Chinese grammar studies, on the history of Chinese as a foreign language learning, and on the history of linguistics in general.

In chapter 8 "Georg von der Gabelentz and Chinese and East Asian Linguistics", Barbara Meisterernst discusses the impact, which the analyses of the Chinese language, and the establishment of the primacy of syntactic studies in Georg von der Gabelentz's work had on general linguistic concepts. The great relevance, Gabelentz attributed to syntactic analysis was evidently based on his encounter with the Chinese language. Georg von der Gabelentz (1840–1893) and his father Hans Conon von der Gabelentz (1807–1874) were two of the most relevant scholars in the research of Chinese and East Asian Linguistics in 19th century Germany. Their influence has been comprehensively discussed in the linguistic literature, mostly with regard to the history of general linguistics, and much less so with regard to the Chinese language and Chinese linguistics. Meisterernst's chapter particularly concentrates on the latter issue. It briefly introduces Gabelentz's general linguistic ideas, presented, e.g., in his major work *Die Sprach-wissenschaft* (Linguistics) (1891), and the theoretical concepts of an *analytic* and a *synthetic* system of grammar behind his 1881 *Grammar of Written Chinese*. Particular focus is on Gabelentz's influence on the development of syntactic concepts such as topicalization in Chinese linguistics. Meisterernst briefly discusses the history of the term 'Topic', 'Psychological Subject' in Gabelentz's terminology, and the different realization of the Psychological Subject, identified in Gabelentz's grammar. Other linguistic issues, including Gabelentz's ideas with respect to the process of grammaticalization, are additionally mentioned. Gabelentz proposed a 'spiral course of language history' (Spirallauf der Sprachgeschichte), i.e., a constant change from an analytic to a synthetic, then back again to an analytic language in the grammaticalization of languages. Gabelentz's concept of grammaticalization has become quite influential in 20th century linguistic research. Another aspect, in which Gabelentz proved to be truly innovative and influential, is the concentration on cross-linguistic syntactic analysis. Gabelentz also developed a program for cross-linguistic typological research, which made him the founder of the, in present-day research quite prominent, field of typological linguistics.

In chapter 9, "Chinese in Sogdian script and Sogdian in Chinese characters", Yutaka Yoshida discusses the influence the Sogdian presence in China during the Tang Dynasty had on the Chinese language, and the relevance of the study of Sogdian for Chinese linguistics. Sogdians were an Iranian speaking people who once lived in what is now Uzbekistan and northern Tajikistan, in particular the area surrounding Samarqand. Sogdians are famous for their trade activities along the Silk Roads before the Islamization of Central Asia. Before the Tang period, many Sogdians came to China and some of them settled there. In his chapter, Yoshida discusses the relationship between the Sogdians and their language on the one hand, and the Chinese and the Chinese language on the other. In particular, problems surrounding one Chinese text transcribed in Sogdian script, and Sogdians' personal names transcribed in Chinese characters are surveyed. The chapter shows, among other things, the relevance, Sogdian transcriptions of Chinese have for the analysis of the phonology of Tang period Chinese. Yoshida demonstrates that the pronunciation of the Chinese characters found in one particular manuscript represents the same as that of the poems of the most famous Tang poets, Li Bai and Du Fu. Yoshida also discusses the history of some Sogdian loanwords in Chinese. The chapter is concluded by a discussion of two Sogdians whom Xuanzang came across when he left China for India in 629 CE.

Due to unfortunate circumstances, not all of the articles collected in this volume have actually be presented at the conference in 2018. I am grateful that the authors who were not able to present their research at the conference nevertheless agreed to contribute their work to this volume. I also want to thank all the authors of this volume for supporting its publication by helping in the peer review process, and for patiently accepting all changes in the schedule of the preparation of this volume. Additionally, I would like to thank James McElvenny for reading the manuscript. One of the PhD students of the linguistics institute at National Tsing Hua University, Kye Shibeta, was so kind to copy-edit all chapters of the volume. Many thanks for your great and meticulous work, Kye. I also want to thank Lukas Betz, a former MA student of the linguistics institute for translating Uchida Keiichi's article from Chinese into English. That was of very great help. I am also particularly grateful to Chinfa Lien, one of the co-organizers of the conference and contributor to this volume, who allowed his assistant Yang Yuju to help with the formatting of the chapters.

My very special thanks go to the Institute of Linguistics of National Tsing Hua University and to Prof. Yueh-chin Chang, who supported every step of the publication process and who helped with the application for the funding of the volume.

Barbara Meisterernst
Hsinchu, May 2023

Chapter 1

In Search for the Dialectal Variants of Hokkien Based on the Early Bilingual Hokkien-Spanish Dictionary[1*]

Chinfa Lien
National Tsing Hua University

Abstract

This paper aims to track down subdialectal variations of Hokkien based on a Spanish-Hokkien-Sinitic bilingual dictionary, a seventeenth century manuscript dubbed Libro Tomo 215 (LT215) in the historical setting when the Hokkiense diaspora encountered the Spaniards in Luzon during the heyday of the Spanish maritime era. There are two kinds of telltale linguistic evidence that can be adduced to pin down the subdialectal variation: (1) phonological patterns of finals, and (2) the use of functional words. A careful examination of phonological patterning of finals and key functional words coupled with our knowledge of the present-day distribution of dialectal elements helps us pinpoint the dialect represented in LT215 as a Zhangzhou variety. Furthermore, there is a concomitant benefit of mapping out the early modern Spanish consonantal values by tackling the Hokkien diaspora's strategy of learning seventeenth century Spanish based on Chinese characters for the spelling of Spanish words.

1. Introduction

This paper aims at pinning down the dialectal variants of Hokkien (Hokkien Southern Min for short) as recorded in an anonymous handwritten bilingual Hokkien-Spanish dictionary catalogued as Libros Tomo 215 (LT215) in the Archives of the University of Santo Tomas.[2] The paper starts with the issue of paleography. When two different linguistic systems meet, how do they cope with the problem of writing an unfamiliar language? In particular, how did the Spaniards use their alphabet to render Hokkien words? I take the rendition of

---

1* The research on which this paper is based is partially supported by MOST 106-2420-H-007-009. I am indebted to Barbara Meisterernst, Alain Peyraube and Kye Shibata for helpful comments and suggestions. Thanks are also due to Yu-ju Yang for his editorial help.

2 For the full name of Libros Tomo 215 see Lee et al. (2019a).

the voiced affricate /dz/ in Hokkien by /x/ in Spanish as a point of departure
to tease out the intricate factors surrounding the choice of symbols for
phonological purposes. The dialectal variation of Hokkien is revealed most
saliently in the contrast of rime patterns and the use of functional words.
Taiwanese Southern Min (TSM) as a descendant of Hokkien has two major
variants: Zhangzhou and Quanzhou. Relying on the strength of previous studies
of rime books, nineteenth century dictionaries, and modern dialectal investigations,
the paper draws on LT 215 and sets up a set of contrasts in rime patterns uniquely
found in Zhangzhou rather than Quanzhou dialects. The variants recorded in
LT215 can be pinpointed with certainty as the Zhangzhou dialect. Functional
categories as the spine of a linguistic system comprise pronouns, demonstratives,
modals, negation, aktionsart/aspect, and preposition/conjunction as well as
grammatical markers such as agent and patient markers of core semantic roles and
the markers of source, goal, and beneficiary as the oblique semantic roles. Although
functional words are useful means of identifying dialectal identity, it is less salient
than phonological criteria. Still there are some telltale expressions that can provide
a pretty straightforward litmus test. *Tsi-tsui* 是誰 'who', a lexicalized human-
denoting WH-word, for example, is a key word for ascertaining the dialectal variant
of Zhangzhou. An attempt will also be made to compare demotic characters used
to render functional words in various contemporary Hokkien texts.

The 17th century or a little bit earlier saw the emergence of bilingual Hokkien-
Spanish dictionaries and Hokkien or Spanish learners including *Doctrina Christiana*
(1593 C.E.) [3], *Arte de la Lengua Chio Chiu* (Ms. 1027) (1620 C.E.), and *Dictionarium
Sino-Hispanicum* (1604 C.E.) among many others.[4] Even since the pioneer works
of van der Loon (1966-67) and Fang (1973), there has been scanty attention to
these manuscripts and early xylographic printing, until toward the end of the 20th
century, when there emerged a renewed interest in studies on the ingenious use
of using Spanish alphabetic script to render Hokkien and the reconstruction of
early Hokkien grammar based on extant colloquial manuscripts by western
missionaries: Yue (1999), Chappell (2000), Ishizaki (2002, 2006), Chen (2003),
Chappell & Peyraube (2006), Takata (2009), Klöter (2009, 2011), Lien (2011),
and Hong (2014) among others.

---

3   This is a Chinese version of Doctrina Christiana dating 1593 compiled by the ministers of the
    Sangleyes (Chinese expatriates in Luzon) of the Dominican Order. It is a book of xylographic
    printing licensed by Keng Yong from the parian (Chinese community) in Manila. An extant copy
    is kept in the Vatican library. See the reproductions of Doctrina Chrsitiana in Gayo Aragón and
    Domínguez (eds.) (1951) and Appendix II in van der Loon (1967: 143 - 186). The dating of
    Doctrina Christiana is in dispute; van der Loon (1966: 11 & 43) estimates it to be 1605.
4   For *Arte de la Lengua Chio Chiu,* a Spanish-Chinese parallel manuscript for learning Hokkien
    (Zhangzhou variety), see Klöter (2011) and Lee et al. (2019b).

The paper examines a handwritten manuscript catalogued as *Libros Tomo* 215 in the Archives of the University of Santo Tomas. It would not be wide off the mark to take it as a 16–17th century document. I will focus on three aspects of the manuscript: (1) how the Spanish alphabet is adjusted to render the Hokkien sounds absent in early modern Spanish, (2) comparison of functional categories among similar Hokkien texts, and (3) the reliance on the key words to ascertain dialectal variants of Hokkinese. Between the introduction and closing words, the paper is structured as follows: Section 2 features the phonological system of Hokkiense and Spanish in synchronic and diachronic perspectives. Section 3 focuses on the functional categories of Hokkien. Finally, Section 4 furnishes two telltale cases of the geographical distribution of functional words shedding light on their subdialectal grouping of Hokkien.

2. Phonological aspects

2.1. The encounter of two phonological systems

For a quick grasp of the difference between the two languages let's compare the consonantal charts in Hokkien and Medieval Spanish in Table 1 and Table 2, respectively.[5]

Table 1. Consonantal Chart in Hokkien

	Voicing	Aspiration	Bilabial	Dental	Velar	Glottal
Stop	Voiceless	Unaspirated	p	t	k	
		Aspirated	pʰ	tʰ	kʰ	
	Voiced		b		g	
Affricate	Voiceless	Unaspirated		ts		
		Aspirated		tsʰ		
	Voiced			dz		
Fricative	Voiceless			s		h
Nasal	Voiced		m	n	ŋ	
Lateral	Voiced			l		

---

5 Hokkien refers to Southern Min dialects including the Quanzhou 泉州 and Zhangzhou 漳州 varieties in southern Fujian as well as the Chao-shan 潮汕 variety in eastern Guangdong. The same language group also migrated to Taiwan, the Philippines, Malaysia, Singapore, and Indonesia as well as many other parts of the world. Southern Min as spoken in Taiwan is referred to as Taiwanese Southern Min (TSM).

Table 2. Consonantal Chart in Medieval Spanish

	Voicing	Bilabial	Dental	Prepalatal	Midpalatal	Velar
Stop	Voiceless	p	t			k
	Voiced	b	d			g
Affricate	Voiceless		ts	tʃ		
	Voiced		dz			
Fricative	Voiceless		s	ʃ		h
	Voiced		z	ʒ	j̡	
Nasal		m	n	ɲ		
Lateral			l	ʎ		
Trill			r			
Flap			ɾ			

Obstruents show a voicing contrast of stops and affricates in both Medieval Spanish and Hokkien. We can see a gap in the stop series in Hokkien in that /d/ is missing, as it merges with /l/. Note that the voiced obstruents are reflexes of early nasals, as in *bi²* 米 'rice' (cf. *mi³* M.), *lam⁵* 南 'south' (cf. *nan²* M.) and *gu⁵* 牛 'cattle' (*niu²* M.). The difference lies in the fricatives: unlike Hokkien, Medieval Spanish exhibits a contrast in dental and palatal fricatives.

2.1.1 Major consonantal shifts from Latin to Medieval Spanish

Latin has no affricates, but stops show a voicing contrast.[6] All fricatives are voiceless. Stops, velar or dental, in Latin, underwent palatalization when they are followed by high and mid front vowels yielding affricates, which comprise four pairs of sibilants in Medieval Spanish: (1) dental affricates /ts/ and /dz/, (2) palatal affricates /tʃ/ and /dʒ/, (3) /s/ and /z/, and (4) /ʃ/ and /ʒ/. Some affricates further developed into fricatives. In later stages the voiced sibilants were devoiced with the result that all of the sibilants became voiceless. Compare the following two consonantal tables:

---

6   In what follows, the discussion of the Spanish phonological system in diachronic and
    synchronic perspective is based mainly on Penny (1991), Lapesa (2004), and Pharies (2007).
    Medieval Spanish refers to the Spanish in the timeline of the thirteenth century to the first half
    of the fifteen century. Early Modern Spanish covers the period from the end of the fifth century
    to the seventeenth century.

Table 3. Sibilants in Medieval Spanish

Sibilants	Voicing	Dental	Palatal
Affricate	Voiceless	ç, c [ts]	ch [tʃ]
	Voiced	z [dz]	j, g [dʒ]
Fricative	Voiceless	-ss- [s]	x [ʃ]
	Voiced	-s- [z]	j, g [ʒ]

Table 4.Early Modern Spanish (15th – 17th century)

		Voicing	Dental	Palatal
Sibilants	Affricate	Voiceless	ç, c [ts]	ch [tʃ]
	Fricative	Voiceless	-ss- [s]	x [ʃ]
Approximant	Lateral			ʎ
	Central			j

Sibilants including affricates and fricatives experience two kinds of phonological changes: (1) deaffrication (viz., spirantization) of affricates, and (2) devoicing of each pair of the three sets of sibilants (dental fricatives /s̄/ vs. /z̄/, alveolar fricatives /s/ vs. /z/, and prepalatal fricatives /ʃ/ vs. /ʒ/).

(1)   Deaffrication (Spirantization)

$$\left. \begin{array}{l} /ts/ \\ /dz/ \end{array} \right\} >^{①} \left\{ \begin{array}{l} \bar{s} \\ \bar{z} \end{array} \right\} >^{②} /\bar{s}/$$

(2)   Devoicing

a. $\left\{ \begin{array}{l} \bar{s} \\ \bar{z} \end{array} \right\} > /\bar{s}/$

b. $\left\{ \begin{array}{l} s \\ z \end{array} \right\} > /s/$

c. $\left\{ \begin{array}{l} ʃ \\ ʒ \end{array} \right\} > /ʃ/$

The two phonological processes, which could have occurred in the sixteenth century, yield three pairs of fricatives distinguishable only in terms of place of articulation (dental, alveolar, and prepalatal) (Penny 1991:88-89).

When Hokkien and Early Modern Spanish (EMS) came into contact in the sixteenth century, devoicing of sibilants had occurred –resulting in the loss of voiced sibilants in Spanish– whereas /dz/, a voiced affricate, was still in existence in early Hokkien. EMS has no voiced affricate in its consonantal inventory to render /dz/ in Hokkien since EMS had developed to the stage at which the voicing contrast of /j/ [ʒ] and /x/ [ʃ] as /ʃ/ was neutralized. However, the letter *x* as well as *y* usually with the superscript /s/ in Spanish was adopted as a measure of expediency to represent /dz/ in Hokkien (van der Loon 1967). In contrast, the letter /j/ is occasionally used to represent /s/ in Hokkien, as in Juan Cobo *ko bo suan* 高母羨 (c. 1546-1593) where Juan 羨 is pronounced /suan/ in Hokkien[7]. This shows that the letter /j/ may have taken the value of voiceless palatal fricative, which later develops into voiceless velar fricative /x/ in modern Spanish. Further phonological changes following deaffrication, or rather spirantization, occur.

The effect of devoicing the sibilants yields two results:

(1) The dental voiceless /s/ resulting from deaffrication and devoicing was further fronted to interdental /θ/.

(2) The voiceless alveolar and prepalatal fricatives merged and turned into velar fricative /x/

2.2. The contrast of rime patterns

Whereas consonants, except the reflex of the initial in Middle Chinese 日, do not show subdialectal variation,[8] the difference between Zhangzhou and Quanzhou varieties is shown in the contrast of vowels.[9]

2.2.1. The contrast of front mid vowels in Zhangzhou

Hokkien mid front vowels show a contrast not only in the lower and higher mid, but also between monophthong and diphthong, as in /ɛ/ vs. /ey/. /ɛ/ in Zhangzhou corresponds to /e/ in Quanzhou, and /ei/ in Zhangzhou to /ɣe/ in Quanzhou.

	Zhangzhou	Quanzhou	Mandarin
家茶	ɛ	e	a
題雞	ei	ue	i

---

7   Juan Cobo rendered as 嗃呣嗹 is said to author *The Veritable Record of the Authentic Tradition of the True Faith in the Infinite God* 無極天主教真傳實錄. It was also rendered as 羨高茂 in another document (van der Loon 1966: 3 & 24). Despite different characters in the two renditions, there is no difference in Hokkiense pronunciation: /kobo suan/. For Jesus 西士 rendered as /se su/ in Hokkiensese see van der Loon (1967: 144).

8   The 日 initial may be realized as /dz-/, /l-/ or /g-/ depending on the subdialect. There are also quite rare cases of subdialectal variation, as in /bak⁴/ 捌 (Zhangzhou) vs. /pat⁴/ (Quanzhou) 'know' (or an experiential marker).

9   Data of Quanzhou and Zhangzhou varieties can be found in Douglas (1873), Dong (1959), Lin (1993), and Ma (2008).

There is a contrast of vowel height, viz. the lower mid /ɛ/ vs. the higher mid /e/, in Zhangzhou, whereas the contrast of vowel height is neutralized in Quanzhou. Nevertheless, the contrast between monophthong and diphthong also plays an important role. The Zhangzhou dialect seems to show more affinity to Mandarin in that the contrast between /ɛ/ and /e/ in the former corresponds to the contrast between /a/ and /i/ in the latter.

2.2.2. The diphthong /ue/ in Zhangzhou corresponding to the monophthong /ɤ/ in Quanzhou

	Zhangzhou	Quanzhou	Mandarin
火	ue	ɤ	uo

The diphthong /ue/ in the Zhangzhou dialect corresponds to /ɤ/, a mid back unrounded vowel, in the Quanzhou dialect. We can see that unlike Quanzhou, both Zhangzhou and Mandarin share the diphthongs even though there is a difference in vowel height. This again shows the closer relationship between Zhangzhou and Mandarin.

There are two more corresponding diphthongs in Mandarin. This lends more support to the affinity of Zhangzhou and Mandarin.

	Zhangzhou	Quanzhou	Mandarin
吹稅尾	ue	ɤ	uei
飛配	ue	ɤ	ei

There is, however, rare cases where a diphthong in Zhangzhou corresponds to a monophthong in Quanzhou and Mandarin.

	Zhangzhou	Quanzhou	Mandarin
皮糜	ue	ɤ	i

*2.2.3. The reflexes of *uan*

The nasal finals, viz., the rimes with nasal codas (-m, -n, -ŋ), show a contrast between /uiⁿⁿ/ in Zhangzhou and /ng/ in Quanzhou. The corresponding reflexes in Mandarin are /-uan/ or rarely /-uang/.

	Zhangzhou	Quanzhou	Mandarin
軟	ui^{nn}	ng	uan
黃	ui^{nn}	ng	uang

It should be noted that there is a group of lexemes sharing the common reflex of /-ng/ which corresponds to /-uang/ in Mandarin.[10]

2.2.4.   *The contrast of /ε^{nn}/ in Zhangzhou and /i^{nn}/ in Quanzhou*

There is another class of nasal finals which exhibits a contrast between /ε^{nn}/ in Zhangzhou and /i^{nn}/ in Quanzhou.

	Zhangzhou	Quanzhou	Mandarin
青	ε^{nn}	i^{nn}	ing
棚	ε^{nn}	i^{nn}	əng

But there is a set of lexemes sharing the reflex of /i^{nn}/ in Zhangzhou and Quanzhou.

	Zhangzhou	Quanzhou	Mandarin
錢天	i^{nn}	i^{nn}	ian
染	i^{nn}	i^{nn}	an

We can see that the contrast between /ε^{nn}/ and /i^{nn}/ is parallel to a contrast between the velar and dental coda in Mandarin.

2.2.5.   *The contrast of /$i\mathopen{}\mathclose{}\mathopen{}\mathclose{}ɔ^{nn}$/ in Zhangzhou and /$iu^{nn}$/ in Quanzhou*

The reflexes of /$iɔ^{nn}$/ in Zhangzhou and /iu^{nn}/ in Quanzhou correspond to the same final /ang/ or /iang/ in Mandarin.

	Zhangzhou	Quanzhou	Mandarin
羊	$iɔ^{nn}$	iu^{nn}	iang
張	$iɔ^{nn}$	iu^{nn}	ang

2.2.6.   *The contrast of /iang/ in Zhangzhou and /iong/ in Quanzhou*

/iang/ in Zhangzhou corresponds to /iong/ in Quanzhou. If the medial /-i-/ is not considered, the reflex of both Zhangzhou and Mandarin are the same. This again shows the affinity of Zhangzhou and Quanzhou.

	Zhangzhou	Quanzhou	Mandarin
香	iang	iong	iang
常	iang	iong	ang

---

10 黃 and 光 are rare items with the nasal coda which spills over into this category.

2.2.7.   The contrast of /in/ in Zhangzhou and /un/ in Quanzhou

There are only a couple of lexemes featuring /-un/ or more conservative /-ən/[11], such as 根, 筋, 巾, 斤, 銀, 近, 勤, 芹 in Quanzhou. Both Zhangzhou and Mandarin shows /in/.[12]

	Zhangzhou	Quanzhou	Mandarin
銀斤近芹	in	un/ən	in

2.2.8.   Two-way vocalic distinction in Zhangzhou vs. neutralized vowel in Quanzhou

Parallel to the two-way distinction of front mid vowels, the back mid vowels also show a contrast between front upper mid vowel /o/ and the lower mid vowel in Zhangzhou, as shown in the following table.

	Zhangzhou	Quanzhou	Mandarin
高	o	ɔ	au
姑	ɔ	ɔ	u

However, /o/ has merged into /ɔ/ in Quanzhou, as attested in the Chin-chew (晉州) dialect recorded in Douglas (1873).

2.2.9.   The transformed 魚/虞 distinction in Zhangzhou vs. its early distinction in Quanzhou

The 魚/虞 distinction of rime categories, which has engaged much attention in recent literature, is kept well in Quanzhou. As shown below, the distinctive lip-rounding feature in Quanzhou has been shifted to a front and back opposition in Zhangzhou.

	Zhangzhou	Quanzhou	Mandarin
鋤	i	ɯ	u
鋸	i	ɯ	y
廚	u	u	u
舅	u	u	iou

If Quanzhou represents an earlier stage of development, then the /i/ form in Zhangzhou must have been a result of fronting the back unrounded vowel to the front unrounded vowel. The shift of /ɯ/ to /i/ may proceed via an intermediate change of /u/. We can see the effect of lexical diffusion caught in mid-stream.

---

11 An alternative reconstructed vocal value could be /ɯ/.
12 All items in Mandarin have the final /in/ except /kən/ 根.

The process has not been completed yet. It means that the realization of the lexemes in the 魚 categories is not neat and uniform. Some reflexes in Mandarin show a neutralization of the two erstwhile contrastive rimes.

2.2.10. *Interim Summary*

To summarize, dialectal variations in Hokkien are manifested in the colloquial (rather than literary) stratum. The latter stratum does not exhibit much difference. Leaving the rimes with stop codas aside, we have concentrated on two types of rimes above: (1) the rimes with no codas (*Yin shengyun* 陰聲韻), and (2) the rimes with nasal codas (*Yang shengyun* 陽聲韻).

In the first place, let us examine the rimes with no codas (*Yin shengyun* 陰聲韻): Consider first the front mid vowels. Zhangzhou shows a contrast between upper and lower mid vowels, whereas Quanzhou features a contrast of the monophthong /e/ and the diphthong /ue/, where /e/ is held in common. Second, the back mid vowels follow a similar pattern: Zhangzhou indicates a contrast between the upper and lower mid vowels, /ɔ/ vs. /o/, whereas Quanzhou experiences a neutralization of the two vowels via the merger of /o/ into /ɔ/. Zhangzhou is more akin to Mandarin in phonological categories in both cases. The third case involving *Yin shengyun* is the correspondence of the diphthong /ue/ in Zhangzhou to the monophthong /ɤ/ in Quanzhou. Both Zhangzhou and Mandarin share the common feature of diphthongs, showing their closer relationship. Fourth, we touch on the contrast of /ɯ/ and /u/ based on lip rounding in Quanzhou, a conservative trait uniquely found in modern southern Sinitic dialects. The contrast transforms itself as a contrast in terms of frontness. The contrast has been obliterated in Mandarin as well.

Next, let us explore the rimes with the nasal codas (*Yang shengyun* 陽聲韻). First, the salient contrast between the Zhangzhou and Quanzhou varieties is shown in the correspondence of /uiⁿⁿ/ and /ng/. In terms of vocalic value, we can see that both Zhangzhou and Mandarin have /u/ in common. Second, another tangible difference between Zhangzhou and Quanzhou is the contrast of /ɛⁿⁿ/ and /iⁿⁿ/. The contrastive nasalized vowels correspond to the rimes with the velar nasal coda in Mandarin rather than the rimes with the dental nasal coda. For example, 姓 'surname', a word with the velar coda */-ŋ/ historically, is /sɛⁿⁿ/ in Zhangzhou but /siⁿⁿ/ in Quangzhou. However, a word like 錢 'money' with the dental coda /-n/ is /tsiⁿⁿ/ in both dialects.

Third, there are a small set of lexemes which still stick to /un/ or even more conservative /ən/ whereas other dialects have shifted to /in/, engulfing even Zhangzhou and Mandarin. Fourth, on the one hand /iɔⁿⁿ/ in Zhangzhou corresponds to /iuⁿⁿ/ in Quanzhou, while on the other hand, /iang/ in

Zhangzhou has its counterpart /iong/ in Quanzhou. Evidently in both cases, the vowel values of Zhangzhou shows a grade lower than counterparts in Quanzhou. The two types of rimes are neutralized in Mandarin. Another noteworthy feature of Zhangzhou is that it is identical to Mandarin in its realization of the rime /(i)ang/. This again shows the affinity of Zhangzhou and Mandarin.

Three types of the rimes with nasal codas (-m, -n, -ŋ) have each of their counterparts with their respective homorganic stop codas (-p, -t, -k). The stop codas have been merged into the glottal stop /-ʔ/ in the colloquial stratum.

	Zhangzhou	Quanzhou	Mandarin
月	ueʔ	əʔ	ye
襪	ueʔ	əʔ	ua
八	eʔ	ueʔ	ia
挾	eʔ	ueʔ	a
血	ueʔ	uiʔ	ie

Both nasalization and glottalization impact the phonological patterning of finals. The finals with zero codas show a two-way contrast of the vowels which are neutralized by nasalization and glottalization. As shown above, glottalization seems to show less impact on the vowel quality. The dialectal variation, in terms of vowel values in glottalized finals, pattern with finals with zero codas than with the nasalized finals.

There are some sporadic lexemes whose phonological value carries the tell-tale dialectal trait. When 花, 瓜, and 話 are realized as /hua1/, /kua1/, /ua7/ in the colloquial stratum, the dialect can be ascertained as the Zhangzhou variety.

We have in this section teased out the subdialectal (Zhangzhou vs. Quanzhou) variation by examining the different patterning of phonological realization, in particular with respect to the final system. Subdialectal variation is manifested not only in the phonological dimension but also in the use of functional words. Section 3 will focus on a range of functional words which reflect subdialectal variation.

3.   Functional Words

Functional words, unlike lexemes, are listable and carry no lexical meaning. They have an important role in determining syntactic structure. In the following we will deal with functional words such as pronouns, demonstratives, interrogatives, and modals, as well as words denoting negation, aktionsart, and aspect, prepositions, and conjunctions.

3.1. *Pronouns*

Pronouns are classified in terms of person and number. The first person plurals fall into two types: (1) *guan²* 阮· exclusive types denoting the speaker and the person(s) on his or her side, and (2) *lan²* 俺/咱, inclusive types including both speaker(s) and addressee(s). The plural forms distinct from the singular forms are fusional forms featuring the plurality denoting coda /-n/. The third person plural forms are not attested.

3.2.　*Demonstratives*

There are two kinds of demonstratives: (1) the proximal demonstrative *tsy²* 只 'this', and (2) the distal demonstrative *hu²* 許 'that'. Unlike 'this' or 'that' in English, they never occur alone. They can be followed immediately by a noun phrase and the demonstratives and noun phrases can be mediated by numerals. They may function as determiners in combination with noun phrases like *ionn* 樣 and *ua* 夥 'many, much'. Proximal and distal demonstratives can merge with the manner noun phrases to form fusional forms *tsionn* 障 'so' (< *tsi² ionn⁷* 只樣 'this way') and *hionn* 向 'so' (<*hu² ionn⁷* 許樣 'that way'). Since our focus is on the functional words found in the dictionary Libros Tomo 215, we have no information that can help us determine the syntactic behavior of the proximal and distal demonstratives in sentences. Nevertheless, a cursory look at Doctrina Christiana, a Chinese text written in Hokkien (Gayo Aragón and Domínguez (eds.) 1951), shows that there are more instances of 只/許-marked determiner phrases in subject position than object position.

3.3.　*Interrogatives*

Interrogative words can be classified in term of the core variables: (1) *mih⁴* 乜, (2) *ti⁷* 值 (<底), *gua⁷/jua⁷* 幾/多/偌, and *tsui⁵* 誰. When coupled with nouns, many types of interrogative words can be formed: (1) *si⁷-mih⁴* 是乜 'what', (2) *tso³ mih⁴* 做乜 'how, why', (3) *ui⁷ mih⁴* 為乜 'why', (4) *tsai³/⁷* 偌 'how, why', (5) *jua⁷ tse⁷* 多 (濟) 'how much', and (6) *si⁷ tsui⁷* 是誰 'who'. *Ti⁷* 值 often functions as the modifier of a noun phrase, as in *ti⁷te³* 值處 'where' and *ti⁷si⁵* 值時 'when'.

3.4.　*Modals*

Modals fall into at least four classes: (1) epistemic modals, (2) deontic modals, (3) dynamic modals, and (4) boulomaic modals.

3.4.1.　*Epistemic modals*

Two types of epistemic modals can be captured in terms of the notion of possibility: (1) modals denoting possibility, and (2) modals denoting necessity. Necessity is a subset of possibility since necessary worlds are derived from possible worlds universally quantified. Epistemic modals of both necessity, as in *tiann⁷tioh⁸* 定著 'must, necessarily' and *tiann⁷tou⁷* 定度 'must', and possibility, as in *ey³/⁷* 會 (<解) 'may, possible'[13], involve subjective evaluation of the world on the part of speakers. In a nutshell, epistemic modality denotes the speaker's coming to grips with the world with his or her assessment of the possibility or necessity of a certain state of affairs.

3.4.2. *Deontic modals*

Deontic modals can also be classified in terms of the notion of possibility. In addition, they feature the duty or obligation for the execution of actions imposed by an authority. Deontic modals of necessity are exemplified by *ai³* 愛 'must, should', *tioh⁸* 著, *cay¹* 該, *cay¹tung¹ / tung¹* 該當, *su¹tong¹* 須當, *hap⁸cay¹tioh⁸* 合該著, *tsiu⁷ay³iong⁷* ?就愛用, whereas deontic modals of possibility feature *thang¹* 可 (< 通) 'can, may', *ey⁷say²tet⁴* 會使得, and *ey⁷tso³tet⁴* 會做得.

3.4.3. *Dynamic modals*

Dynamic modals, as in *ey³/⁷* 會 'can', *cham¹iong³* 堪用 'can', and *cann²* ?敢 'dare', denotes the inherent capability of an animate entity and are subject-oriented (rather than speaker-oriented).

3.4.4. *Boulomaic modals*

Boulomaic modals denoting desire, wish, and volition embrace *bueh⁴* 卜 / 要 'want', *cam¹* 甘 'be willing'[14], *quheng²(guan⁷)* 肯 (願) 'be willing', and *guan⁷/y³guan⁷* 願/意願 'wish'.[15]

3.5. *Negation*

There is an intimate relationship between negation and modality and aspect (or even mood). There are two kinds of relationships between negative modals and their positive counterparts. Type one shows that negative modals are compositional and derived from adding a negative element to positive modals often yielding a fusional form, as in *bey⁷* 袂 and its positive counterpart *ey⁷* 會. Type two indicates a suppletive relationship as exemplified in *bien²* 免 and *tioh⁸* 著.[16]

---

13 會 as a semantic loan character is etymologically derived from 解 as a result of grammaticalization (Yang 2001).

14 *Cam¹* 甘 as a negative polarity item often occurs in negative contexts or irrogatives.

15 There are many aspects in which dynamic and boulomaic modals can be distinguished. For example, *bueh⁴ lim¹ tsiu²* 要飲酒 'want to drink wine' is not the same as *ey⁷ lim¹ tsiu²* 會飲酒 'can drink wine/have a high alcohol tolerance'.

16 The necessity deontic modal *tioh⁸* 著 'must' cannot be negated. Of course, *tioh⁸* 著 can be preceded by a negative word like *m⁷* 不 yielding the meaning of 'not correct', but it is an adjective rather than a modal.

3.5.1.   Epistemic negation

Bey⁷ 袂 is a phonetic loan character featuring the fusion of the negative element 勿 and the modal *ey⁷* 會 (<解) 'may', an epistemic modal of possibility: *bo⁵tiann⁷tioh⁸* 無定著 'may not' is the negative counterpart of *tiann⁷tioh⁸* 定著 'must' an epistemic modal of necessity.

3.5.2.   Deontic negation

Bien² 免 'need not' is the negative counterpart of the deontic modal of necessity *tioh⁸* 著 'must', a deontic modal of necessity. The positive *tioh⁸* 著 and the negative *bien²* 免 are in a suppletive relationship. Unlike *bien²* 免, which shows a suppletive relationship with its positive counterpart *tioh⁸* 著, *m⁷thang¹* 不通, alternatively written as *m⁷thang¹* 不可 'may not', is derived from merging the negative element and the positive modal *thang¹* 通 'can, may'. *bey⁷say²tet⁴* / *bey⁷tso³tet⁴* 袂使得 / 袂做得 'may not' is the negation of the deontic modal *ey⁷say²tet⁴* / *ey⁷tso³tet⁴* 會使得 / 會做得 'may not'.

3.5.3.   Boulomaic negation

M⁷ 不 (<毋) 'will not' is the negative counterpart of the boulomaic modal *bueh⁴* 卜/要 'want'.[17] Thus, *m⁷* 不 and *bueh⁴* 卜/要 are suppletive. *M⁷ cam¹* 不甘 'be not willing, grudge' is the negation of *cam¹* 甘 'be willing'[18]. Similarly, *bo⁵ai³* 無愛, and *m⁷ai³* ?不愛 'will not' are the negation of *ai³* 愛 'want'.

3.5.4.   Dynamic negation

Bey⁷ 袂 'cannot, be unable to' is the negative counterpart of the dynamic modal *ey³/⁷* 會 'can'. Be it positive or negative, they are ambiguous between epistemic and dynamic. *Bey⁷ cham¹* 袂堪 'cannot bear' is a more elaborate form of dynamic negation.

3.5.5.   Prohibitive negation

The relevance of mood to the use of negative modals can be seen in the exclusive use of *moh⁸* 莫 'don't' in imperatives. *moh⁸ tit⁴* ?莫得 'don't' is a more elaborate form of prohibitive negation.

We can see that there is a fine distinction of the four types of positive modals; it

---

17 Boulomaic modals may well be subsumed under dynamic modals or even deontic modals. However, we opt for a finer distinction. Boulomaic modals involve desire and wish, whereas dynamic modals concern ability and capacity. Deontic modals always feature the imposition of an authority's will on the addressee for the execution of an action. These distinctions may have syntactic consequences.

18 *Cam¹* 甘 as a negative polarity item often occurs in negative contexts or interrogatives.

is naturally expected that, given the principle of compositionality, their negative counterparts will remain distinct. Prohibitive negation is the negative modal that takes on an imperative force.

3.6. *Aktionsart and Aspect*

Aktionsart concerns kinds of action (Vendler 1957). Aspect deals with situation types. Aktionsart and aspect correspond to lexical and grammatical aspect, or situation and viewpoint aspect respectively (MacDonald 2008 and Travis 2010). In terms of linear sequence, aktionsart is closer to the verb root than aspect, reflecting a distinction between inner and outer aspect. The inner aspect exhibits richer and more variegated paradigmatic items than the outer aspect. This is shown in the contrast between accomplishment and achievement markers, on the one hand, and the progressive and continuative aspect markers as well as the inchoative marker on the other (Lien 1995). The accomplishment marker features a set of forms in a paradigmatic relationship, viz. *liau²* 了, *suah⁴* 煞, *tit⁴* 得, *khi³* 去, and *uan⁵* 完. The achievement markers are *tioh⁸* 著 and *kinn³* 見. The latter is more limited in its distribution and can only occur with the visual and auditory verbs. Unlike progressives and continuatives, both accomplishment and achievement constructions are telic and have a culmination at the end. However, the former is durative whereas the latter is punctual. The progressive marker may come from the contraction of the locative head *ti⁷* 佇 and the inherent localizer *te³* 處 (Lien 2015b). The continuative marker *teh⁸ / leh⁸* 著 in postverbal position may well share same source as the continuative marker. The inchoative marker may evolve from two sources: (1) *lai⁵* 來 yielding *lo* 嘮/朥, and (2) *liau²* 了 neutralized as *lah⁰* or *d⁰*. Aspectual negation *bue⁷* 未 'not yet' emerges as a negation of a perfect aspectual marker.

3.7. *Preposition and Conjunction*

The preposition *cang⁷* 共 'to, from, for' is underspecified in that the noun phrase that it licenses can bear the semantic role of source, goal, and benefactee depending on the verb types (Chappell 2000, Lien 2002). Further, in contrast with *cab⁴* 甲/合 'with, and', it is unidirectional since the event always involves non-reciprocity. The patient marker in disposals is *tsiong¹* 將 rather than 把 (Lien 2015a). In terms of chronology profile, 將 and 把 date back to the seventh and tenth century (Wei 1997). Another patient marker, *liah⁸* 力, is uniquely found in Southern Min (Lien 2010). *Quhit⁴* 乞 and *thou⁷* 度 are two prepositions evolving from ditransitive verbs. Both 乞 and 度 are agent markers in passives, but they can also be root verbs in directive-causative constructions.

4.   Telltale expressions or functional categories for identifying dialectal variants

The identity of dialectal variants is revealed not only in the selection of types of functional words, but also in patterns of phonological traits. First, we furnish a pretty informative example of the functional words, such as human-denoting wh-words, as a giveaway for subdialectal variation. Second, we will provide a clear-cut example of the phonological contrast between the Zhongzhou and Quanzhou varieties in Hokkien.

4.1.   Humans-denoting wh-words

A cursory look at the dialectal survey of Hokkien dialects (FDBW 1998: 545-547) turns up three types of humans-denoting wh-words: (1) $tsua^5$ 誰阿 / tsi^7 $tsua^5$ 是誰, (2) ti^2 $lang^5$ 底儂, and (3) $siann^2$ $lang^5$ 啥儂. Type (1) is closer to $shei^2$ / $shui^2$ 誰 in Mandarin and belongs to the Modern Chinese stratum. Type (2) belongs to the North-South Dynasties stratum, and Type (3) belongs to the Tang stratum.

The geographic distribution of the three kinds of human-denoting wh-words as well as their chronological strata are shown in Table 5.

Table 5. Geographic distribution of Humans-denoting wh-Words

Human-denoting wh-words	Dialectal sites	Chronological strata
$tsua^5$ 誰阿	Zhongzhou 漳州, Longhai 龍海, Changtai 長泰, Nanjing 南靖, Pinghe 平和, Zhangpu 漳浦, Yunxiao 雲霄	誰 stratum
tsi^7 $tsua^5$ 是誰	Dongshan 東山	
ti^7 $lang^5$ 底儂	Yongchun 永春, Dehua 德化, Changping 漳平, Datian 大田, Longyan 龍岩	底 stratum
$siann^2$ $lang^5$ 啥儂	Xiamen 廈門, Jinmen 金門, Tong-an 同安, Quanzhou 泉州, Jinjiang 晉江, Shishi 石獅, Nan-an 南安, Anxi 安溪	物 stratum

We can see that *tsua⁵* 誰阿 and *tsi⁷ tsua²* 是誰 as a type belong in the pan-Zhangzhou variant, *sia² lang⁵* 啥儂 to the pan-Quanzhou variant, and *ti⁷ lang⁵* 底儂 to peripheral varieties (See Lien (2017) for more details).[19]

4.2. Key Phonological contrast

As shown in the following table based on (FDBW 1998: 464-466), the syllabic nasal /ŋ/ can be found in the Quanzhou variant as the Northern group of Hokkien, whereas /uiⁿⁿ/ in realized in the Zhangzhou variant as the Southern group of Hokkien.

---

19 A bilingual learner of Mandarin compiled by Cai (1747) from Zhangzhou for Southern Min speakers shows 萃萃 'who' as the reflex of 是誰 in the Zhangzhou variety, corresponding to 誰阿 in Mandarin in the section devoted to *Shishi Changtan* 時事常談 'everyday expressions'. According to my field survey, *tsui tsui* 萃萃 is a humans-denoting wh-word uniquely found in Penang Hokkiense as a reflex of the Zhangzhou variety. To the best of my knowledge, there is no modern reflex of /tsui tsui/ in the homeland of Hokkien. Why was 萃萃 registered in the eighteenth century learner? Did the compiler Cai Bolong 蔡伯龍, a native of Zhangzhou, have an overseas experience in his lifetime? That is an exceedingly intriguing puzzle to be solved in the future.

飯	Dialectal site
ŋ̍	Yongchun 永春, Anxi 安溪, Nan-an 南安, Dehua 德化, Quanzhou 泉州, Jinjiang 晉江, Shishi 石獅, Xiamen 廈門, Jinmen 金門, Tong-an 同安, Changtai 長泰
uiⁿⁿ	Changping 漳平, Longyan 龍岩, Changzhou 漳州, Hua-an 華安, Longhai 龍海, Nanjing 南靖, Heping 平和, Changpu 漳浦, Yunxiao 雲霄, Zhao-an 詔安, Dongshan 東山

From the above map, we can grasp a neat geographical distribution of /uiⁿⁿ/ and and /ŋ̍/ in pan-Zhangzhou and pan-Quanzhou variants.

5. Closing Words

We have tried to bring the manuscript Libro Tomo (215) to bear on the issue of how the people with different linguistic backgrounds and writing systems managed to cope with the problem of communication. In this paper, we first take this interactive situation into consideration by thinking about how the Spaniards devised an ingenious way of rendering the Hokkien sounds absent in their linguistic system. Secondly, we attempt to pin down the dialectal variant in terms of a set of contrasts of rime patterns uniquely found in Zhangzhou absent in Quanzhou.

Thirdly, we look into the functional categories as the spine of a linguistic system focusing on common functional words exclusively found in Hokkien. Fourthly, two cases of telltale expressions (vis. key words and reflexes of phonological category) are furnished as two pieces of evidence attesting to the validity of the language recorded in Libros Tomo 215 as a Zhanzhou variant.

References

Cai, Bolong 蔡伯龍（蔡奭）. 1747. *Guanyin Huijie* 官音彙解 [Mandarin-Hokkien Parallel Texts]. Xiazhang Da Wentang Cang Ban 霞漳大文堂藏版.

Chappell, Hilary. 2000. Dialect grammar in two early Southern Min texts: a comparative study of dative *kit* 乞, comitative *cang* 共 and diminutive *–guia* 仔. *Journal of Chinese Linguistics* 28.2: 247-302.

Chappell, Hilary and Peyraube, Alain. 2006. The diachronic syntax of causative structures in Early Modern Southern Min. In Dah-an Ho (ed.), *Festschrift for Ting Pang-Hsin*, 973-1011. Taipei: Academia Sinica.

Chen, Matthew Y. 2003. Unsung trailblazers of China-West cultural encounter. Ex/Chang (Hong Kong) 8: 4-12.

Chirino, P. Petrus. 1604. *Dictionarium Sino Hispanicum* [Chinese-Spanish Dictionary]. Rome: Biblioteca Angelica.

Dong, Tonghe 董同龢. 1959. Si Ge Minnan Fangyan 四個閩南方言 [Four Southern Min Dialects]. *Bulletin of the Insitute of History and Philology, Academia Sinica*, vol.30, 729-1042.

Douglas, Rev. Cartairs. 1873. *Chinese-English dictionary of the vernacular or spoken language of Amoy with the principal variations of the Chang-chew and Chin-chew dialects*. London: Trubner and Co.

Fang, Hao 方豪 (Fr. Maurus). 1973. Mingmo Manila huaqiao jiaohui zhi teshu yongyu yu xisu (xinkan Liaoshi Zhengjiao bianlan yu Doctrina Christiana en lengua China ershu zhi zonghe yanjiu) 明末馬尼拉華僑教會之特殊用語與習俗: "新刊僚氏正教便覽"與 *Doctrina Christiana en lengua China* 二書之綜合研究 [Special Words and Customs of Minila overseas Chinese Church at the end of Ming Dynasty: an integrated study of the two books entitlted: *Memorial de la vida christiana en Lengua China* and *Doctrina Christiana en lengua China*]. *Xiandai Xueyuan* 現代學苑 10.5: 177-193.

Fujiansheng Difangzhi Bianzuan Weiyuanhui 福建省地方誌編纂委員會 (FDBW). 1998. *Fujian shengzhi: Fangyanzhi* 福建省誌：方言誌 [Local gazetteers of Fujian Province: Dialects]. Beijing: Fangzhi Press.

Gayo Aragón, J., and Antonio Domínguez (eds.) 1951. *Doctrina Christiana: Primer libro impreso en Filipinas*. Manila: Imprenta de la Real y Pontificia de Universidad de Santo Tomas de Manila.

Hong, Weijen (aka Ang Uijin) 洪惟仁. 2014. Shiliuqi shiji zhijian Lüsong de Zhangzhou fangyan 十六七世紀之間呂宋的漳州方言 [The Zhangzhou dialect in Luzon in the sixteenth and seventeenth century]. *Lishi Dili* 歷史地理 30: 215-238.

Ishizaki, Hiroshi 石崎博志. 2002. Mvsevm Sinicvm niokeru hoogen kijiutsu-bunpoo wo chusin ni MVSEVM SINICVM における方言記述-文法を中心に [A grammatical description of the dialect in MVSEVM SINICVM]. *Nihon Tooyoo Bunka Ronshuu Ryukyu Daigaku Hoo Bungakubu Kiyoo* 日本東洋文化論集琉球大学法文学部紀要 [Bulletin of the Faculty of Law and Letters, University of the Ryukyus] 8: 1-21.

Ishizaki, Hiroshi 石崎博志. 2006. Honkoku shiryoo Barcelona Daigakuzoo 'Arte de la Lengua Chin Cheu 翻刻資料 Barcelona 大学蔵"Arte de la lengua chin cheu" [Arte de la Lengua Chin Cheu in the University of Barcelona]. *Nihon Tooyoo Bunka Ronshuu Ryukyu Daigaku Hoo Bungakubu Kiyoo* 日本東洋文化論集琉球大学法文学部紀要 [Bulletin of the Faculty of Law and Letters, University of the Ryukyus] 12: 151-206.

Klöter, Henning. 2009. The earliest Hokkien dictionaries. In Otto Zwartjes, Ramón Arzápalo Marín & Thomas Smith-Stark (eds.), *Missionary linguistics IV: Lexicography. Selected papers from the Fifth International Conference on Missionary Linguistics, Mérida-Yucatán, 14–17 March 2007*, 303–330. Amsterdam: John Benjamins.

Klöter, Henning. 2011. *The language of the Sangleys: A Chinese vernacular in missionary sources of the seventeenth century*. Leiden, Boston: Brill.

Lapesa, Rafael ラペサ・ラファエル. 2004. *Historia de la lengua Española* スペイン語の歴史 [The history of the Spanish language]. (Edited by Yoshirou Yamada 山田善郎 and translated by Shoji Nakaoka 中岡省治 & Jiunosuke Miyoshi 三好準之助). 京都 Kyoto: 昭和堂 Showado.

Lee, Fabio Yuechung, Tsung-jen Chen, Regalado Trota José, and José Caño Ortigosa (Eds.). 2019a. *Dictionario Hispanico Sinicum*. Part 1, 2 & 3. Hokkien Spanish Historical Document Series I. Hsinchu: National Tsing Hua University Press.

Lee, Fabio Yuechung, Tsung-jen Chen, Regalado Trota José, and José Caño Ortigosa (Eds.). 2019b. *Arte de la Lengua Chio Chiu*. Hokkien Spanish Historical Document Series I. Hsinchu: National Tsing Hua University Press.

Lien, Chinfa 連金發. 1995. Taiwan Minnanyu wanjie shixiangci shilun 臺灣閩南語完結時相詞試論 [Phase words in Taiwan Southern Min]. In Fengfu Tsao 曹逢甫 and Meihui Tsai 蔡美慧 (eds.), *Papers from the 1994 Conference on Language Teaching and Linguistics in Taiwan*. Volume I: Southern Min, 121-140. Taipei: The Crane Publishing Co., Ltd.

Lien, Chinfa. 2002. Grammatical function words 乞, 度, 共, 甲, 將 and 力 in Li[4] Jing[4] Ji[4] 荔鏡記 and their Development in Southern Min. In Dah-an Ho (ed.), *Papers from the Third International Conference on Sinology: Linguistic Section. Dialect Variations in Chinese*, 179-216. Taipei: Institute of Linguistics, Preparatory Office, Academia Sinica.

Lien, Chinfa. 2010. The dual function of *liah[8]* 力 in Li Jing Ji. *Journal of Chinese Linguistics*. 38.1: 45-69.

Lien, Chinfa. 2011. East-West encounter: Comparing earlier romanized and Chinese-character Southern Min texts: The development of interrogative words in Southern Min. In Zbigniew Wesolowski (ed.), *The Sixth Fu Jen University International Sinological Symposium: "Early European (1552-1814) Acquisition and Research on Chinese Languages" Symposium Papers*, 385-410, 411-432. New Taipei: Fu Jen Catholic University Press.

Lien, Chinfa. 2015a. The condition and change of 共 vis-à-vis 合 in Southern Min with a sidelight on intra-dialectal variation. *Journal of Chinese Linguistics* 43.1A: 1-33.

Lien, Chinfa. 2015b. Zaoqi Minnayuzhong duogongnengci chu de tansuo: cong fangwei dao timao 早期閩南語中多重功能詞「處」的探索：從方位到體貌 [Polyfunctionality of 處 in early Southern Min: from location to aspect]. *Tunghai Journal of Chinese Literature* 29: 249-268.

Lien, Chinfa. 2017. Humans-denoting interrogative words in Early Southern Min: Coexistence and evolution. In Gang Peng and Feng Wang (eds.), *New horizons in evolutionary linguistics*, 130-158. The Chinese Uniersity Press of Hong Kong.

Lin, Liantong 林連通. 1993. *Quanzhou fangyanzhi* 泉州方言志 [A description of Quanzhou dialect]. Beijing: Shehui Kexue Wenxian Chubanshe.

van der Loon, Piet. 1966. The Manila incunabula and early Hokkien studies Pt. 1. *Asia Major*, new series, XII.95-186.

van der Loon, Piet. 1967. The Manila incunabula and early Hokkien studies Pt. 2. *Asia Major*, new series, XIII.1-43.

Ma, Chongqi 馬重奇. 2008. *Min Tai Minnan fangyan yunshu bijiao yanjiu* 閩台閩南方言韻書比較研究 [A Comparative Study of Southern Min Rime Books in Fujian and Taiwan]. Beijing: Zhongguo Shehui Kexue Chubanshe.

MacDonald, Jonathan E. 2008. *The syntactic nature of inner aspect: A minimalist perspective.* Amsterdam: John Benjamins Publishing Company.

Mançano, Melchior de. 1620. *Arte de la Lengua Chio Chiu* [Grammar of the Language of Changchiu]. Biblioteca de la Universidad de Barcelona.

Penny, Kalph. 1991. *A history of the Spanish language.* Cambridge: Cambridge University Press.

Pharies, David A. 2007. *A brief history of the Spanish language.* Chicago: The University of Chicago Press.

Takata, Tokio 高田時雄 2009. Sangley yu yanjiu de yi zhong ziliao Sangley 語研究的一種資料 [A manuscript relating to the study on Sangley language]. In Yiyuan Chen 陳益源 (ed.), *Minnan Wenhua Guoji Xueshu Yantaohui Lunwenji* 閩南文化國際學術研討會論文集 [Internal Conference on Min-nan Culture], 663-671. Kinmen: Cultural Affairs Bureau of Kinmen County.

Travis, Lisa de Mena. 2010. *Inner aspect: The articulation of VP.* Dordrecht: Springer.

Vendler, Zero. 1957. *Verbs and times. The Philosophical Review* 66.2: 143-160.

Wei, Peichuan 魏培泉. 1997. Lun gudai hanyu zhong jizhong chuzhishi zai fazhan zhong de fen yu he 論古代漢語中幾種處置式在發展中的分與合 [Split and merger in the development of several disposals in early Chinese]. *Chinese Language and Linguistics* 4: 555-594.

Yang, Hsiufang 楊秀芳. 2001. The forms and meaning of the word「解」jie: A historical perspective. *Language and Linguistics* 2.2: 261-297.

Yue, Anne O. 1999. The Min translation of the Doctrina Christiana. *Journal of Chinese Monograph Series* 14: 42-76.

Chapter 2

Language contact, wishful thinking or bad fieldwork? How to make sense of consistent language documentation in missionary sources

Henning Klöter
Humboldt-Universität zu Berlin – Department of Asian and African Studies
henning.kloeter@hu-berlin.de

Abstract

In the first part of the chapter, some of the earliest missionary sources documenting the Hokkien variety spoken by Chinese settlers in Manila during the 17th century will be introduced. By looking at the contents and explanatory devices found in these sources, I will then examine the purpose behind the compilation of these grammars and dictionaries. Were they analytical treatises, teaching manuals or field notes or a bit of everything? Finally, I will point out that some data in the sources display a remarkably high degree of consistency. For example, the second person singular pronoun is almost always transcribed as *lu*. In modern dialects, however, the forms of this and other examples vary considerably. How can this be explained? Do the sources consistently describe the language as it was spoken, or did the missionary compilers 'manipulate' their data? If the latter was the case, what would have been the reason for doing so?
Keywords: Missionary linguistics, Early Manila Hokkien, fieldwork, language and metalanguage

1. Introduction

This paper builds on previous research on the earliest linguistic documentation of Southern Min dialects by Western missionaries (Ang 2014; Klöter 2009, 2011, 2016, 2017; Kwok 2018: 157–160; Loon 1966, 1967).[1] These documents, together with Chinese documents of the same period (Lien 2009, 2010, 2013), are

---

1   Two types of sources can be distinguished: dictionaries and grammars. The former include the *Bocabulario de la lengua sangleya por las letraz de el A.B.C.* (anonymous, 222 ff. British Library, London), the *Dictionario Hispanico Sinicum* (anonymous, UST Archives, Manila), the *Vocabulario*

valuable materials for the study of Southern Min language history, including Taiwanese. Without exception, the Western documents are manuscripts written by European missionaries, presumably in the first half of the seventeenth century. These missionaries, mostly Spaniards, were part of the Spanish colonial administration in the Philippines. The fact that the beginning of the seventeenth century also witnessed a rapid growth of the Chinese population in the Philippines explains why Spanish missionaries became interested in the Chinese language, or, more precisely, the Southern Min dialects spoken by the Chinese settlers (referred to as 'Sangleys' in western documents). Although only one document contains solid bibliographical information with regard to the year of compilation and authorship, internal textual evidence helps us to narrow down the compilation period to the first half of the seventeenth century (Klöter 2011). In a previous publication (Klöter 2011, chapter 6), I have argued that the language of the Sangleys is a contact variety with features of different Southern Min dialects, including Zhangzhou, Quanzhou, and Chaozhou, and I proposed to label it as 'Early Manila Hokkien'. Later Kwok (2018: 160) has convincingly argued in favor of a stronger Zhangzhou identity of the data.

In terms of genre, the Chinese and Western sources are fundamentally different. The former are mostly printed editions of early stage plays; they abound with dialogic examples but lack explanations on language use or any kind of metalinguistic hint as to how the sentences were actually pronounced some 400 years ago. Western sources, on the other hand, are fairly explicit on a metalinguistic level, but lack the wealth of example sentences found in Chinese sources. The use of transcription systems and explicit explanations of pronunciation, word formation, and sentence structure may give a misleading impression of obviousness. A close reading of the sources reveals, however, that explicitness is not the same as obviousness. The main argument of this chapter is therefore that a proper understanding of the linguistic information documented in early Western sources requires a good understanding of their nature. By 'nature', I refer to the interplay of three interrelated features, i.e. materiality of the sources, intentionality of the author, and accessibility of language data. I argue that the combination of these three factors helps us to better distinguish missionary linguistics in this period from later periods. It is also argued that an understanding of the nature of missionary documents as defined here is necessary if we want to make sense of their contents, notably the way certain linguistic phenomena are described.

Hispanico y Chinico (anonymous, UST Archives, Manila), and the *Dictionarium Sino Hispanicum* (P. Petrus Chirino, 1604. Biblioteca Angelica, Rome). The only extant grammar is the anonymous *Arte de la lengua Chio Chiu*, one copy of which is kept at the British Library in London and one in the library of the University of Barcelona.

My analysis remains restricted to Sinitic sources and thus to the (Western) history of Chinese linguistics. In terms of their material properties, the sources are, as mentioned, all manuscripts. To state the obvious, manuscripts usually exist in much smaller numbers than printed books, and their dissemination therefore remains much more restricted. From the perspective of the missionaries, dissemination beyond the local church was by no means intended, since the manuscripts were compiled for didactic purposes. Nonetheless, scholars in Europe had a keen interest in these sources, since they were the only access to language data. By contrast, two hundred years later, grammars and dictionaries were written by missionaries and printed and published by missionary presses. This happened with the explicit purpose to contribute to European scholarship. At the same time, due to the growing presence of Europeans of various professional backgrounds in China after the middle of the nineteenth century, language data became much more accessible and, by implication, missionaries lost their monopoly as the sole gatherers and analyzers of language data.

2. Missionaries as fieldworkers?

The Norwegian linguist Even Hovdhaugen once referred to missionaries as "the first professional field workers" (1996: 14): "They listened to the new languages and tried to speak them ... from the very beginning and with a rudimentary knowledge of the language in question, they worked with informants ... and they started to collect words ranging from small handwritten vocabularies for their fellow brethren to extensive dictionaries" (ibid.). As a result, a huge body of linguistic documentation, such as wordlists, dictionaries, grammars and teaching manuals, were produced by missionaries who had learned hitherto unknown languages through direct intercourse with native speakers in remote regions of the Americas, Africa and Asia, including the Hokkien documents discussed in this paper.

Hovdhaugen's missionary/fieldworker comparison certainly sheds some light on neglected aspects of a missionary's sideline job. At the same time, however, if taken literally, it invites some critical questions: If language documentation by missionaries is comparable to fieldwork, to what extent does this fieldwork qualify as "professional"? What is the difference between a "missionary linguist" and a "non-missionary linguist"? Is it justified at all to speak of "missionary linguistics" as a distinct chapter in the history of linguistics? When it comes to the access to original language data, the missionary/fieldworker comparison is fully justified. As a matter of fact, before the middle of the nineteenth century, the most crucial difference between missionary linguists and secular language scholars lay in the degree of access to first hand language data. Whereas early language scholars based at European academies resembled "armchair linguists" who typically do not "conduct original research on any language" (cf. Crowley 2007: 12), missionaries are closer to the notion of "dirty-feet linguists" who "provide the fodder upon which many armchair linguists depend" (ibid.). The question of accessibility should not be underestimated. Even after reports about hitherto unknown peoples, cultures and languages had shaken the European worldview after the sixteenth century, it was beyond imagination for the overwhelming majority of people in Europe to even think of travelling to those remote places by themselves. To be sure, missionaries were not the only monopoly holders of access to remote areas. Stolz and Warnke rightly point out that "a noticeable number of linguists of the times did not belong to any missionary society or religious order" (2015: 4). On the other hand, however, since the main focus of relevant research during the past two decades has been on missionaries and their contributions to language documentation and linguistic analysis, this paper will not pursue the question as to how to distinguish missionary linguistics from colonial linguistics. More importantly, when it comes to the history of Chinese linguistics in Europe after the sixteenth and before the late nineteenth century, it becomes obvious that the major contributions came from missionaries (cf. Uchida 2017, chapter 2; Harbsmeier 1998: 9).

Whereas similarities between missionaries and fieldworkers cannot be denied, the comparison should not be stretched too far. Differences between the two are significant insofar as they shed light on the nature of documents left behind by missionaries and, related to this, help us to better understand how to read the documents. One important difference between missionaries and fieldworkers lies in the intention behind learning and documenting languages. Modern linguistic fieldworkers, although willing to get their feet dirty, are still devoted to linguistics as an academic field, with its theories, terminologies, questions, and hypotheses. The devotions of early missionaries in the fields, on the other hand, were completely different. They needed to achieve a good command of a language in order to succeed in their proselytizing efforts; language learning and documentation were thus by definition subordinate to the success of the mission. And, more importantly, they had the liberty not to care at all about linguistic theories in faraway Europe. Another important difference lies in the verifiability of the documented data. To be sure, comparing a missionary equipped only with his ears, his mouth and a quill with a fieldworker of the digital era is in itself lopsided. Nonetheless, it has to be kept in mind that the absence of modern recording and reproduction techniques and the monopoly of contact with native speakers invited inaccuracy and even forgery.

If the documents discussed in this paper were not written with the intention to contribute to an academic discipline, then we have to ask: For what purpose were they written? Generally speaking, it is broadly accepted that the "purpose of missionary linguistics is mainly didactic" (Zwartjes and Hovdhaugen 2004: 2). To a great extent, the linguistic competence of missionaries was shaped through concrete experience, such as spoken interaction with members of the indigenous population and exchange of goods. Just as importantly, it was shaped through formal teaching by tutors, which included members of the indigenous population and/or missionaries who had succeeded in acquiring a sufficient language competence. Thus, when looking at linguistic documents written by missionaries, notably manuscripts, we have to keep in mind that these were typically written with the purpose to help newly arriving missionaries learn the language. As I will discuss in the next paragraph, this does not rule out that they were received as grammatical treatises or other kinds of linguistic documents to be cited and analyzed by European scholars. We thus have to be aware of the fact that these manuscripts represent a convergence of what are nowadays considered very different types of texts, i.e. fieldnotes, teaching manuals and reference works, such as grammars and dictionaries. As emphasized above, from the perspective of intentionality, these manuscripts were teaching manuals. This does, however, not rule out the possibility of manuscripts unintendedly turning into reference works of European scholars.

It is impossible to state with certainty how many manuscripts documenting a Chinese language were written prior to the nineteenth century. As pointed out above, manuscripts were hardly ever written with the intention to be used outside the 'inner circle' of the mission, and many manuscripts largely remained undiscovered and unnoticed by the outside world. An example of such a case is the Portuguese-Chinese manuscript dictionary attributed to the famous Jesuit missionaries Matteo Ricci (1552–1610) and Michele Ruggieri (1543–1607).[2] Compiled during the late sixteenth century, the manuscript was brought to the Jesuit archives in Rome and remained unnoticed for some 200 years, until it was discovered by Pasquale D'Elia (1890–1963) in the first half of the twentieth century (Zwartjes 2011: 286). Against this background, the "fate" of the Hokkien *Arte de la lengua chio chiu* (hereafter: *Arte*) must be considered an exception rather than a rule, since it became known to European scholarship at a very early stage. It was the German proto-sinologist Gottlieb Bayer (1694–1738), a scholar at the St. Petersburg Academy of Sciences, who published a Latin translation in his book *Museum Sinicum* in 1730. The *Museum Sinicum* is "a collection of theoretical essays,

---

2   Authorship of Ricci and Ruggieri should not be taken for granted, cf. Barreto (2002).

long and short, on the Chinese language, literature, grammar, origins of the script, lexicography, dialects, and materials leading towards a full-fledged dictionary, based largely on the works of earlier Jesuits" (Honey 2001: 24). It is noteworthy that the flow of linguistic information from China to Russia had not been as smooth as Bayer had hoped for. For a long time, he had asked Jesuit missionaries in China to send him the first-hand sources he needed, but to no avail. They only arrived when the *Museum Sinicum* had been ready for printing. Lundbæk ironically describes "the situation of the young scholar who had conceived of the idea of writing a book on Chinese language and literature in the wilderness of Peter the Great's Russia. The book is finished and being printed; there is no time to make corrections or additions. And now the material is arriving which he should have had all the time – the fundamental texts and dictionaries" (Lundbæk 1986: 100). The *Museum Sinicum* must be considered the first printed book in the history of Chinese linguistics in Europe that contains a Hokkien grammar, i.e. the *Arte* (London ms.). According to Lundbæk, Bayer included the grammar, as he "felt it was important as an example of a language or dialect in which the sounds and the tonal system were very different from those of the standard Mandarin" (1986: 129). The *Museum Sinicum* is presumably also the first European publication representing a functional change of a manuscript written by a missionary: Handwritten by a missionary "in the field" as a teaching manual, it became a part of an academic treatise to be read by European scholars. This functional change came along with a transformation from manuscript to print and a translation from Spanish to Latin, the language of European scholarship. It needs to be emphasized that Bayer's translation contains many mistakes, since he was unable to establish meaningful matches between the Spanish metalanguage and the Southern Min examples. Bayer acknowledged his inability to make sense of the source text. The fact that he nonetheless included it in his *Museum Sinicum* shows his eagerness to present examples of authentic language use. In his days, these were scarce, and for European scholars, availability was a matter of chance, persistence, and even boldness.

3. Reading the *Arte de la langua chio chiu*

As stated above, the prime purpose behind the compilation of manuscript grammars and dictionaries in the early period of Chinese missionary linguistics was the teaching of newly arriving missionaries. The *Arte* contains many pieces of textual evidence in support of this claim. An example in case is the explanation following the section on pronunciation, which reads as follows (*Arte*, Barcelona ms., f. 2v, left column, English translation in Klöter 2011: 187):

todas las diferençias dichas sen / tenderan claramente açiendo a / un chino pronunçiar los exen / plos puestos y los que se siguin / Para quel que comiença[n] sea / perfecta lengua procure desde / al prinçipio aprender con perfec / tion estas tonadas y luego le dé / un sanglei el exerçiçio / aunque la pratica [se la ensene] / el padre ministro en el bocabu / lario se pondran todas las ton / adas para aprender desde / el prinçipio con per-fection[3]

This short passage gives relatively clear instructions on how to use the *Arte* in teaching/learning contexts. It is not entirely clear, however, what kind of "practice" is referred to in the sentence "a Father Minister will teach the practice". Is it a particular way of instructing learners that could be distinguished from *exerçiçio* 'exercise'? Or is this sentence hinting at the religious practice, i.e. the performance of religious rituals in the local language, which was an essential part of missionary work. In the case of the Chinese in the Philippines, some of the documents used in Church services, such as translations of Christian prayer texts into Early Manila Hokkien, have been reproduced in Loon (1967). Irrespective of the sort of 'practice' mentioned here, the paragraph gives a clear indication that language teaching involved native speakers and non-native speakers of Early Manila Hokkien (EMH). This division of tasks is also visible in the arrangement of the text, as exemplified by Figure 1.

A short explanation of a linguistic phenomenon (the upper half) is typically followed by a few examples. For the examples, three levels of representation must be distinguished: (1) Transcription, (2) Chinese characters, (3) gloss/translation. The fact that the EMH example has a digraphic representation (romanization combined with characters, columns 1 & 2) is noteworthy, since such an arrangement only makes sense if a native speaker was indeed involved in the teaching practice. To be sure, one could also argue that Chinese characters are culturally authentic and therefore the 'default script'. But then, on the other hand, the *Arte* does not contain a single sentence about Chinese characters and whether or how they should be learned. Chinese writing and relevant cultural knowledge were obviously not part of the curriculum.

---

3   All these differences will be understood clearly when these and the following examples are pronounced by a Chinese speaker. In order for the beginner to learn the language with perfection he should try from the beginning to learn these tones perfectly. Then he should be given a Sangley for exercise, although a Father Minister will teach the practice. In order to learn with perfection from the beginning, all tones are indicated in the vocabulary.

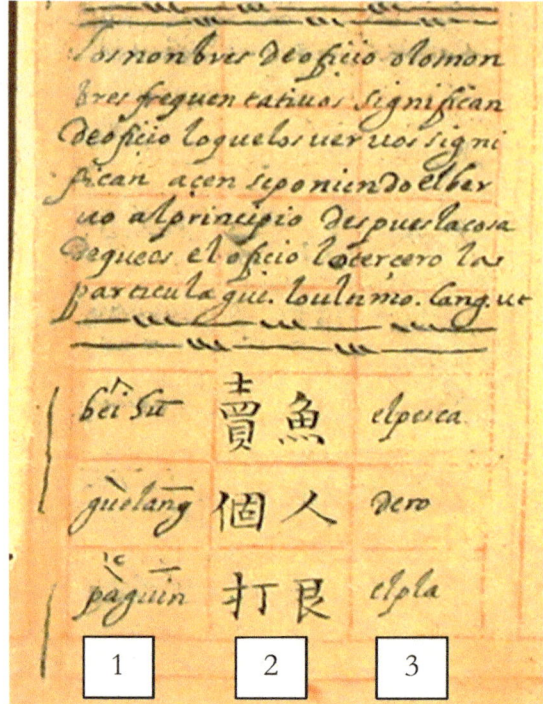

Figure 1: *Arte*, f. 5r, left column (excerpt)

This particular arrangement therefore needs to be distinguished from later attempts by Bayer and others to print Chinese characters, following the belief that characters were the (only) culturally legitimate Chinese script. As DeFrancis points out, until the middle of the nineteenth century, "there was still almost unanimous agreement among experts and amateurs alike that the Chinese language should be characterized as exceedingly difficult, uniquely monosyllabic, and, most important of all, necessarily ideographic in its written form" (1950: 18). Instead, we may imagine a small group of newly arrived missionaries being taught by two teachers. The native speakers would recite the characters, and the student(s) would match the pronunciation to the transcription. Although there is no textual evidence in proof of this scenario, it seems the most obvious assumption. We may even go a step further and claim that a native tutor also wrote the characters, since they were obviously not written by a western hand.

The presentation of examples shows that when reading a missionary document, one has to make sense of and explain details which are simply there, without obvious significance. Vice versa, one often has to critically question the obviousness of details which are claimed explicitly. As stated in the introduction, when reading missionary documents, we have to keep in mind that explicitness is not the same as obviousness. To give one example: From the sources I have consulted so far, the system of personal pronouns in Early Manila Hokkien seems to be very regular, as shown in Table 1.

Table 1: EMH personal pronouns

Pronoun	EMH
1.sg	gua^2
2.sg	lu^2
3.sg	i^1
1.pl exclusive	$guan^2$
1.pl inclusive	lan^2
2.pl	lun^3
3.pl	in^1

The high degree of consistency between the sources seems to suggest a regular pattern, i.e. a final <-n> indicating the plural. However, if we accept that explicitness is not the same as obviousness, we have to ask whether it is obvious that EMH displayed this sort of regularity in the formation of plural personal pronouns. The question suggests itself, since most (if not all) Hokkien dialects documented elsewhere do not display this kind of regularity. Since it seems impossible to provide an unambiguous answer to this question, I will briefly discuss four different arguments in support of two different answers. First, we accept the transcription as it stands and assume that the system of EMH personal pronouns corresponded to the data in Table 1. Language contact could be a possible explanation for the differences between EMH and other Hokkien dialects. Second, we question the transcription and assume that the missionaries simply misheard linguistic details. This would bring us back to the missionary/ fieldworker comparison. As Crowley points out, linguistic fieldworkers today run a similar risk. He writes that "we would like to believe that our field notes are completely free of judgements and that they contain nothing but objective reality. While we may readily jump to the conclusion that some other linguist's notes may be inaccurate, we sometimes seem to be less willing to say the same about our own notes" (Crowley 2007: 136f.). One reason for mishearing details, according to Crowley, is that "our perceptions of what we are hearing may sometimes be influenced by what we were expecting to hear in the first place" (2007: 137). Third, we question the transcription and assume that the missionary who wrote the *Arte* 'manipulated' the data on purpose. He could have done so out of didactic considerations, since regular patterns are easier to teach than irregular patterns. Since Hokkien speakers in Manila had different dialectal backgrounds, the missionary linguist also could have manipulated the data with the intention to define a (regular) standard to be superimposed on different competing forms. As I have pointed out elsewhere (Klöter 2011, chapter 4), personal pronouns are by no means the only 'questionable' examples in the *Arte*. On the basis of these examples we can argue that "any kind of structural parallelism in the target language fits better to an approach that looks for rules and regularities" (Klöter 2011: 110). If supporting evidence for the last two explanations could be found, the data as presented in the *Arte*, at least to some extent, would reflect wishful thinking rather than objective reality.

4. Concluding remarks: Missionaries as witnesses or contributors?[4]

On the basis of the comparison of missionaries with fieldworkers, this chapter has tried to sketch the nature of early missionary linguistics by elaborating on the materiality of the sources, the intentionality of the author, and the accessibility of language data in different historical periods. The argumentation has brought up a new question: Did missionaries 'manipulate' language data? Whereas a definite answer cannot be provided in this chapter, I want to conclude by emphasizing the importance of the question for document-based research on Sinitic language history. As fieldworkers, missionaries would qualify as witnesses of language use, and we would expect a high degree of 'objectivity'. There is, however, solid evidence of missionaries playing an active role as contributors to language change. In the history of Chinese linguistics, missionaries as contributors to language change have mostly been analyzed in the context of lexical innovations and their introduction through translation of Western scientific works (*inter alia* in Amelung 2001, Kurtz 2001, Shen 2001, Xiong 2001). The question whether missionaries may have considered themselves as language planners and whether this may have included the standardization of 'invented' linguistic features would require a broader comparative approach. An interesting case in this regard is discussed by Zwartjes (2011: 45). Analyzing the língua geral ('general language') of Brazil during the seventeenth century he asks whether "a certain 'general language' already existed as a lingua franca of the region before the Europeans arrived, or was such a 'general language' the product of European missionary activities?"

---

4   The question "missionaries as witnesses or contributors" goes back to Benjamin Tsou and his keynote speech at the 10th International Conference of Missionary Linguistics in Rome (Tsou 2018).

References

Amelung, Iwo. 2001. Weights and Forces: The reception of Western mechanics in late imperial China. In: Lackner, Michael, Iwo Amelung and Joachim Kurtz (eds.), *New Terms for New Ideas: Western knowledge and lexical change in late imperial China*. Leiden, Boston: Brill, pp. 197–232.

Ang, Uijin 洪惟仁. 2014. Shíliù, qī shìjì zhījiān Lǚsòng de Zhāngzhōu fāngyán 十六、七世紀之間呂宋的漳州方言 [The Zhāngzhōu dialect of Luzon between the 16th and the 17th century]. *Lìshǐ dìlǐ* 歷史地理 vol. 30, pp. 215–238.

Barreto, Luís Filipe. 2002. Reseña de "Dicionário Português-Chinês" de John W. Witek (ed.). *Bulletin of Portuguese/Japanese Studies* vol. 5: pp. 117–26.

Crowley, Terry. 2007. *Field Linguistics: A Beginner's Guide*. Oxford: Oxford University Press.

DeFrancis, John. 1950. Nationalism and Language Reform in China. Princeton: Princeton University Press.

Harbsmeier, Christoph. 1998. *Language and logic in traditional China* [= Science and Civilisation in China, vol. 7.3]. Cambridge: Cambridge University Press.

Honey, David B. 2001. *Incense at the altar: Pioneering sinologists and the development of classical Chinese philology*. New Haven: American Oriental Society.

Hovdhaugen, Even. 1996. Missionary Grammars: An attempt at defining a field of research. In: Even Hovdhaugen (ed.), *...and the Word was God: Missionary linguistics and missionary grammar*. Münster: Nodus Publikationen, pp. 9–22.

Klöter, Henning. 2009. The earliest Hokkien dictionaries. In Zwartjes, Otto, Ramón Arzápalo Marín & Thomas Smith-Stark (eds.), *Missionary linguistics IV: Lexicography. Selected papers from the Fifth International Conference on Missionary Linguistics, Mérida-Yucatán, 14–17 March 2007*. Amsterdam: John Benjamins, pp. 303–330.

Klöter, Henning. 2011. *The language of the Sangleys: A Chinese vernacular in missionary sources of the seventeenth century*. Leiden, Boston: Brill.

Klöter, Henning. 2016. Missionary Linguistics. In Sybesma, Rint, et al. (eds.), *Encyclopedia of Chinese Language and Linguistics* (ECLL), vol. 3. Leiden, Boston: Brill, pp. 41–46.

Klöter, Henning. 2017. China mission and linguistics: Early contributions by Catholic missionaries. Davor Antonucci & Pieter Ackerman (eds.), *Chinese Missionary Linguistics*. Leuven: Ferdinand Verbiest Institute, pp. 73–92.

Kwok, Bit-Chee. 2018. *Southern Mǐn: Comparative phonology and subgrouping*. London and New York: Routledge.

Kurtz, Joachim. 2001. Coming to terms with logic: The naturalization of an occidental notion in China. In: Lackner, Michael, Iwo Amelung and Joachim Kurtz (eds.), *New Terms for New Ideas: Western knowledge and lexical change in late imperial China*. Leiden, Boston: Brill, pp. 147–175.

Lien, Chinfa. 2009. The focus marker *si⁷* 是 and lexicalization of *si⁷ mih⁸* 是乜 into *what* WH-words in earlier Southern Min texts. *Language and Linguistics* vol. 10, no. 4, pp. 745–764.

Lien, Chinfa. 2010. The dual function of *liah⁸* 力 in *Li Jing Ji* 荔鏡記. *Journal of Chinese Linguistics* vol. 38, no. 1, pp. 45 – 69.

Lien, Chinfa. 2013. 'Why' and 'How' WH-words in Earlier Southern Min Texts: Interface of Inherent Properties of 'why/how' WH-words and their Syntactic Positions, *Language and Linguistics* vol. 14, no. 4, pp. 633–661.

Loon, Piet van der. 1966. The Manila incunabula and early Hokkien Studies (part 1). *Asia Major* vol. 12, pp. 1–43.

Loon, Piet van der. 1967. The Manila incunabula and early Hokkien Studies (part 2). *Asia Major* vol. 13, pp. 95–186.

Lundbæk, Knud. 1986. *T.S. Bayer (1694–1734): Pioneer Sinologist.* London and Malmö: Curzon Press.

Stolz, Thomas and Ingo H. Warnke. 2015. From missionary linguistics to colonial linguistics. In Zimmermann, Klaus and Birte Kellermeier-Rehbein (eds.), *Colonialism and Missionary Linguistics.* Berlin: De Gruyter, pp. 3–25.

Uchida, Keiichi. 2017. *A Study of Cultural Interaction and Linguistic Contact: Approaching Chinese linguistics from the periphery.* Göttingen: V&R unipress.

Shen, Guowei. 2001. The creation of Technical Terms in English-Chinese Dictionaries from the Nineteenth Century. In: Lackner, Michael, Iwo Amelung and Joachim Kurtz (eds.), *New Terms for New Ideas: Western knowledge and lexical change in late imperial China.* Leiden, Boston: Brill, pp. 287–304.

Tsou, Benjamin. 2018. Missionaries as Witnesses or Contributors to Consequential Changes in China? Dr Benjamin Hobson (1816-1873) in respect of Neologisms and Medicine. Plenary lecture presented at the *10th International Conference of Missionary Linguistics,* University of Rome "la Sapienza", 21–24 March 2018

Xiong, Yuezhi. 2001. 'Liberty', 'Democracy', 'President': The translation and usage of some political terms in late Qing China. In: Lackner, Michael, Iwo Amelung and Joachim Kurtz (eds.), *New Terms for New Ideas: Western knowledge and lexical change in late imperial China.* Leiden, Boston: Brill, pp. 69–93.

Zwartjes, Otto. 2011. *Portuguese Missionary Grammars in Asia, Africa and Brazil, 1550–1800.* Amsterdam, Philadelphia: John Benjamins.

Zwartjes, Otto, and Even Hovdhaugen, eds. 2004. *Missionary Linguistics / Lingüística misionera. Selected papers from the First International Conference on Missionary Linguistics, Oslo, 13–16 March 2003.* Amsterdam, Philadelphia: John Benjamins.

Chapter 3

West meets East
The influence of Dutch clergymen in 17th century Taiwan

Alexander Adelaar
Palacký University, Olomouc[1] Asia Institute, University of Melbourne

Abstract

This paper begins with a brief historical overview of the Dutch in Formosa (1627-1661) detailing the reasons they were there, the things they observed, and the ways they altered the local cultural and political landscape. It then concentrates on the Protestant clergymen who came in the wake of the Dutch East India Company. As a by-product of their missionary activities they collected data on some of the languages and cultures of western Taiwan which would become invaluable for a better understanding of that part of the island. Their scholarly achievements include the 'Discourse', a detailed ethnographic description written in 1628 by Georgius Candidius, and various texts and vocabularies documenting two Formosan languages, Siraya and Favorlang. The linguistic materials clearly signal some of the challenges the clergymen must have encountered while learning these languages and trying to use them in their religious teachings. They not only had to master the outlandish structures of these languages but also had to learn how they reflected a rather different conceptualisation of the world and all it contains. Finally, they had to figure out how they could adapt these languages in order to represent concepts and values that were typical of 17th century European culture as well as of the biblical world at the time of Christ. The chapter provides examples of some neologisms and linguistic circumscriptions used by the clergymen to that effect. It also relates a theological misunderstanding which occurred between a Favorlanger and a clergyman as a consequence of the latter's limited understanding of the former's speech.

1. The Dutch in Formosa: historical setting

The Dutch East India Company established a colony in Taiwan between 1624 and 1662. At the time, the island was known in Europe by its Portuguese name,

---

1 This publication was supported by the European Regional Development Fund Project "Sinophone Borderlands – Interaction at the Edges" CZ.02.1.01/0.0/0.0/16_019/0000791, and by the Institute of Linguistics, University of Cologne, where I was a visiting research fellow during Spring 2019.

Formosa. Initially, the reason why the Dutch came to Taiwan had little to do with the island itself. They were primarily interested in the trade between China and Japan, and had previously tried to get a foothold in Macau and in Fujian province. However, the Portuguese had already established trading posts in these areas before they arrived. The Dutch tried to oust them, but failed. They also made a series of diplomatic blunders towards the local Chinese authorities, after which they were forced to leave China. They decided to bide their time in a region nearby which was outside Chinese and Japanese territorial waters. They built Fort Zeelandia, a stronghold on Taiwan's southwest coast, in a place which would eventually become the city of Tainan. Their motive to be there was to stand by, waiting for a second chance to forge trade relations with the Chinese on the mainland. In the meantime, they wanted to establish some limited contact with the local population in order to obtain fresh food and other logistical support. They were also interested in the trade of deer skins. However, they would soon be dragged into local politics, eventually leading to the colonisation of parts of western and northern Taiwan.

2. Clergymen and their role in the colonisation process

The East India Company staff included some Protestant pastors, who were strongly motivated to engage with the locals and convert them to Christianity. They were also better organised than the other members of the staff and carried out their own regional and ethnic surveys. Through their scouting activities and local knowledge, they managed to make the general East India Company staff dependent on them, and gradually manipulated them into a more systematic colonisation of Southwest Taiwan.

In their missionary activities these clergymen sought to make an impact on the Siraya, a local Formosan population, through a combination of medical aid, education and religious instruction. They also tried to teach them improved agricultural techniques, and although the application of these techniques was successful in itself, it left the Siraya indifferent. It soon became clear to the clergymen that the only way to impress them was by giving them military support. After a series of incidents between the Dutch and various local Formosan communities, the East India Company joined the warriors of Sinkan village in their headhunting raids and helped them secure a head. They did so on the instigation of the clergymen (who incidentally were acting in blatant contravention of the rules of their Protestant home congregation). Their participation in a local war brought the Dutch instant acceptance and a willingness to convert among the residents of Sinkan. Through their alliance with the latter, they gradually conquered large parts of western and south-eastern Taiwan. They also added north-ern regions to their occupied territory by defeating the Spanish strongholds in Keelung and Tamsuy in 1642. Once their power was consolidated they intro-duced some changes that would have far-reaching social consequences for the Siraya and other local Formosans. In the Siraya-speaking regions of southwestern Taiwan, they merged sovereign villages, broke the power of the *inib*s (female shamans), and made drastic changes to marital law. *Inib*s were in control of reli-gious affairs and were the guardians of Siraya traditions and customary law. They were banished to an island off the coast of Taiwan, where most perished. Newly-weds were from then onwards encouraged to live together, and the young wives were allowed to bear children. Before, the communities had been matrilocal: brides would stay with their family, whereas bridegrooms stayed in a men's house and were only allowed to visit their wives on the sly. The latter were not allowed to have children until very late, and if they became pregnant, they had to undergo abortion, which was carried out by the *inib*s (Shepherd 1995a).

The Dutch changed a lot in the short period of their rule, and one wonders how they got away with such far-reaching acts of social engineering. Heartland Protestants in the Netherlands used to refer to the Formosan mission as one of their most successful conversion activities (Ginsel 1931), notwithstanding the fact that after the Dutch had left, Christianity disappeared in the area and was re-introduced centuries later by British missionaries. Interpretations like these are influenced by religious righteousness and chauvinism, and ask for an ethnograph-ically more informed explanation. The willingness of the Siraya to convert to Christianity and accept Dutch interference in their daily activities, which became part of Dutch domination, probably had little to do with the attraction of Chris-tianity as a doctrine. As the anthropologist John Shepherd (1995b:61-63) indi-cates, it was primarily motivated by Dutch military power and the prospect to make use of it in the ongoing headhunting activities of the Siraya. Success in local warfare and headhunting was the primary goal of the latter, and mandatory abor-tion as well as matrilocal residence, men's houses, and age groups were structur-ally dependent on a successful outcome of their expeditions against neighbouring communities. However, the Dutch with their new religion, new technology, and military strength, had managed to discredit the old Siraya religion. They were now recognised as an attractive alternative, which explains why the Siraya opened themselves to Dutch authority and religion. Shepherd (1995a) furthermore shows that the extremity of some of the practices abolished by the Dutch may have been a concomitant factor in their success. That is, there may have been unease among the Siraya about mandatory abortion and the fact that married couples were not allowed to live together. The power of the *inib*s was seemingly unchallenged when the Dutch arrived, and it is possible that their grip on society had become too extreme and therefore susceptible to change. A change would sooner or later have emerged from within Siraya society itself, but it is not difficult to imagine how it could have been precipitated through external intervention. From this vantage point, the "success" of the Dutch in intervening in local practices could also be explained by the likelihood that some of their reforms were overdue.

Candidius (1628) informs us that the Siraya practiced systematic abortion on women until they were in their mid-thirties or even older. Shepherd (1995a) tries to explain the reasons for this "mandatory abortion" as described in Candidius' Discourse and other 17th century Dutch sources. He also uses comparative evidence involving the Amis, currently one of the largest and best known Formosan ethnic groups with a language that is closely related to Siraya. He shows that population control, as advanced by Montesquieu (1758), Malthus (1803), and the anthropologist Ferrell (1971), cannot have been a motivation at any level for mandatory abortion among the Siraya. The population density in the Siraya region was very low (5.2 persons per square kilometre), people were healthy and tall, and there was a large supply of agricultural products and animal protein (the island was teeming with deer). Nor does Freudian psychology or gender inequality supply adequate explanations. Shepherd convincingly shows that in Siraya society mandatory abortion was intrinsically linked to the existence of male age grades and matrifocal households. In Siraya cosmology, anything to do with menstruation, pregnancy, childbirth and child rearing was considered as diminishing the chances of success in headhunting and warfare. Marriage at a young age was allowed but husband and wife continued to live separated for as long as the husband was still a warrior (until the age of forty). The wife stayed with her family, and the husband lived in a men's house, only being allowed to visit his wife in secret, who, as already mentioned, was not allowed to have children. In performing abortions, the *inibs* applied massage rather than using tools or foreign objects. Their method was less dangerous, although it was still hazardous and painful to the victim.

This marital arrangement would end when the man turned forty, at which point he stopped being a warrior and became a member of the community council for the next two years. From that period onwards, husband and wife would live together and have children. There has been uncertainty in the literature about the age at which Siraya women were allowed to have children, as the ethnographic sources mention figures varying between 39 and 36 or slightly younger. Shepherd (1995a:31-34) solves this riddle by showing that the critical factor here is not the absolute age of the women, but that of their husbands, who as a rule were older than their wives by a small but varying number of years. When they stopped being warriors at the age of forty, their wives' pregnancies were no longer a threat to their military career, and they could have children. Shepherd notes that this mystical link between wife and husband which is created by pregnancy and endangers head-hunting, also exists in many other Austronesian-speaking societies. Many of these also practice abortion by massage. (However, only among the Siraya had abortion become a mandatory way to prevent pregnancy from interfering with success in head-hunting [Shepherd 1995a:47fn.10]).

In 1662 the Dutch were defeated by the Chinese warlord Zheng Chenggong (also called Guo Xingye or Koxinga), who prohibited the Christian religion. When two centuries later the British Reverend William Campbell took up missionary work among the Siraya Christianity was no longer practiced in Taiwan. Zheng Chenggong's prohibition was no doubt an important factor in this end result. However, another factor may have been the way Siraya had responded to Dutch influence, which was basically utilitarian. They opened themselves to Christianity only after the Dutch had given support to their headhunting expeditions and had led them to victory. They hitherto had counted on their traditional deities for support in warfare but then discovered that the Dutch were a more solid guarantee of success. The adoption of Christianity did not necessarily mean that the old deities were rejected, but rather that they were relegated to the background in a pantheon-like arrangement. The defeat of the Dutch showed that their God was also not infallible: as He no longer provided protection in the new circumstances that had arisen under Zheng Chenggong's occupation, it was His turn to be shifted to the background. As years went by with no sign of the Dutch coming back, their God may have gradually disappeared from the Siraya pantheon.

3. Ethnographic legacy

The primary source of information on Taiwan left by the 17th-century Dutch is Georgius Candidius' (1628) *Discourse*. Shepherd (1995a:1; 1995b:454fn.1) and Blussé et al. (1999:ix) are impressed with its accuracy and eye for detail, and they generally do not doubt its ethnographic precision. Its information is moreover corroborated by that of other sources, including an earlier account from Jacob Constant and Barent Pessaert, two merchants who paid a short visit to the village of Sulang in 1623 (see below).

The *Discourse* is a detailed description of parts of South West Taiwan and its people. It has remained a major ethnographic and historical source ever since it was written. It gives an account of the region's geography, flora, and fauna. It also describes the agricultural, fishing, and hunting practices of the Siraya people and their social organisation, including a gender-based labour division, the role of age groups and councils, the exertion of authority, marital practices, religion and the institution of *inibs*, weddings, death and burial practices, headhunting, and local warfare. It also gives information on local trade and its prospects, and on the influence of the Chinese and the Japanese.

The 1623 account of Jacob Constant and Barent Pessaert is part of the daily records of *Fort Zeelandia* (Blussé and Roessingh 1984; Blussé et al. 1999:4-22). While interesting, it is less detailed than the *Discourse*.

4. Linguistic legacy

The Dutch clergymen left a large corpus of material for two languages, Siraya and Favorlang, which belong to separate branches of Austronesian and differ considerably from one another. Siraya is represented in two dialects, the Gospel dialect and the Utrecht Manuscript dialect. Apart from a few odd developments (such as "lexical prefixes" and "anticipating sequences" in the Gospel dialect) it is typologically not unlike many other Austronesian languages, and as such its appearance and structure has much in common with Philippine languages. By comparison, Favorlang seems more idiosyncratic in both its phonology and grammar.

Five main linguistic sources of Siraya and Favorlang have survived the last 360 years:

1) a Siraya translation of the Gospels of Saint Matthew and Saint John (174 + 141 pages of Siraya-Dutch text, published by Gravius [1661]);
2) a Siraya translation of a catechism (288 pages of Siraya-Dutch text, published by Gravius [1662]);
3) an extensive wordlist and five short conversations in the Utrecht Manuscript dialect, kept in the Utrecht municipal library for almost two centuries before it was published by Vlis (1842);
4) a Favorlang-Dutch dictionary of 77 pages compiled by Happart (1650);
5) a corpus of 101 pages of Favorlang texts, of which 75 pages have a Dutch translation; they were collected by Vertrecht between 1647 and 1651 (Vertrecht no date, 1888).

The Gospel of Saint John was considered lost or even non-existent until 2019, when it was rediscovered in the Royal Library of Denmark.[2] Both the Favorlang dictionary and Favorlang texts were kept as manuscripts in the Batavia Church Council, where they were rediscovered in 1839. Happart's dictionary was subsequently published by Hoëvell (1842). Meanwhile, a new version augmented with

---

2   It was rediscovered by Christopher Joby from Adam Mickiewicz University, Poznań (Posen).

English glosses was prepared by Medhurst (1840). Vertrecht's texts were published in 1888 by an unknown editor (see Vertrecht [no date]).

At the end of the 19th century, Campbell published some of the Siraya and Favorlang sources again in annotated form. Campbell (1888) is a new edition of Gravius' Gospel of Saint Matthew augmented with a parallel text in English. The latter is simply the King James version of Saint Matthew's Gospel and therefore of limited use for comparison with the Siraya text. Campbell (1896) combines the works of Happart and Vertrecht, adding Medhurst's English translation to the dictionary.

The 17th century Siraya and Favorlang materials left behind by the Dutch have been discussed more recently in several scholarly publications concerning the grammar, texts, and lexicon of these languages, including Adelaar (2011, 2013), Ogawa (2003) and Li (2019).

The Siraya materials have also been the basis for an impressive language revitalisation effort by Edgar Macapili, Uma Talavan, Jimmy Huang, Shih Chao-kai, Te Nga-gi and others, resulting in the publication of various Siraya teaching materials (see below).

The original 17th century sources are difficult to access. The following account concentrates on Siraya, which is the language I am most familiar with, but in general, it also applies to the Favorlang data (Ogawa 2003: Introduction; Li 2019: Introduction).

A major problem with the Siraya materials is that they are not linguistically uniform. The wordlist is fairly extensive but it represents the Utrecht Manuscript dialect. It therefore can only partly be used to decode the Gospel text or the Catechism, and often only through the application of comparative linguistic methodology.

Another issue involving the Siraya materials is their unstable spelling, which is moreover based on 17th century Dutch orthography. Dutch has a very different phonology from Siraya, and it is to be expected that some relevant Siraya sound distinctions may have become lost when this language was transcribed in the Dutch orthography. That is not the only problem: as well as being ill-equipped to cater to the phonological peculiarities of Siraya, Dutch spelling also had some instability of its own. The (northern) Netherlands had recently become independent and was still trying to achieve its own national spelling unification, which was plagued by competing traditions. Although the official Dutch translation of the Bible, the Statenbijbel, had been published around that time (1637) and would have a certain influence on spelling unification, its influence was probably still too early to play a regulating role in the spelling of the Siraya texts. Although the two Gospels and Catechism were published under Daniel Gravius' name, from the archival materials of the Dutch in Taiwan it is clear that Gravius was only the last in a line of translators/editors, including, among others, Candidius. Reading the Gospel of Matthew easily gives the impression that there is some random spelling variation. However, a careful counting of instances of each different spelling form shows that the initial chapters are consistently different from later chapters in their choice of spelling, and that the turning point is roughly around chapter 21, showing that from here onwards a new editor must have taken over from a previous one.

Also cumbersome was the habit of the authors to use hyphens between parts of a word where one part looked like an affix but was in fact part of the root. Segmenting a derived word between the root and a real affix can be helpful, as with *mu-*[3] 'movement towards', which is distinguished with a hyphen from the root *kua* 'going/being' in the derivation *mu-kua* 'to go to'. But it can seriously wrong-foot the uninitiated in cases like *mu-tus* ('mou-tous' in the original spelling), where *mu-* is no affix but part of the root *mutus* 'mouth'. Here, the hyphen has no function at all and is misleading.

A final problem is the language of the Siraya Gospel and Catechism. The difficulties when reading 360-year old texts are sometimes daunting enough, but but here it is complicated even further by the style of the original Dutch bible and catechism translations which served as a basis for the Siraya texts. Compared to the King James Bible with its relatively loose style, the Statenbijbel is closer to the original Hebrew and Greek, and more difficult to appreciate and comprehend. This too had its effect on the Siraya texts as final products.

5. Importance of the linguistic legacy.

While the efforts of the clergymen to convert the Siraya eventually did not amount to much, their educational efforts left a more lasting legacy. After the Dutch had left Taiwan, the Siraya continued to use their Dutch-based orthography in bilingual Chinese-Siraya land contracts for another 120 years. These contracts protected them to some extent against Chinese migrants, who needed land and were expanding at the expense of the locals. They are important specimens of 18th century Siraya. They were composed by Siraya speakers themselves and may therefore claim a greater authenticity than that of the 17th century liturgical texts, which were composed by Dutch clergymen and show a great deal of language engineering in the coining of biblical terms. On the other hand, the contracts are highly formulaic and lack the grammatical and lexical variation of the gospel text, which makes

---

3   In order to avoid possible confusion caused by spelling variation in the 17th century Siraya texts, I write Siraya words in the rationalised spelling that I devised in Adelaar (2011).

their reading very difficult. They have been studied by the historian Weng Chia-yin (1989, 1990a, 1990b) and the linguist Paul Jen-kuei Li (2010).

Another after-effect of the clergymen's efforts to educate the Siraya, albeit a very indirect one, is the Siraya revitalisation project that has been going on since 1999. In that year, various members of the Siraya community (both Christians and traditional believers) founded the Tainan Pepo Siraya Cultural Association, in an endeavour to retrieve their cultural heritage and to obtain official tribal status from the Taiwanese government. The Association is chaired by Mrs. Uma Talavan. It has become the leading activist group in the Siraya renaissance movement and has been active in many projects, such as the organization of various summer camps for the promotion of Siraya language and culture (since 2007), as well as teacher-training seminars and language classes in various elementary and secondary schools (since 2009), the compilation of various trilingual Siraya-Chinese-English dictionaries (Macapili 2008, 2021), and the development of other language course material (including Macapili 2002, 2008; Macapili et al. 2010).

The 17th century Siraya and Favorlang materials are also invaluable for pure linguistic research. Typologically, they not only broaden our understanding of the structure of Austronesian languages, but they also enrich our insights into language diversity in general. For historical linguistics, they are an essential missing link in the historical study of Austronesian languages, providing various clues for the classification of these languages and for the reconstruction of their common (hypothetical) stock language, Proto Austronesian. They also provide critical evidence for the study of Taiwan's prehistory and culture history more generally. The reason why they are so important for the history of the Austronesian language family is that they are Formosan languages. There are about 1200 Austronesian languages. However, whereas almost all Austronesian languages (whether they are spoken in South East Asia, Madagascar or the Pacific) belong to one single branch of Austronesian (called Malayo-Polynesian), there are only a handful of other languages (about 20 in total) which belong to other branches that had split off (very early onwards) from the "Austronesian language tree". These are the Formosan languages. They are genetically not only very different from Malayo-Polynesian languages, but often also from one another. The fact that Formosan languages belong to separate "primary branches" makes them of great value for language classification and for the reconstruction of the Proto Austronesian language, material culture, and social organisation, especially if this evidence is combined with data from history, archaeology, and anthropology.

6. A theological misunderstanding

The Favorlang texts are largely meant for religious education. They include sermons, prayers, religious instruction about baptisms, and other theological teaching materials. One text stands out because it gives us a glimpse of the difficulties faced by the Dutch clergymen in their effort to convert the Favorlang tribespeople, no matter how much they may have believed in their chances to succeed. In it, a clergyman is presented as a 'Stranger' (Dutch '*Vreemdeling*') and his Favorlang conversation partner as '*Terner*' (? meaning unknown). The Stranger warns the Terner against believing in *Haibos*, the Favorlang main deity, and in the songs of a little bird called *Adam*. "All lies", the Stranger says, "because the birds sing without discrimination: how can such a little bird be the prophet of *Haibos*?" "But why then", the Terner replies, "should *Haibos* have given the name of *Adam* to this little bird?" The Stranger explains that "by mocking the first man, the villain might have led him to the path of terror."

In order to understand the underlying misunderstanding in this conversion, one should know that in Favorlang, *aðam* is a general word for omen birds and has nothing to do with the biblical figure Adam. Once that becomes clear, one might still wonder who was causing the confusion, and who was being confused: the Dutch Stranger, the Favorlang clansman, or the translator?[4]

7. Polysemy in Siraya

When the Dutch arrived in southwestern Taiwan, they had to familiarise themselves with the local languages, which were very different from the European languages they were used to. A completely different grammar and phonology were not the only difficulties they were facing. Siraya vocabulary was also rather unusual, caused by the fact that Siraya speakers had different ways of dividing up the world around them, singling out what was important to them, and backgrounding what was not. The meaning associations they used to make must also have been outlandish and difficult to follow to the Dutch.

---

4   The word *aðam* has many cognates in Austronesian languages and derives from Proto Austronesian *qayam 'bird'. In Malayo-Polynesian languages (Austronesian languages outside Taiwan) the meaning of *qayam basically shifted to that of 'domestic animal' and developed further into cognate forms usually referring to 'fowl' but occasionally also to 'pet' (in Iban, Borneo), 'animal' (Palauan), 'dog' (Old Tagalog and some other Philippine languages), or 'pig' (Murik, in Borneo). In Old Javanese, the word is also reflected in *Hayam Wuruk*, the name of a famous 14th century Javanese king. Those familiar with Indonesian and Malaysian cuisines will no doubt recognise *ayam* 'chicken', which features prominently on the menu list in Indonesian and Malaysian restaurants.

For instance, Siraya makes a direct association between darkness and thinking, as seen in the following set of derivations based on *dendem/rendem*: compare *ma-remdem* 'dark' with *pax-demdem* 'to think' and *na da-remdem* 'thoughts'.[5]

Another example is the root *iup*. It means 'trumpet' and reflects an earlier (Proto Austronesian) *Seyup 'to blow'. It has the following derivations: *m-iup* 'to extinguish, go out (fire)' and *iup-an* 'ghost, spirit'. The latter word also refers to the Holy Spirit in the phrase *Iup-an ka dīlix ma-tiktik* ('the Spirit which is truly just/honest') in the Siraya Gospel.

The root *litu* or *litäw* refers to demons, spirits, and devils. In conjunction with the verb *pa-ato* ('produce smoke'), *litäw ka pa-ato* (literally 'spirit producing smoke') it means 'incense'. The verbal derivation *m-u-litu* means 'to enter, take possession (of a demon)'. The relation between spirit, in the sense of demon or ghost, and spirit, for alcohol or perfume, is relatively easy to follow for speakers of English (compare 'Holy Spirit' and 'alcoholic spirits') and for Dutchmen provided they are familiar with English or classical languages. Whether this also applied to Siraya speakers is not obvious. More likely than not, incense was a concept introduced by non-Formosans (Dutch or Chinese), and so was its name *litäw ka pa-ato*, even if its constituent parts are Siraya.

An interesting peek into the way Siraya thought of the body and mind are the associations made with the words referring to these notions. The root *xinawa* basically means 'breath' but it is also used for 'mind'. So is *rix*, which primarily means 'neck' but is also used for 'mind' and 'centre of the senses'.[6] Derivations with *rix* are *p-u-ra-rix* 'to have in mind' (also *pukidi p-u-ra-rix* 'to think, have an idea') and *ka-rix-aŋ* 'sacred period, monthly period of ten days during which conjugal relations are taboo'. The latter term is discussed in Shepherd [1995a:25, 42] but does not occur in the 17th century Dutch language materials. Its rather narrow meaning should probably be interpreted as the semantic specification of a more general notion of "mindfulness" (in its original sense of attentiveness, and watchfulness). It is not clear whether it also refers to menstruation (although the inference is difficult to avoid).

The bound verb *smaki-* has the meaning of throwing. For instance, *smaki-mala* 'throw out', and *smaki-vauŋ* 'throw into the sea', where *-mala* means 'outside, and *vauŋ* 'sea'. However, prefixation to the root *nanaŋ* 'name' yields *smaki-nanaŋ* 'to cast a name, call', indicating a different relationship between a person (or object) and its designation than in a western context.

---

5   'x' was presumably pronounced as a soft (voiced) counterpart of the 'g' in Dutch, or the 'ch' in German *ich* 'I' etc.

6   In the same way as such extended meanings apply to the heart in European languages, and to the liver (*hati*) in Malay.

The root *vuil* 'belly' also occurs in the derivation *ka-vuil-an* (and in the reduplicated forms *ka-vui-vuil-an* and *ka-va-vui-vuil-an*), where it means 'lineage, tribe'
or 'generation'. A similar association between 'belly' (or, more precisely, 'womb')
and matrilinear 'lineage' exists in the Minangkabau language (Sumatra) and in
matrilineal societies of central Africa (Vuyk 1991).[7]

Finally, the term *täi-apara* stands for 'brother' in the Gospel text. It consists
of a verbal element *täi-* 'reside, be with' and a complement *a-para* 'be together',
and its literal meaning must be '(those) living together'. It is never used for 'sister'.
This suggests that it refers to the relationship between members of a men's house
rather than to real siblings.

8. The creation of new Siraya concepts through bible translation:

The Siraya language material contains many words (neologisms) that were created by the Dutch - and more particularly the translators of the Gospel of Saint
Matthew - in order to adapt Siraya to their own purposes.

Introducing the Holy Scripture to the Siraya must have involved an endless
number of semantic complications. To understand the Bible was already complicated enough for Europeans who had a different material culture and social organisation, and who lived in a moderate climate. Now, some of the religiously-
minded among them had come to Taiwan to preach the Bible to people who
lived in a sub-tropical environment and who were totally preoccupied with headhunting. These people had moreover a matrilineal organisation. Their sexual
habits were very free compared to those of the Dutch, and they considered
abortion to be mandatory.

Some of the difficulties the clergymen of the East India Company had in
teaching the Bible can be seen in the collocations they used to convey particular
meanings with which the Siraya were not familiar. A term like *dinar* (from Latin
denarius denoting a Roman coin) was translated into Siraya as *malitok ka ni-patax-
ən* 'money that is engraved on', in reference to the picture of the Roman emperor
engraved ("*ni-patax-ən*") on it. 'Desert' was translated as *päwlä-päwläx*, a reduplicated word derived from the root *puläx* 'uncultivated field'. A theologically more
complicated notion is that of 'heaven'. The clergymen translating the Gospels
into Siraya created a somewhat awkward compound combining *tunun* 'multitude'
with a reduplicated form of *vulŭm* 'cloud', hence *tunun ki vulŭ-vulŭm*, literally 'a
large number of clouds'. The noun *tunun* also comes up in the derivation *ka-
tunun-an* 'thousand', which in turn became part of the compound *saat katununan*

---

7   I am grateful to John Shepherd for pointing out this association to me (in email correspondence)
    and to Jos Platenkamp for directing my attention to the central African evidence.

ki na ka-arux ki rapal. The latter literally means 'one thousand movements across, of the leg' and stands for 'mile', a European notion. As to the concept of century, it is simply expressed by the phrase *sa[a]t kaxatuxang ki tawil* 'one hundred of years' (Vlis 1842), and by *i-da-rinux-an*, in the Gospel text (Adelaar 2011). The root of the latter is *dinux* (also *rinux* or *rĭnux*) conveying the notion of unlimited time or space, and the derivation *i-da-rinux-an* was used both temporally (with the meanings 'century' and 'eternity') and spatially (with the meaning 'world'). Other derivations are *ma-rĭnux* 'constantly', *mĭ-darĭnux* 'eternal'; *tu ĭ-darĭnux-an* (literally 'in eternity') is used in the sense of 'forever'.

In addition to *sa[a]t kaxatuxang ki tawil* 'one hundred of years', the notion 'hundred' also appears in the compound *ma-i-sa-su ki saat kaätuxan*, literally meaning 'be in charge of one hundred' and referring to a centurion.[8]

The notion of 'teaching' is expressed in derivations based on the root *täwx*, compare *ma-täwx* 'to tell'; *ma-ta-täw-täwx* both meaning 'to teach' and 'teacher'; and *pä-ta-täw-täwx-an* ('who is being taught to' =) 'disciple'.

The new testamentary notion of 'synagogue' was ultimately derived from *saal* 'together', a root which was used as a base for the derived phrase *na p-äw-i-sa-saal* 'the entire council'. This phrase in turn was used as a base for the causative verb *pa-pa-äw-i-sa-saal* 'to bring together, assemble' and for the noun *p-äw-i-sa-saal-an* 'synagogue'. Semantically, *p-äw-i-sa-saal-an*[9] is a calque based on the original Greek *sunagōgé* 'gathering, assembly'. It is different with the Siraya word for church, which is *sasongdaxang*: this is a locative derivation from the root *soŋdax*, reflecting in turn the Dutch word *zondag* 'Sunday'. Consequently, the literal meaning of *sasongdaxang* must have been 'place of Sunday', or 'place where the Sunday is observed'.

In matters of vice and moral turpitude, the clergymen were apparently very knowledgeable and had a lot to teach to the Siraya, who lacked the terminology to refer to various forms of misbehaviour the clergymen wanted them to be aware of. The Siraya Gospel translation makes frequent mention of the word *rbu-rbo* in order to render the notion of committing adultery, which is a reduplicated form of *rbu* 'inside'. It also emerges in a further compound *tama-rbu-rbo* (literally a person committing *rbu-rbo*) which is labelled in Vlis' list as 'hoereerder' ('whore-monger' in modern Dutch, but in 17th century Dutch it also meant 'fornicator' and 'adulterer'). The word *rbu-rbo* is probably an inherited Siraya term and not a neologism introduced by Dutch clergymen. One might imagine that it stands for the act of sexual penetration. However, a more culturally informed interpretation

---

8   *Kaätuxan* occurs in the Gospel text and is slightly different from *kaxatuxang* (spelled 'kagatougang'), which is listed in Vlis (1842).

9   Note that *pa-* is a causative prefix, and *-an* is a locative suffix.

is that it was related to the circumstance that Siraya males under the age of forty did not have direct access to women. In order to be with the woman they desired they had to wait till night time and steal their way into her parental house. A primary meaning 'to try to go in, find one's way in (a woman's house)' of *rbu-rbo* would be more in agreement with this practice.

In the Gospel text, the root *urung* or *uzung* refers to shameful or spiteful activities, or to secret activities. In this way, *uz-uzung* means 'illicit sexual activity', which is further specified as *uz-uzung ki na asi makakitil* (secret activities among unmarried people =) 'fornication' and *uz-uzung ki na makakitil* (secret activities among married people =) 'adultery'. A parallel semantic connection between secrecy and having sex expressed by one and the same root is *veyung*: with *ma-* (a verbal prefix) it forms *ma-veyung* 'to fornicate'; a combination of reduplication and various affixes yields *äw-vä-väwung-en* 'secrecy'. The notion of a 'robber' is expressed by *tama-riung* ('person who demands'), which is derived from the root *riung* 'urging, demanding'.

One way to reconcile the semantic divergence between *uzung* 1) 'secret activity', 2) 'illicit sexual activity', and *husong* 3) 'stealing', is to realise that neither fornicating nor stealing may have had the same social stigma among the Siraya as they did among the clergymen. Considering that the Siraya men resided in communal men's houses for most of their lives, the principle of private property must have been largely immaterial to them. Most objects were common property, and the lack of domestic privacy must have made it "difficult" for them to commit an act of theft anyway. As to fornication, the Siraya were sexually much more promiscuous than the Dutch, and they were certainly less concerned about it, as described by Constant and Pessaert in 1623 (see Blussé et al. 1999:4-22) and Candidius (1628). This may explain why the terms referring to these moral vices are both vague ('do in secret') and long winded (do in secret before marriage', 'do in secret standing marriage'). The clergymen may have found it very difficult to find (and create) the right words for notions that were of less consequence to the Siraya.

Other cases of "lexical wrestling" in the Gospel text are the following terms. The phrase *pa-ni-ni-en ki rix ki su* literally means 'differing in mind and word' and was used to render the meaning 'hypocrite'. Note again the use of *rix* (basically 'neck') with its associated sense of 'mind'.

Concepts of authority and rule are often derived from *su*, which means 'word', as well as 'language' and 'order, command'. *ma-i-sa-su*, meaning both 'to speak' and 'to be in charge' became the basis of the further derivations *ma-i-sa-su ka Sibavaw* ('who is in charge and on top' =) 'king', *pa-i-sa-su-an* 'kingdom', and also *ma-i-sa-su ki saat kaätuxan* ('be in charge of one hundred' =) which refers to 'centurion' (as already mentioned).

References

Adelaar, Alexander. 2011. *Siraya. Retrieving the phonology, grammar and lexicon of a dormant Formosan language*. Berlin: De Gruyter Mouton.

Adelaar, Alexander. 2013. Reviving Siraya: a case for language engineering, *Language Documentation and Conservation* (Honolulu) 7:12-34.

Blussé, Leonard and Marius P. H. Roessingh. 1984. A visit to the past: Soulang, a Formosan village anno 1623. *Archipel* vol. 27, pp. 63-80.

Blussé, Leonard, Natalie Everts, and Evelien Frech. 1999. *The Formosan Encounter. Volume I: 1623–1635*. Taipei: Shung Ye Museum of Formosan Aborigines.

Campbell, William. 1888. *The Gospel of St. Matthew in Formosan (Sinkang dialect)*. London: Trübner & Co.

Campbell, William. 1896. *The articles of Christian instruction in Favorlang-Formosan, Dutch, and English, from Vertrecht's MS of 1650; with Psalmanazar's dialogue between a Japanese and a Formosan, and Happart's Favorlang vocabulary*. London: Kegan Paul.

Candidius, Georgius. 1628. *Discourse. Family Archive Huydecoper R. 67–68*. Utrecht: Rijksarchief (reprinted and provided with a translation in Blussé et al. 1999).

Ferrell, Raleigh. 1971. Aboriginal peoples of the southwestern Taiwan plain. *Bulletin of the Institute of Ethnology* (Academia Sinica) vol. 32, pp. 217-235.

Ginsel, Willy Abraham. 1931. *De Gereformeerde Kerk op Formosa of de lotgevallen eener handelskerk onder de Oost-Indische-Compagnie 1627-1662* [History of the Dutch Reformed Church in Formosa 1627-1662]. Leiden University, PhD dissertation.

Gospel of Saint John. The Royal Danish Library, http://www.kb.dk/e-mat/dod/130023646693_color.pdf (originally published by Daniel Gravius in 1661).

Gravius, Daniel. 1661. *Het heylige Euangelium Matthei en Johannis. Ofte Hagnau ka d'llig matiktik ka na sasoulat ti Mattheus ti Johannes appa* [Gospels of Matthew and John]. Amsterdam: M. Hartogh.

Gravius, Daniel. 1662. *Patar ki tna-'msing-an ki Christang ofte 't Formulier des Christendoms* [Siraya translation of Catechism]. Amsterdam: Michiel Hartogh.

Happart, Gilbertus. 1650. *Woord-boek der Favorlangse taal, waarin het Favorlangs voor, het Duitsch achter gestelt is* [Favorlang – Dutch dictionary]. (Published in Batavia and provided with an Introduction by W.R. van Hoëvell in 1842).

Hoëvell, W. R. van (ed.). 1842. See Happart, Gilbertus (1650).

Li, Paul Jen-kuei. 2010. Studies of Sinkang manuscripts. *Languages and Linguistics Monograph Series* vol. 39. Taipei: Institute of Linguistics. Academia Sinica.

Li, Paul Jen-kuei. 2019. Text analysis of Favorlang. *Language and Linguistics Monograph Series* vol. 61. Taipei: Institute of Linguistics, Academia Sinica.

Macapili, Edgar L. 2002. *Ta avang ki Noe-an. Noah's Ark in Siraya*. Tainan (A newer version to appear under the title *Na avang ti Noe ki Su ka Maka-Siraya*).

Macapili, Edgar L. 2008. *Siraya Glossary. Based on the Gospel of St. Matthew in Formosan (Sinkan Dialect): A Preliminary Survey*. Tainan: Tainan Pe-po Siraya Culture Association.

Macapili, Edgar L. 2021. *Su ka maka Siraya ka Hagnau ka dilig matiktik [kana sasulat] ti Joannes.* [Siraya lexicon from the Gospel written by John]. Tainan: Tainan Siraya Culture Association.

Macapili, Edgar L., Shih Chao-kai, Uma Talavan, Te Nga-gi, and Jimmy Huang. 2010. *Sulat ki Su ka Maka-Siraya ki kakuting-an* (*Siraya Language Learning Book*, a bilingual English and Chinese manual).

Malthus, T. R. 1803. *An essay on the principle of population, Volume I.* (New edition by Patricia James, 1989, Cambridge [UK]: Cambridge University Press).

Medhurst, W.H. 1840. *Dictionary of the Favorlang dialect of the Formosan language, by Gilbertus Happart: written in 1650.* Batavia: [printed at Papattan].

Montesquieu, Charles-Louis Baron de. 1758. *The spirit of the laws.*

Ogawa, Naoyoshi (with an introduction by Paul Li). 2003. *English-Favorlang Vocabulary.* Asian and African Lexicon Series No. 43. Tokyo: Tokyo University of Foreign Studies, Research Institute for Languages and Cultures of Asia and Africa.

Shepherd, John R. 1995a. *Marriage and Mandatory Abortion Among the 17th-Century Siraya.* Arlington, VA: American Anthropological Association.

Shepherd, John R. 1995b. *Statecraft and Political Economy on the Taiwan Frontier, 1600- 1800.* Taipei: SMC Publishing Inc (2nd edition; 1st ed. 1993 by Stanford UP).

Statenbijbel. 1637. (Dutch bible translation authorised by the States General of the Dutch Republic).

Vlis, Christianus Jacobus van der. 1842. Formosaansche woorden-lijst, volgens een Utrechts Handschrift [Siraya wordlist, Manuscript in the Archive of the University of Utrecht. In *Verhandelingen van het Bataviaasch Genootschap* vol. 18.

Vertrecht, Jacobus. (no date). *Leerstukken en preeken in de Favorlangse taal (eiland Formosa).* Afgedrukt naar een handschrift uit de 17de eeuw [Doctrines and prayers: print version of a 17th century manuscript]. Uitgave Brandes [Brandes edition], 1888. Batavia: Landsdrukkerij.

Vuyk, Trudeke. 1991. *Children of One Womb: Descent, Marriage and Gender in Central African Societies.* CNWS Publications 3. Leiden: Centrum voor Niet-Westerse Studies.

Weng, Chia-yin. 1989. An attempt at reading Siraya document No. 22 In *Newsletter of Taiwan History Field Research* vol. 12, pp. 27-28. [in Chinese]

Weng, Chia-yin. 1990a. An attempt at reading a Siraya document. In *Field Materials, Institute of Ethnology* vol. 1, pp. 143–152. Taipei: Academia Sinica. [in Chinese]

Weng, Chia-yin. 1990b. List of prices in Siraya documents. In *Taiwan Folkways* vol. 40, no. 1, pp. 133-137. [in Chinese]

Chapter 4

The 18th century Siraya – songs from "A Tour of Duty on the Raft in the Taiwan Sea"[*]

Izumi Ochiai and Chao-Kai Shih

Abstract

To date, there have been limited attempts to decipher Siraya songs recorded in the early 18th century due to several difficulties, including the fact that the language is extinct. The songs were transcribed in Chinese characters using Southern-Min pronunciation; the Chinese transcription has neither word boundaries nor word-by-word glossing. There were Chinese translations by phrase or by clause, however, these provided free translations rather than literal translations in some cases; and finally, there is no large-scale Siraya dictionary. Progress was made in overcoming these difficulties by identifying Siraya words from Chinese characters. The present paper shows these results alongside the relevant grammatical observations.

1. Background

Siraya is among the Austronesian languages spoken by indigenous peoples in Taiwan, also referred to as the Formosans. There are more than 20 Formosan tribes in Taiwan. The Siraya have resided on the southwest plains of Taiwan. From the 17th century, they underwent acculturation to Dutch culture, the Dutch having occupied the southwest plains of Taiwan. Since the Dutch left Taiwan, the Siraya have undergone acculturation to Chinese culture. When Japanese linguists visited Siraya villages in the early 20th century, the Siraya spoke Southern Min, and their native language was highly endangered. Siraya is now considered a dormant language.

---

[*]   In 2018, the authors found they had been independently working on identifying words in Siraya songs from "A Tour of Duty on the Raft in the Taiwan Sea". Then, the second author kindly provided his manuscript to the first author. In this paper, the first author adopts some of the analyses by the second author while providing some of her own analyses. The authors benefited from the comments and suggestions of two reviewers. However, the first author is solely responsible for any errors remaining in this paper.

This paper presents the results of a preliminary decipherment of the words to Siraya songs recorded in the 18th century, when Taiwan, excluding the mountainous areas where non-Sinicized aboriginal people lived, was under the rule of the Qing dynasty.[1] The songs that this paper addresses are, to the best of the authors' knowledge, from the oldest document of Siraya songs. They were compiled as appendices in "Barbarian Customs Under Six Heads" (*Fan-su Liu-K'ao* 番俗六考), which is included as a chapter in the book "A Tour on Duty on the Raft in the Taiwan Sea" (*Taihai Shichalu* 臺海使槎錄), published in 1722. Later, "Barbarian Customs Under Six Heads" were cited in the "Reedited Gazetteer of Taiwan Prefecture" (*Xuxiu Taiwan Fuzhi* 續修臺灣府志) by Yu (1764), to which Florenz (1898) and Sato (1936) referred when they transliterated and analysed Siraya songs and other Formosan songs.[2]

In "A Tour on Duty on the Raft in the Taiwan Sea," 14 Siraya songs were recorded in different Siraya villages.[3] These songs could have been recorded by the author of the book, Shu-Ching Huang himself or by the magistrates of the two districts (*hsien*) under the control of Qing dynasty, Chu-lo *hsien* and Feng-shan *hsien*. According to Thompson (1969: 44), Shu-Ching Huang was the first supervisor dispatched to Taiwan by the Qing government immediately after the anti-Qing government rebellion of 1721 by ethnic Chinese in Taiwan.

Despite our utmost efforts, we were able to identify only a few words in some of the songs, such as those in Sections 2.1, 2.2, 2.3, 2.5, 2.6, 2.12, and 2.14, and we were unable to identify any words in other songs, such as those in Sections 2.4, 2.7, 2.8, 2.9, 2.11, and 2.13. A song from Ta-lou village (Section 2.10) was the one in which we were able to identify the most words.

The transcriptions of the songs have a drawback that hindered our linguistic analysis: they were transcribed using Chinese characters. These syllabary characters are not the best tool for transcribing languages that differ in syllable structures from Chinese. Regarding this point, Thompson (1969: 47), in his Chinese-to-English translation of "Fan-su Liu-k'ao", says "We may get some conception of the sound of the languages from the Chinese transliteration (although that is no doubt only a distant approximation). The compiler's purpose in including the

---

1   Sinicized Formosans who mainly live on the plains are also referred to as "cooked savages" (熟番), whereas non-Sinicized Formosans who mainly live in the mountains are also referred to as "raw savages" (生番).

2   This paper adopts the transliteration of Chinese characters by Thompson (1969) whenever available. Thompson used Wade-Giles romanization.

3   Other songs in "A Tour on Duty on the Raft in the Taiwan Sea" were recorded in villages of other Formosan tribes, such as Hoayna, Babuza, Papora, and Taokas. These songs have not been deciphered excepting an attempt by Ochiai (2018) that identified a few words in Babuza songs.

songs was, of course, to illustrate the sentiments of the barbarians, in the hoary tradition of *Shih Ching*." Therefore, the results of the decipherment in this paper should not be considered serious linguistic work. In many cases, our decipherment is only speculation based on the loose Chinese translations of the Siraya songs. In addition, it is uncertain whether the loose translations properly represent the meanings of the songs.

Thompson (1969) transliterated indigenous songs written in Chinese characters into the Latin alphabet, according to the pronunciation of the characters in Mandarin Chinese. However, these Formosan songs should have been transliterated not according to the Mandarin Chinese pronunciation, but according to the Southern Min pronunciation of the characters. Florenz (1898), a specialist on oriental literature, provided transliterations of Formosan songs according to the Southern Min pronunciation, which was probably the idea of Naoyoshi Ogawa, a student of Florenz at the University of Tokyo, who was a linguist specializing in Formosan languages.[4]

The authors found manuscripts by Ogawa in which he attempted to decipher these Formosan songs. They were stored at the Research Institute for Languages and Cultures in Asia and Africa, of the Tokyo University of Foreign Studies, under the file number OA068. Ogawa transliterated the Chinese characters of the songs into their Southern Min pronunciation and made some notes on the possible identification of some words. Sato (1936), an anthropologist, also attempted to partly decipher one of the Siraya songs (a song from Ta-chieh-tien village). However, these remain far from complete. We have to admit that these songs have received superficial treatment.

Although our study adds only a few more identified words to the previous study, we have attempted to provide a comprehensive presentation of the songs. We present the original text, including the songs written in Chinese characters and their translations in Chinese, followed by the transliteration of the Chinese characters according to their Southern Min pronunciation by Florenz (1898),[5] the authors' analysis including transcriptions and interlinear glosses, and the Mandarin-to-English translation of the meaning of the song by Thompson (1969).

---

4   Lin (2012: 594) mentioned that Florenz instructed Naoyoshi Ogawa in Linguistics at the University of Tokyo.

5   The Florenz (1898) transliterations are sometimes inconsistent. For example, he writes "ba(mo)" in some cases and "ba(moa)" in other cases for the Chinese letter 麻. The form in brackets means that it is a variant. In this paper, his transliteration is shown as it appeared in Florenz (1898). In addition, his transliterations seem not to distinguish /o/ and /ɔ/, different phonemes in Southern Min, both phonemes being transliterated as *o*. However, we did not correct these in this paper because it was not particularly relevant to our study.

The authors referred to the Siraya glossaries in Adelaar (2011), the glossary in the Utrecht Manuscript (Van der Vlis 1842) excerpted by Murakami (1933), the glossary in *Zhuluoxianzhi* 諸羅縣志 (Zhou 1717)[6] and Bullock (1874), and a collection of Siraya vocabulary from many different sources (Tsuchida and Yamada 1991) which include words recorded by Japanese people during the Japanese colonization of Taiwan (1895–1945). In what follows, the identified Siraya words are based on Adelaar (2011) unless cited otherwise.

2. Siraya songs

This section provides the Siraya songs and their transcriptions. First, a sample of the original text and its transcription are shown below.

(i) 塔樓社念祖被水歌
(ii) …
　　 磨葛多務根 《走上山內》
　　　 …

(iii)　　　MO-KAT-TO-BU-KIN
(iv)　　　*mu-kua*　　　　　*tu*　　　　　*vukin*
(V)　　　AV.MOT-go　　　　LOC　　　mountain
(vi)　　　"And fled into the mountains"

The first line (i) is the title of the Siraya song, and it includes the village name and the theme of the song; in this case, "From Ta-lou: Song recalling how the ancestors suffered from floodind" (Section 2.10). The Thompson translation of this title is presented as the title of each subsection in Section 2. The following lines in (ii) are the verses of the songs transcribed into Chinese characters, which are followed by the Chinese translations in brackets. The Chinese characters for the songs are characterized by their frequent use of the mouth radical (e.g., 咳, 呵).[7] This mouth radical was likely used in order to show that only the pronunciation of the character is relevant and that the meaning of the Chinese character as a whole is irrelevant. For some Chinese characters with a mouth radical, it was technically difficult to show them as one character. In these cases, the character is separated into two, the mouth radical and the phonetic component, with the two characters surrounded by angle brackets (e.g., <口甬>).

6　This glossary from *Zhuluoxianzhi* needs to be used with caution, since the words were collected from different tribes, among which Hoanya had the most words followed by Siraya, according to Ogawa (1999).

7　A reviewer pointed out that this use of the mouth radical is a typical feature of writing non-Standard Chinese, that is also observed in Cantonese.

Following these lines, the transliteration of the Chinese characters into the Latin alphabet according to their Southern Min pronunciation (Florenz 1898) is presented verse by verse as in line (iii). The Florenz transliteration is shown in the upper-case in this paper. When there are multiple possible pronunciations for a particular Chinese character in Southern Min, the variants are separated by a slash. The transliteration for each Chinese character is separated by a hyphen. Under the transliteration of a verse, a transcription into Siraya by the authors and interlinear glosses are presented as in lines (iv) and (v), respectively, followed by a translation of the meaning of the verse by Thompson (1969) as in line (vi). When no word in a verse is identifiable, the Siraya transcription is omitted. In Siraya transcriptions by the authors, the forms in italic font indicate that these words have been identified; that is, these words have been found in previous Siraya literature. Non-italic font indicates that the word remains unidentified. The meanings of these unidentified words are uncertain in some cases, but they can be inferred from the meaning of the song in other cases. When the provided meaning is inferred, it is followed by a question mark.

The abbreviations used in the interlinear glosses are as follows: 1 (first person), 2 (second person), AV (actor voice), CAUS (causative), COMP (complementizer), INC (inclusive plural), IRR (irrealis), LNK (linker), LOC (locative), MOT (motion), NOM (nominative), OBL (oblique), PN (personal marker), POSS (possessive), RDP (reduplication), SG (singular), STAT (stative), UVP (undergoer voice patient subject).

2.1 From Hsin-kang Village: Song on parting from one's wife

新港社別婦歌

　　馬無艾幾唎 《我愛汝美貌》
　　唅無晃米哖 《不能忘》
　　加麻無知各交 《實實想念》
　　麻各巴圭里文蘭彌勞 《我今去捕鹿》
　　查美狡呵呵孛沈沈唅無晃米哖 《心中輾轉愈不能忘》
　　奚如直落圭哩其文蘭 《待捕得鹿》
　　查下力柔下麻勾 《囬來便相贈》

MA-BU-GAI-KI-LI
　　"I love your beauty"

YOK-BU-HONG-BI-LO
　　yokbuhong　　　bilo[8]

8　This form could be related to *mila* "to do again, again." This form appears three times at the

cannot.forget   ---
"I cannot forget"

KA-BA/MO-BU-TI-KOK-KAU
ka   ma-butira⁹   kaw
CONJ STAT-beautiful   2SG
"I shall truly keep [you] in my thoughts"[10]

BA/MO-KOK-PA-KE-LI-BUN-LAN-BI/MI-LO
m-u-kua   keli[11]   bunlan[12]   bilo
AV-MOT-go.out ---   deer   ---
"Now I am going to hunt deer"

TS'A-BI-KAU-O/A-O/A-PUT/PUI-TIM-TIM-YOK-BU-HONG-BI-LO
ts'abi kawa   aput/apui   *tintin*   yokbuhong   bilo
---   ---   ---   heart   can.not.forget   ---
"Thoughts of you turning over and over in my mind, still less can I forget"

HE-JI-TIT-LOK-KE-LI-KI-BUN-LAN
heiru titlok   keli[13]   *ki*   *bunran*
when ---   ---   OBL   deer
"When I have hunted down the deer"

TS'A-HA-LEK-JU-HA-BA/MO-KA/KYA/KAU
ts'ahalek   *ru*   haba/hamo   *kau*
come.back?   when   give?   2SG?
"I'll return and give it to you"

2.2 From Hsiao-lung Village: Rice planting song
蕭壠社種稻歌
    呵搭<口甬>其礁《同伴在此》
    加朱馬池喇唭麻如《及時播種》

---

9   *mabutira* "pretty" is from Bullock (1874: 42).

10   According to the interlinear glosses, the verse would mean "that you are beautiful", however,
     this meaning does not match the translation for this verse.

11   This word could be related to a similar form *koli*, which is reported in the Sinkang manuscript
     (Li 2010: 250–251) as a word meaning "I".

12   This word seems to be identical to *fnang* "antelope" in Van der Vlis (1842).

13   This could be related to *kirix*, which means "to bind".

包烏投烏達《要求降雨》
符加量其斗逸《保祐好年冬》
知葉搭著礁斗逸《到冬熟後》
投滿生唭<口迦>僉藍《都須備祭品》
被離離帶明音免單《到田間謝田神》

O/A-TAH-YONG-KI-TSAU/TA
   ata-un   *kita*
   this-UVP   1INC
   "Our comrades are here"

KA-TSU-MA-TI-LI-KI-BA/MOA-JI/ZU
   ka   *du*   *ma-diri*   *ki*   *maru*
   LNK when   STAT-sow OBL   corn
   "Now is the planting season"[14]

PAU-O-TAU-O-TAT
   pau   *uda-udal*
   pray.for? RDP-rain
   "We entreat the rainfall"

HU-KA-LYANG/LYONG-KI-TO/TAU-IT
   hu-*ka-riang*   *ki*   *tawil*
   ?-STAT-good OBL   year
   "And a good winter season to protect [the sprouts]"

TI-HYAP-TAH-CHAK-TSAU/TA-TO/TAU-IT
   tihyap   tahchak   *ta*   *tawil*[15]
   ---   ---   NOM   year
   "After the winter ripening"

TAU-BOAN-SENG-KI-KYA-TS'YAM-LAM
   tauboanseng   *ki*   kyats'yamlam
   must.prepare OBL   oblation
   "All must prepare offerings"

---

14 According to our transcription, the verse begins with a subordinate clause. Its meaning would be "when we sow corn".

15 This word also means "agricultural cycle, harvest year", as pointed out by one of the reviewers.

PI-LI-LI-TAI-BENG-IM-BEN-TAN

pilili[16] taibeng   *imitan*
pray   god.of.the.fields?   1INC.POSS
"Go to the fields and thank the god of the fields"

2.3 From Ma-tou Village: Thinking of spring
麻豆社思春歌
　　唉加安呂燕《夜間難寐》
　　音那馬無力圭吱腰《從前遇著美女子》
　　礁嗎圭礁勞音毛嘈《我昨晚夢見伊》
　　沒生交耶音毛夫《今尋至伊門前》
　　孩如未生吱連《心中歡喜難說》

SU/AI-KA-AN-LI/LU-EN
"During the night it is hard to go to sleep"

IM-NA-MA-BU-LEK-KE-TSI-YAU

ina   mabulek *ki*   *ti*   *yau*
woman   ---   OBL   PN   1SG
"I have met a pretty girl"

TSAU/TA-MA-KE-TSAU/TA-LO-IM-MO-HOAN

dama   *kita*   lo   *imuhu-an*
morning   see   ---   2SG-OBL
"Last night I saw her in my dreams"[17]

BUT-SENG-KAU-YA-IM-MO-HU

butseng   kauya   *imuhu*
arrive?   ---   2SG
"Now I seek her in front of her door"

---

16 In his translation of Fan-su Liu-k'ao, Thompson (1969: 75) says "…in giving congratulations
    for a wedding one says *pei-li-i-ch'i-ta-hsüeh* 備力力其塔學." The transliteration by Thompson
    is based on a Mandarin Chinese pronunciation that should be re-transliterated into Southern
    Min pronunciation. The Siraya transcription would be *pilili ki tau* (congratulate OBL person).

17 There is a mismatch in the use of the pronoun. The translation for the verse has the 3rd person,
    "her" corresponding to 伊. However, the transcription shows that the pronoun used here is
    the 2nd person.

HAI-JI/ZU-BI-SENG-TSI-LEN

hairu   mising   tsilen

if   truly   happy?

"The joy in my heart is inexpressible!"

2.4 From Wan-li Village: Song enjoining one's wife

灣裏社誠婦歌[18]

朱連麼吱匏裏乞《娶汝眾人皆知》

加直老巴縣煙《原為傳代》

加年呀嘎加犁蠻《須要好名聲》

拙年巴恩勞勞呀《切勿做出壞事》

車加犁未礁嘮描《彼此便覺好看》

TSU-LIEN-MOʔ-KI-PAU/PU-LI-KI

"Everyone knows I have taken you for my wife"

KA-TIT-LO/NO-PA-BENG-IEN

"For the purpose of carrying on the family"

KA-NI-GA-HA-KA-LI-BAN

"You must have a good reputation"

TSOAT-NI-PA-UN-LO-LO-GA

"And never do anything bad"

CHHIA-KA-LI-BI-TA-LO-BA/BIAU

"Then you and I can be proud of ourselves!"

2.5 From Ta-chieh-tien: Song of prayer for the new year

大傑巔社祝年歌

臨臨其斗寅《今過年》

尋<口耶>唭什剝格唭圭甲《為粉餐殺雞》

施里西奇文林《祭天地》

匏打鄰其斗寅麻亮其斗寅《祝新年勝去年》

嗒學嘎葛唭唔因《倍收穫食不盡》

---

18 Florenz (1898) failed to include this song. Therefore, the authors of this paper have added the transliteration based on the Southern Min dictionary by Douglas (1873).

LIM-LIM-KI-TO/TAU-IN

limulimu	*ki*	*tawil*
end	OBL	year

"Now we are celebrating the new year"

SIM-YA-KI-SIP-PAK-KEK-KI-KE-KAH

si-mia[19]	*ki*	*si-pakek*[20]	*ki*	*huka*[21]
do-prepare	OBL	si-kill	OBL	chicken

"Grinding [rice] and killing chickens"

SI-LI-SE-KI-BUN-LIM

silise	*ki*	*vulum*
worship?	OBL	sky

"To sacrifice to Heaven and Earth"

PAU/PU-TA-LIM-KI-TO/TAU-IN-BA/MO-LYANG-KI-TO/TAU-IN

pa-u-talim	*ki*	*tawil*	*ma-riang*	*ki*	*tawil*
CAUS-MOT-plant?	OBL	year	STAT-big	OBL	year

"Praying that the new year may be better than the past year"

TAH-HAK-HA-KAT-KI-I/O-IN

tau	hakat	*ki*	oin?
people	?	OBL	?

"That our harvest may be doubled, and we may eat all we want!"

2.6 From Ta-wu-lung Village: Drinking-party song about tilling and hunting
大武壠社耕捕會飲歌

毛務麻亮其斗寅《耕種勝往年》

遏投嗎<口录>務那其壘《同去打鹿，莫遇生番》

嫣毛買仍艾奇打<口录>《社眾呼釀美酒》

美樂哄密嗒奇打<口录>嗎萌《齊來乘興飲酒至醉》

---

19 *simia* "to prepare" is based on *simimia* "to do, make" (Adelaar 2011: 372). The authors guess that these are cognates even though the forms do not match, since *simia* appears to be a form of *simimia* undergoing haplology.

20 *si-pakek* "to kill" is based on 剝抉 *pak-koat* "to kill" (Zhu 1765).

21 *huka* "chicken" is from Tsuchida and Yamada (1911: 95). A cognate form was reported as *tahuka* in Bullock (1874: 41).

MO-BU-BA/MO-LYANG-KI-TO/TAU-IN

mobu	ma-riang	ki	tawil
harvest?	STAT-good	OBL	year

"Our farming was better than in former years"

HAT/AT-TAU-MA-LYOK-BU-NA-KI-LUI

atu	maliok	buna[22]	kilui
PERF?	---	deer	K'uei-lei.savage

"And when we went together to hunt deer we didn't met the raw barbarians"

MA-MO-MAI-JENG/GENG-GAI-KI-TA-LYOK

mamu	mareng	gai	ki	talak
elder	officer?	make?	OBL	wine

"The villages have been summoned to brew good liquor"

BI-GAK/LOK-HANG-BIT-TAP-KI-TA-LYOK-MA-BENG

bigakhangbittap	ki	talak	mabeng
---	OBL	wine	drunk?

"We've all come joyfully to drink until we're drunk!"

2.7 From Shang Tan-shui: Song of working in the fields

上淡水社力田歌
　　咳呵呵里慢里慢那毛呵埋《此時係畊田之後》
　　唭唹老唭描嘎咳《天今下雨》
　　唭吧伊加圭朗烟《及時畊種》
　　唭麻列唭呵女門《下秧耡草》
　　唭描螺螺嘎連《好雨節次來了》
　　唭麻萬列其嘻列《播田明白好來飲酒》

HAI/AI-O-O-LI-BAN-LI-BAN-NA-MO-O-BAI

"Now it is weather for plowing the fields"

KI-I/U-LO/NO-KI-BA/BYAU-HA-HAI/AI

"Today it is raining"

KI-PA-I-KA-KE/KI-LONG-EN

"The time having arrived we'll plow and sow"

---

22 This word seems to be identical to *fnang* "antelope" in Van der Vlis (1842).

KI-BA/MO-LET-KI-O/A-LI/LU-BUN
  "We'll [trans]plant the seedlings and hoe the weeds"

KI-BA/BYAU-LE-LE-HA-LEN
  "The good rains have come again and again"

KI-BA/MO-BAN-LET-KI-HI-LIET
  "When the sowing of the fields is clearly finished, it will be good for us to drink!"

2.8 From Hsia Tan-shui: Song in praise of the ancestor
下淡水社頌祖歌
　　巴干拉呀拉呀留《請爾等坐聽》
　　礁眉<口迦><口迦>漢連多羅我洛《論我祖先如同大魚》
　　礁眉呵干洛呵連《凡行走必在前》
　　呵吱媽描歪呵連刀《何等英雄》
　　唦嗎礁卓擧呀連呵吱嗎《如今我輩子孫不肖》
　　無羅嘎連《如風隨舞》
　　巴干拉呀拉呀留《請爾等坐聽》

PA-KAN-LYAP/NA-GA-LYAP/NA-GA-LYU
  "I invite you all to sit and listen"

TSAU/TA-BI/MI-KYA/KA-KYA/KA-HAN-LEN-TO-LO-GO-LOK
  "While I tell of my ancestor who was like a great fish"

TSAU/TA-BI/MI-O/A-KAN-LOK-O/A-LEN
  "Whenever he ran he was bound to be in front"

O/A-TSI-MA-BA/BYAU-OAI-O/A-LEN-TO
  "What a great hero!"

I/U͞-MA-TSAU/TA-TOK-KI-GA-LEN-O-TSI-MA
  "Nowadays the sons and grandsons of my generation are worthless"

BU-LO-HA-LEN
  "They dance whichever way the wind blows!"

PA-KAN-LYAP/NA-GA-LYAP/NA-GA-LYU͞
  "I invite you all to sit and listen"

2.9 From A-hou: Song in praise of the ancestor

阿猴社頌祖歌
　　咳呵呵咳仔滴唹老 《論我祖》
　　振芒嘆糾連 《實是好漢》
　　礁呵留的乜乜 《眾番無敵》
　　礁留乜乜連 《誰敢相爭》

HAI/AI-O-O-HAI/AI-A-TEK/TIT-I/U-LO/NO
　　"I tell of my ancestor"

TSIN-BONG-KI-KYU-LEN
　　"He was really a man!"

TSAU/TA-A/O-LYU-TEK-MIH-MIH
　　"None among the barbarians was his match"

TSAU/TA-LYU-MIH-MIH-LEN
　　"Who would dare to fight him!"

2.10 From Ta-lou: Song recalling how the ancestors suffered from flood

塔樓社念祖被水歌
　　咳呵呵咳呵嘎 《此係起曲之調》
　　加斗寅 《祖公時》
　　嗎搏嘆嘮濃 《被水沖擊》
　　搭學嘆施仔捧 《眾番就起》
　　磨葛多務根 《走上山內》
　　佳史其加顯加<口幽> 《無有柴米》
　　佳史嘆唹嗎 《也無田園》
　　麻踏堀其搭學 《眾番好艱苦》

HAI-O-O-HAI-O-HA
　　"(This is the tune of the first song)"

KA-TO-IN
　　ka-*tawil*
　　PST?-year
　　"In the time of our ancestors"

MA-PHOK-KI-LO-LONG
| *ma-buk*[23] | *ki* | *ralum* |
| STAT-hit | OBL | water |

"We were inundated by the floodwaters"

TAH/TAO-HAK-KI-SI-A-HONG
| *tau* | *ki* | siahong |
| people | OBL | rise? |

"All the barbarians arose"

MO-KAT-TO-BU-KIN
| *mu-kua* | *tu* | *vukin* |
| AV.MOT-go | LOC | mountain |

"And fled into the mountains"

KA-SU-KI-KA-HEN-KA-HYU͞
| kasu[24] | *ki* | *kahien*[25] | *kayu*[26] |
| not.have | OBL | rice | firewood |

"They had no firewood or rice"

KA-SU-KI-I/U͞-MA
| kasu | *ki* | *uma* |
| not.have | OBL | field |

"Nor any fields"

BA/MO-TAP-KUT-KI-TAH-HAK
| *ma-takut* | *ki* | *tau* |
| STAT-fear | OBL | people |

"The barbarians suffered greatly"

---

23 *ma-buk* "to beat" is likely related to *bukbuk* "to beat" (Adelaar 2011: 397), which is the reduplicated form of *buk*.

24 *kasu* "not have" could be related to *ausi* "to be absent" (Adelaar 2011: 304), Li (2010: xx) points out that it derives from *akou-si* (probably pronounced as *aku-si*) "have-not."

25 Tsuchida and Yamada (1911: 83) have *khai-seng* "rice", which is based on the transcription 開生 seen in 諸羅縣志. Its cognate, *qaising*, is seen in Bunun (a Northern dialect based on the first author's field notes).

26 *kayu* "wood" is from Tsuchida and Yamada (1991: 138).

2.11 From Chia-t'eng: Drinking song

笻藤社飲酒歌

　　近呵欸其歪《請同來飲酒》

　　礁年臨萬臨萬其歪《同坐同飲》

　　描呵那哆描呵欸《不醉無歸》

　　代來那其歪《答曰多謝汝》

　　嘻哆萬那呵欸其歪《如今好去遊戲》

　　龜描呵滿礁欸其歪《若不同去遊戲便回家去》

KIN-O/A-K'OAN-KI-OAI

"Please all come together and drink!"

TSAU/TA-LEN-LIM-BAN-LIM-BAN-KI-OAI

"Sit down together and drink together"

BA/BYAU-O-NA-TO-BA/BYAU-O-K'OAN

"Don't go home until you're drunk!"

TAI-LAI-NA-KI-OAI

"The answer: We thank you very much!"

HI-TO-BAN-NA-O-K'OAN-KI-OAI

"Now we'd like to go out and have some fun"

KUI/KU-BA/BYAU-O/A-BOAN-TASU/TA-K'OAN-KI-OAI

"If you do not go with us, then we'll go back home!"

2.12 From Fang-so: Song about planting ginger

放<糸索>社種薑歌

　　粘粘到落其武難馬凉道毛呀覓其嗾馬《此時是三月天好去犁田》

　　武郎弋礁拉老歪礁嗎嘆《不論男女老幼》

　　免洗溫毛雅覓刀嗎林唭萬萬《同去犁園好種薑》

　　嗎米唭萬萬吧唎陽午凉藹米唭唎呵《俟薑出後，再來飲酒》

LYAM-LYAM-TO-LOK-KI-BU-LAN-MA-LYANG-TO-MO-GA-BEK-KI-I/U-MA

limulimu	*turu*[27]	*ki*	*buran*[28]	*ma-riang*	tomoga
end	three	DF	moon	STAT-good	cultivate?

ki	*uma*
OBL	field

"These are the days of the third month, right for planting the gardens"

BU-LONG-EK-TSAU/TA-LYAP/NA-LO/NO-OAI-TSAU/TA-MA-BOK

"Men and women, old and young"

BEN-SEN/SE-UN-MO-GA-BEK-TO-MA-LIM-KI-BAN-BAN

bensenun	mugabek	tomalim	*ki*	*banban*
together?	Arake?	plant?	OBL	ginger

"Go out together to plow the gardens for planting ginger"

MA-BI-KI-BAN-BAN-PA-LI-YANG/YONG-GO-LYANG/LYONG-AI-BI-KI-LI-O

mabi	*ki*	*banban*	pariang	goriangay	*mit*	*ki*	*lihu*[29]
wait?	OBL	ginger	---	---	AV.drink	OBL	wine

"After the ginger has sprouted we'll drink again!"

2.13 From Wu-lo: Song in praise of the ancestors

武洛社頌祖歌

嘻呵浩孩耶嘎 《此句係起曲之調》
乜連糾 《先時節》
鎮唎烏留岐跌<口耶> 《我祖先能敵傀儡》
那唎平奇腰眉 《聞風可畏》
鎮仔奇腰眉 《如今傀儡尚懼》
唭耳奄耳奄罩散嘎 《不敢侵越我界》

HI/I-A/O-HO-HAI-YA-HA

"(This is the tune of the first song)"

---

27 *turu* "three" is from Bullock (1874: 48).

28 *buran* "moon" is from Bullock (1874: 42).

29 *lihu* "liquor" is from Tsuchida and Yamada (1991: 97).

MIH-LEN-KYU
   "In former times"

TIN-LI-O-LYU-TSI-TET-YA
   "Our ancestors were more than a match for the K'uei-lei"

NA-LI-PENG-KI-YAU-BI/MI
   "Their reputation was fearsome"

TIN-A-KI-YAU-BI/MI
   "To this day the K'uei-lei still fear them"

KI-JI/NI-YAM/AM-JI/NI-YAM/AM-TA/TAU-SAN-HA
   "And do not dare to encroach on our territory!"

2.14 From Li-li: Song about drinking and hunting deer
力力社飲酒捕鹿歌
   文嘮唭啞奢 《來賽戲》
   丹領唭漫漫 《種了薑》
   排裏唭黎唉 《去換糯米》
   伊弄唭嘮力 《來釀酒》
   麻骨裏唭嘮力 《釀成好酒》
   匏黍其麻因刃臨萬唭嘮力 《請土官來飲酒》
   媽良唭嘮力 《酒足後》
   毛丙力唭文蘭 《去捕鹿》
   毛里居唭丙力 《捕鹿回》
   文嘮唭啞奢 《復來賽戲》

BUN-LO-KI-A-TS'YA
   bunlo   *ki*   ats'ya
   come.to.play?   OBL   dance?
   "Come and *sai-hsi*"[30]

TAN-LENG-KI-BAN-BAN
   tanleng   *ki*   *banban*
   sow   OBL   ginger
   "The ginger we grew"

---

30   Thompson (1969: 63) explains that a dance to thank the gods at a harvest festival is called *sai-hsi* 賽戲.

PAI-LI-KI-LE-SU/AI
    paila[31]   *ki*   lesu
    exchange   OBL   sticky.rice?
    "We'll exchange for glutinous rice"

I-LONG-KI-LO-LEK
    ilong   *ki*   lolek
    come.to.brew? OBL   wine
    "To brew liquor"

BA/MO-KUT-LI-KI-LO-LEK
    makutli   *ki*   lolek
    finish.brewing?   OBL   wine
    "After we've brewed the good liquor"

PAU/PŪ-SI/SU-KI-BA/MO-IN-JIM-LIM-BAN-KI-LO-LEK
    pausi *ki*   *main*[32]   jimlimban   *ki*   lolek
    invite?OBL   officer   ---   OBL   wine
    "We'll invite the local headman to come and drink"

MA-LYONG-KI-LO-LEK
    ma-riang   *ki*   lolek
    STAT-good   OBL   wine
    "After we've drunk enough"

MO-PENG-LEK-KI-BUN-LAN
    mu-penglek   *ki*   *bunlan*
    AV.MOT-catch? OBL   deer
    "We go to hunt deer"[33]

MO-LI-KI-KI-PENG-LEK
    mu-rikur   *ki*   penglek
    AV.MOT-go.back OBL   hunting
    "Returning from the hunt"

---

31 *paijla* "buy" and other similar forms are seen in Sinkang manuscripts (Li 2010).

32 Zhu (1765) has *ma-jin* 罵仁, meaning "officer".

33 Thompson (1969) failed to include the translation of the eighth line; therefore the authors have supplemented it.

BUN-LO-KI-A-TS'YA

bunlo	*ki*	ats'ya
come.to.play?	OBL	dance

"Once again we'll *sai-hsi*!"

3. List of Siraya words identified from the songs[34]

Below we list the Siraya words that have been identified from the songs. The words are considered to have been identified when they are recorded in the wordlist in Van der Vlis (1842), Bullock (1874), or Adelaar (2011). In some cases, we found forms in the songs that are similar to the words of the intended meaning listed in Tsuchida and Yamada (1991). We mention this in the footnote for each word. We have not included these words in the following list because the data in Tsuchida and Yamada (1991) were mostly collected from the end of the 19th century to the early 20th century, by which time the Siraya language had likely undergone language attrition.

(1)   List of words that have been identified from the Siraya songs

ataun "here"   呵搭<口甬> o/a-tah-yong (Sec. 2.2)
dama "morning"   礁嗎 ta-ma (Sec. 2.3)
diri "to sow"   池唎 ti-li (Sec. 2.2)
du, ru "when, if"   朱 tsu (Sec. 2.2); 柔 ju (Sec. 2.1)
fnang[35] "antelope"   文蘭 bun-lan (Sec. 2.1, 2.14); 務那 bu-na (Sec. 2.6)
heyru conjugation   奚如 he-ji/zu (Sec. 2.1); 孩如 hai-ji/zu
huka[36] "chicken"   圭甲 ke-kah (Sec. 2.5)
imhu "you" (sg., free form)   音毛夫 im-mo-hu (Sec. 2.3)
imitan "we" (inclusive, oblique)   音免單 im-ben-tan (Sec. 2.2)
imuhuan "you" (sg., oblique)   音毛� im-mo-hoan (Sec. 2.3)
ina "woman"   音那 im-na (Sec. 2.3)
ka linker   加 ka (Sec. 2.1, 2.2, 2.10)

---

34 According to Adelaar (2011: 50–51), Siraya has the following phoneme inventory: consonants /p b t d k m n ŋ l r v s x h w y/, and vowels /i u e ə o a/. In this paper, *ng* corresponds to ŋ. /d/ appears as [d] or [r], as in *du* or *ru* "when." Likewise, /b/ appears as /b/ or /v/.
According to Chappell (2018: 5–6), Southern Min has the following phoneme inventory: consonants are /p pʰ b t tʰ ʦ ʦʰ ʣ k kʰ g ʔ s h l/, and while phonemically [m], [n], and [ŋ] are nonexistent, these are phonetically realized as allophones of /b/, /l/, and /g/, respectively. For vowels, there are monophthongs /i u e o ɔ a/, and diphthongs and triphthongs /ia io iu iau ui ue uai/. In the transliteration by Florenz (1898), the *h* in coda position corresponds to ʔ, *ng* corresponds to ŋ, and *j* and *z* correspond to ʣ. He uses a macron over a vowel in some cases; however, this seems to not be a distinctive feature.

35 This form is from Van der Vlis (1842: 468).

36 It is uncertain why this word with a word-initial *h* was transliterated with a Chinese character with an onset *k*.

kariang "good"   加量 ma-lyang/lyong (Sec. 2.2)
kaw "you" (sg., nominative)   勾 kau (Sec. 2.1)
kayu "wood"   加<口幽> ka-hyū (Sec. 2.10)
ki relation marker   其 ki (Sec. 2.1, 2.2, 2.5, 2.6, 2.10, 2.12, 2.14); 唭 ki (Sec. 2.2, 2.5. 2.10, 2.12, 2.14); 奇 *ki* (Sec. 2.5, 2.6)
kita "to see"   圭礁 ke-ta (Sec. 2.3)
kita "we" (inclusive)   其礁 ki-ta (Sec. 2.2)
limulimu "end"   臨臨 lim-lim (Sec. 2.5); 粘粘 lyam-lyam (Sec. 2.12)
mabutira "pretty"   麻無知各 ba/mo/moa-bu-ti-kok (Sec. 2.1)
mariang "good"   麻亮 mo-lyang (Sec. 2.5, 2.6); 媽良 ma-lyong (Sec. 2.14); 馬凉 ma-lyang (Sec 2.12)
maru "corn"   麻如 ba/mo/moa-ji/zu (Sec. 2.2)
matakut "to be afraid"   麻踏堀 ba/mo/moa-ta-kut (Sec. 2.10)
mukua "to go"   磨葛 mo-kat (Sec. 2.10); 麻各巴 ba/mo-kok-pa (Sec. 2.1)
murikur "to follow from behind"   毛里居 mo-li-ki (Sec. 2.14)
mising "true, really"   未生 bi-seng (Sec. 2.3)
mit "to drink"   米 bi (Sec. 2.12)
ralum "water"   嘮濃 lo-long (Sec. 2.10)
ta nominative   礁 ta (Sec. 2.2)
tau "person"   嗒學 tah-hak (Sec. 2.5); 搭學 (Sec. 2.10)
tawil "year, agricultural season"   斗寅 to-in/tau-in (Sec. 2.5, 2.6, 2.10); 斗逸 to-it/tau-it (Sec. 2.2)
tintin "heart"   沈沈 timtim (Sec. 2.1)
tu locative   多 to (Sec. 2.10)
turo, turu "three"   到落 to-lok (Sec. 2.12)
udal "rain"   烏達 o-tat (Sec. 2.2)
uma "field"   嗁嗎 ū-ma (Sec. 2.10); 嗁馬 ū-ma (Sec. 2.12)
vukin "mountain"   務根 bu-kin (Sec. 2.10)
vulum "sky"   文林 bun-lim (Sec. 2.5)
vural "moon"   武難 bu-lan (Sec. 2.12)

In some cases, a distinct Chinese character is used to transliterate a Siraya word. Overall, it can be said that there are no particular regularities in the selection of Chinese characters. For example, for the function word *ki* (relation marker), either 其 or the form with the mouth radical 唭 is used. Another character, 奇, is also used. Similarly, uma "field" is transliterated either as 嗁嗎 or 嗁馬, with the second Chinese character differing only in the existence or non-existence of the mouth radical.

Other words such as *mariang* "good" (as well as the derived form *kariang*), *tawil* "year", *mukua* "to go to", *limulimu* "end", *fnang*[37] (probably, *bnang* or *vnang*) "deer",

---

37 This form is from Van der Vlis (1842: 468).

heyru "when", and *tau* "person" appear more than once in the songs. Their forms in Chinese characters vary. For instance, for *mariang*, three different Chinese characters were selected to represent the first syllable *ma*: 麻 mo, 媽 ma, and 馬 ma. Foru different Chinese characters were selected to represent the second syllable of *mariang* as well as *kariang*: 亮 lyang, 良 lyong, 凉 lyang, and 量 lyang or lyong. It also seems that the distinction between the vowels *a* and *o* is rather ambiguous in the use of Chinese characters.

Likewise, for some Siraya words, the selection of the vowels for the Chinese characters shows irregularity. For example, for the first syllable of *kita*, a homonym meaning either "to see" or "we" (inclusive) is transliterated either as 其 ki or 圭 ke. The vowel *i* in *limulimu* is transliterated either as *i* or *ya* (or *ia*), included in the rhymes for 臨 lim and 粘 lyam. For the same Siraya word, the vowel *u* is neglected in the Chinese characters. A vowel *u* is also omitted in other transliteration: 磨葛 mo-kat, for *mukua* "to go," where the *u* in the final syllable is not represented in the second Chinese character 葛 kat. For the vowel in the first syllable of *heyru* (conjugation), the corresponding transliteration is either the monophthong *e* in 奚 he or the diphthong *ai* in 孩 hai.

As for the use of consonants, a devoiced stop *t* is used in Chinese characters for Siraya words having a *d*. For example, *dama* and *diri* are transliterated as ta-ma 礁嗎 and *ti-li* 池唎. Similarly, for the onset for *du* "when", the devoiced affricate *ts* is used in the Chinese character *tsu* 朱. According to Adelaar (2011: 52–55), the word-initial *b* in Siraya has *v* as its allophone. However, only *b* is seen in the use of Chinese characters, e.g., 文蘭 bun-lan and 務那 bu-na for *fnang* "antelope," 務根 bu-kin for *vukin* "mountain," 文林 bun-lim for *vulum* "sky," and 武難 bu-lan for *vural* "moon." This is because the phoneme *v* is non-existent in the phoneme inventory of Southern Min.

In Southern Min, *m* in the onset is an allophone of *b* (Chappell 2018). Therefore, in representing the word-initial *m* in Siraya, *b*-initial Chinese characters are used. For example, *mising* "true" and *mit* "to drink" are 未生 bi-seng and 米 bi in Chinese characters. In Southern Min, *r* is not included in the phoneme inventory. The *r* in Siraya is replaced by the *l* of Southern Min in the word *ralum* "water" transliterated as 嘮濃 lo-long and *murikur* transliterated as 毛里居 mo-li-ki. Siraya allows word-final *l*; however, Southern Min does not have *l* in coda position. According to Chappell (2018: 7), the possible codas in Southern Min are the stops /p t k ʔ/ or the nasals /m n ŋ/. The word-final *l* in Siraya is sometimes replaced by the stop *t*, as seen in 斗逸 tau-it for *tawil* "year" and 烏達 o-tat for *udal* "rain," and sometimes by the nasal *n* as seen in 斗寅 tau-in for *tawil* "year". It is unclear why the coda *m* was selected in the Chinese characters 沈沈 timtim for the Siraya word *tintin* "heart," having *n* as its codas. Likewise, for *ataun* "here," the Chinese character with the coda *ng* is used, giving 呵搭<口甬> o/a-tah-yong, rather than a character with the coda *n*.

In the Southern Min transliteration, nasals are doubled across syllable bound-aries. For example, *imhu* "you" (sg.) and *imuhuan* "you" (sg., oblique) are translit-erated as 音毛夫 im-mo-hu and 音毛嘓 im-mo-hoan respectively, in which *m* appears twice as the coda of the first syllable and the onset of the second syllable. The same pattern is seen in *imitan* "we" (inclusive, oblique), which is transliterated as 音免單 im-ben-tan. Although the onset of second Chinese character is *b*, it could be equivalent to *m* to the transcriber of that song. Similarly, for *ina* "woman", its transliteration in Chinese characters shows a doubled nasal, 音那 im-na, the first nasal being *m* and the second being *n*. The second nasal properly represents a Siraya sound.

In some cases, a consonant is doubled across words. The fifth verse in Section 2.10 is repeated below as (2). The second Chinese character 葛 kat ends in *t*, and the third Chinese character 多 to starts with *t*. Even though the rest of the second Chinese character belongs to the final syllable of the first Siraya word *mu-kua*, the coda *t* in 葛 kat as well as the onset of 多 to correspond to the onset of the Siraya function word *tu* (locative).

(2) 磨葛多務根 MO-KA**T-T**O-BU-KIN
    mu-kua   *tu*   *vukin*
    AV.MOT-go   LOC   mountain
    "And fled into the mountains"

A similar pattern is seen in the first verse in Section 2.12, repeated partly here as (3). The fourth Chinese character 落 lok ends in *k*, and the fifth Chinese char-acter 其 ki starts with *k*. Even though the rest of the forth Chinese character belongs to the final syllable of the second Siraya word *turu*, the coda *k* in 落 lok likely corresponds to the following function word *ki*.

(3) 粘粘到落其武難... LYAM-LYAM-TO-LO**K-K**I-BU-LAN...
    limulimu   *turu*[38]   *ki*   *buran*[39]   ...
    end   three   DF   moon
    "These are the days of the third month…"

---

38   *turu* "three" is from Bullock (1874: 48).
39   *buran* "moon" is from Bullock (1874: 42).

In other cases, irrelevant consonants are inserted in the Southern Min transliteration. For example, for *ataun* "here," an unnecessary *y* is seen as the onset of the final word in 呵搭<口甬> o/a-tah-yong. For *kayu* "wood," unnecessary *h* is seen as the onset of the final word in 加<口幽> ka-hyū. For *mukua* "to go," an unnecessary *k* and *p* are seen as the coda and the onset of the second and the final word in 麻各巴 ba/mo-kok-pa.[40] In contrast, a word-final consonant *r* in Siraya is neglected in the Southern Min transliteration for *murikur*, which is 毛里居 mo-li-ki.

Southern Min has two registers: a literary pronunciation and a colloquial pronunciation. In the transliteration of Siraya songs, some words used the colloquial pronunciation, but other words used the literary pronunciation. For 斗 (colloquial *tau* and literary *t*), the colloquial pronunciation is more appropriate in 斗寅, which represents *tawil* "year." However, for 學 (colloquial *oʔ* and reading *hak*), the literary pronunciation is more appropriate in 搭學, which represents *tau* "people."

Overall, it can be said that the transliteration of the Siraya songs using Southern Min pronunciation was not conducted with precision. The purpose of supplementing these songs from "A Tour of Duty on the Raft in the Taiwan Sea" was probably not to accurately present the Siraya pronunciations but to add poetic sentiment to the governmental record, as Thompson (1969: 47) pointed out.

4. Concluding remarks

This paper aimed to decipher Siraya songs recorded in the 18th century using Chinese characters with Southern Min pronunciation by making the best use of available materials relating to Siraya. The results are presented in this paper as a preliminary report. Although the authors were able to identify only a small number of Siraya words, we hope that the unidentified words from the songs will be uncovered in the future as linguistic and historical studies continue to progress.

References

Adelaar, Alexander. 2011. *Siraya: Retrieving the phonology, grammar and lexicon of a dormant Formosan language.* Berlin: De Gruyter Mouton.

Bullock, Thomas L. 1874. Formosan dialects and their connection with the Malay. *China Review, or Notes and Queries on the Far East* vol. 3: 38-46.

Chappell, Hilary. 2018. A sketch of Southern Min grammar. In: Alice Vittrant and Justin Watkins eds. *The Mainland Southeast Asia linguistic area*, 176-233. Berlin: Mouton de Gruyter.

Douglas, Carstairs. 1873. *Chinese-English dictionary of the vernacular or spoken language of Amoy, with the principal variations of the Chang-chew and Chin-chew dialects.* London: Trüber.

---

40 It is also possble that the transcriber intended to represent *w*, which could appear as a glide between the vowel hiatus *u* and *a*, by the use of the onset *p* in the final Chinese character.

Florenz, Karl. 1898. Formosanische Volkslieder, nach Chinesischen Quellen [Formosan folk songs, from Chinese sources]. *Mitteilungen der Deutschen Gesellschaft fur Natur- und Völkerkunde Ostasiens*, vol.7, part 1: 110-158. [in German]

Huang Shujing [黃叔璥]. 1722. *Taihai Shichalu* [Record of Missions to Taiwan and Adjacent Waters 臺海使槎錄]. [in Chinese]

Li, Paul Jen-kuei. 2010. Studies of Sinkang manuscripts. Taipei: Institute of Linguistics, Academia Sinica.

Lin, Chu-Mei. 2012. 小川尚義論文集 *Ogawa Naoyoshi Ronbunshū*. Tokyo: Sangensha. [in Japanese]

Murakami, Naojirô. 1933. *Sinkan Manuscripts (新港文書 Shinkō bunsho)*. Memoirs of the Faculty of Literature and Politics, Taihoku Imperial University, vol.2, no.1. Formosa: Taihoku Imperial University. [in Japanese]

Ochiai, Izumi. 2018. Favorlang songs transcribed in Southern-Hokkien: Decipherment, *Proceedings of the 51st International Conference on Sino-Tibetan Languages and Linguistics*, 723-734. Kyoto: The organizing committee of the 51st International Conference on Sino-Tibetan Languages and Linguistics & The Hakubi Project, Kyoto University.

Ogawa, Naoyoshi. 1999. 台灣府志に出たる蕃語 Taiwanfushi ni idetaru bango [Aboriginal words in Taiwanfuzhi]. 台湾原住民研究 *Taiwan genjyūmin kenkyū* vol. 4: 159-186. [in Japanese]

Ogawa, Naoyoshi. Unknown. Material pertaining to Siraya vocabulary and songs. [Unpublished manuscripts, The Research Institute for Language and Cultures of Asia and Africa, OA068].

Sato, Bunichi. 1936. The songs of the civilized aborigines of Formosa as recorded in the Taiwan fu-chih or Gazetteer of Formosa (「臺灣府志」に見る熟蕃の歌謡 *Taiwanfushi ni miru jukuban no kayo*). *The Japanese journal of ethnology* vol. 2, no. 2, 366-420. [in Japanese]

Thompson, Laurence. 1969. Formosan aborigines in the early eighteenth century: Huang Shu-ching's Fan-su Liu-k'ao. *Monumenta Serica* vol. 28, no. 1: 41-147.

Tsuchida, Shigeru and Yukihiro Yamada. 1991. Ogawa's Siraya/Makatao/Taivoan comparative vocabulary. In Sigeru Tsuchida, Yukihiro Yamada and Tsunekazu Moriguchi (ed.) *Linguistic materials of the Formosan sinicized populations I: Siraya and Basai*, 1-94. Tokyo: The University of Tokyo, Department of Linguistics.

Van der Vlis, Christianus Jacobus. 1842. Formosaansche woorden-lijst, volgens een Utrechts Handschrift [word list of Formosan according to a manuscript from the archives of Utrecht]. In: *Verhandelingen van het Bataviaasch Genootschap*, vol. 18: 437-488. [in Dutch]

Yu, Wenyi [余文儀] ed. 1764. *Xuxiu Taiwanfuzhi* [Reedited gazetteer of Taiwan prefecture 續修臺灣府志].

Zhou, Zhongzuan [周鍾瑄] ed. 1717. *Zhuluozianzhi* [Topographical and historical description of Zhuluoxian 諸羅縣志].

Zhu, Shijie [朱士玠] 1765. *Xiaoliuqiu Manzhi* [Essays on Lesser Liuqiu (Taiwan) 小琉球漫誌].

Chapter 5

Bazin, Edkins and Bi Huazhen's *Yǎnxù cǎotáng bǐjì* (Notes on the abundant heritage of the thatched cottage)

Alain Peyraube & Lin Xiao
Ecole des Hautes Etudes en Sciences Sociales
Centre de recherches linguistiques sur l'Asie Orientale
Paris, France

1. Introduction

It is generally accepted that it was not before 1898 that the first grammar of the Chinese language written by a Chinese scholar was published: the *Mǎ shì wén tōng* 马氏文通 (*Basic principles for writing clearly and coherently from Mister Ma*) by Ma Jianzhong 马建忠 (1844–1900). This grammar, although relying heavily on Chinese tradition, is clearly designed like a Western grammar. The author himself acknowledged in the second preface that his book "has been written in imitation to Western grammars" (*cǐ shū xì fǎng gélángmǎ ér zuò* 此书系仿葛郎玛而作).

When Ma Jianzhong speaks of the model of Western grammars, what he has in mind are obviously grammars on Indo-European languages written by European scholars. After examining several possible sources, Peyraube (1998, 1999, 2001a) has concluded that, among all the grammars that Ma Jianzhong could have had at his disposal, it is likely that the *Grammaire générale et raisonnée* (1660, better known under the name of *Grammaire de Port-Royal*) by Arnauld (1612-1694) and Lancelot (1615-1695) had the most influence on him. The philosophical systems of the *Grammaire de Port-Royal* and that of the *Mǎ shì wén tōng* are quite the same. Moreover, when one compares the terms used in the two books, one finds many similarities, which could hardly have come about by mere chance.[1] However, it has also already been shown that some European grammars

---

[1] See also Gao Mingkai (1953), who acknowledged that "When he studied grammar in France, Ma Jianzhong was more or less influenced by the Grammar of Port-Royal," and more recently Chen Guohua (1997). See also Lü Shuxiang and Wang Haifen (1986).

of the Chinese language - compiled by missionaries or sinologists - could have served as a model for the *Mǎ shì wén tōng*. The *Notitiae Linguae Sinicae* by Prémare (1831) had certainly inspired Ma Jianzhong, but not, curiously and probably unfortunately, Gabelentz's (1881) excellent grammar of Classical Chinese.[2]

In recently re-reading Antoine Bazin's *Grammaire mandarine, ou principes généraux de la langue chinoise parlée* (1856), we noted that in his introduction (p. xxiv), he was referring to Joseph Edkins' important mention in *Grammar of Colloquial Chinese as exhibited in the Shanghai Dialect* (1853, 1868) of Bi Huazhen's 毕华珍 *Yǎnxù cǎotáng bǐjì* 衍绪草堂笔记 (*Notes on the abundant heritage of the thatched cottage*). This is supposed to be the first grammatical book before the *Mǎ shì wén tōng*, since it was written around 1840, half a century earlier than the *Mǎ shì wén tōng*.

Our article will deal mainly with the characteristics of these *Notes on the abundant heritage of the thatched cottage,* to see if it is really a grammar written before *Mǎ shì wén tōng* (Section 3). However, in Section 2, we will first detail the analyses of Bazin, who recognized that he did not have the treaty at his disposal, and Edkins, who clearly had access to this work which later became very difficult to access.

2. Bazin and Edkins' remarks and comments on Bi Huazhen's volume

2.1 Bazin's remarks

Antoine Bazin (1799-1863) was a French sinologist who studied at the Collège de France, where he was a disciple of Abel-Rémusat (1788-1832) and of Stanislas Julien (1797-1873). He contributed numerous articles to the *Journal asiatique* and published several translations of Yuan dynasty (1279-1368) operas. In his *Mémoire sur les principes généraux du chinois vulgaire,* which dates from 1845, he nevertheless considers that Abel-Rémusat's *Élémens de la grammaire chinoise* (1822) "ne sauraient être d'un grand secours ni d'une grande utilité pour l'étude de la langue vulgaire (cannot be of great help or great use for the study of the vernacular language)" (p. 3). He adds:

"On peut croire aussi que M. Abel-Rémusat, malgré sa science, n'est pas sur tous les points d'accord avec les faits (one can also believe that Mr. Abel-Rémusat, despite his science, does not agree on all points with the facts)." (p. 4)

He devotes the first section of his *Mémoire* to the vernacular and its dialects, before tackling again, in the third section (p. 35 *sq.*), the relationship between spoken and written language. He obviously wrongly thought that there are only two dialects, Northern Mandarin (which he calls *Běi guānhuà* 北官话) in Beijing

---

2   Prémare's work was written in 1728, but published for the first time in Malacca in 1831.

and Southern Mandarin (*Nán guānhuà* 南官话) in Nanjing, relegating all other languages to the status of "local idioms or patois."[3] He returned ten years later in detail on this distinction between different language registers in the introduction of his *Grammaire mandarine, ou principes généraux de la langue chinoise parlée* (1856), helped by Chinese scholars who were in Europe at that time (Ou Tanjin, originally from Zhejiang, Wang Ki-yè from Beijing and Tcho Siang-lang from the province of Canton) and who definitively convinced him that:

> "Les Chinois ne reconnaissent pas … deux langues différentes l'une de l'autre, mais deux formes de la même langue, l'une écrite, l'autre parlée, l'une savante, l'autre vulgaire (The Chinese do not recognize… two languages different from each other, but two forms of the same language, one written, the other spoken, one learned, the other vulgar)". (p. ii)

Bazin then specifies above all (pp. xxii - xxiii) that the Chinese grammar consists in making a distinction between *shí zì* 实字 (full words) and *xū zì* 虚字 (empty words), a traditional division that dates back to the Song Dynasty (11th c. CE):[4]

> "Les *shí zì* ont par eux-mêmes une signification propre ; les *xū zì* ou les particules marquent les rapports que les mots pleins ont entre eux (the *shí zì* have their own meaning by themselves; *xū zì* or particles mark the relationships that full words have with each other)" (p. xxiii).

Inside the *shí zì* category, he further distinguishes *huó zì* 活字 (living words, which express an action or a state, like verbs) and *sǐ zì* 死字 (dead words, which only serve to qualify objects, like nouns and adjectives). As for the *xū zì*, these are particles and pronouns:

> "Il y a les particules initiales, les particules conjonctives, les particules disjonctives, les pronoms, les particules collectives, les particules interjectives et les particules finales (There are the initial particles, the conjunctive particles, the disjunctive particles, the pronouns, the collective particles, the interjectional particles, and the final particles)".[5] (p.xxiv)

---

3 In what follows, the transcripts adopted by A. Bazin in his writings have been transformed into *pinyin,* the official transliteration used in China.

4 See Uchida (2011) for an analysis of the evolution of the meanings of *zì* 字 (word), *cí* 词 (word, or sometimes phrase) and *cí* 辞 (phrase, or sometimes sentence) in grammatical treatises before the *Mǎ shì wén tōng.*

5 In his work, A. Bazin adds the Chinese terms corresponding to the different particles he has just

That is when he also mentions that:

"en 1852 le savant M. J. Edkins mit la main sur un traité grammatical, composé par un indigène, dont le nom est Bi Huazhen (in 1852 the scientist M. J. Edkins got hold of a grammatical treatise, composed by a native, whose name is Bi Huazhen)" (pp. xxiv-xxvi).

He considered it as a real grammatical treatise. A. Bazin then details the new distribution proposed by Bi Huanzhen between 'full characters/words' and 'empty characters/words'. He notes that the Chinese author removed the verbs and adjectives from the category of 'full words' to leave only the nouns there, and that he consequently considerably increased the category of 'empty words', which he divided into four subcategories: (1) adjectives; (2) verbs; (3) interrogative and final particles; and (4) conjunctions, negative, and interrogative adverbs. He finds this classification of empty words to be too complicated, but he adds that Bi Huazhen's classification between full and empty words

"... se rapproche beaucoup des classifications européennes. À mon avis, les définitions de l'auteur sont encore plus remarquables que ses divisions. Je n'en citerai que deux, la définition de l'adjectif et la définition du verbe. L'adjectif, dit-il est un mot qui s'ajoute au substantif pour exprimer la manière d'être du substantif. C'est exactement la définition de nos grammairiens (is very close to the European classification. In my opinion, the author's definitions are even more remarkable than his classifications. I will only mention two, the definition of the adjective and the definition of the verb. The adjective, he says, is a word that is added to the noun to express the way of being of the noun. This is exactly the definition of our grammarians)". (pp. xxv-xxvi)

2.2 Edkins' remarks

Joseph Edkins (1823-1905) was a British protestant missionary who spent 57 years in China, 30 of them in Beijing. He was a well-trained linguist and philologist. In his *China's Place in Philology* (1871), he also tried to show that the languages of Europe and Asia have a common origin by comparing the Chinese

---

distinguished: *qǐyǔcí* 起语辞 (initial particles), *jiēyǔcí* 接语辞 (conjunctive particles), *zhuǎnyǔcí* 转语辞 (disjunctive particles), *chènyǔcí* 襯语辞 (pronouns), *shìyǔcí* 束语辞 (collective particles), *tànyǔcí* 叹语辞 (interjectional particles), and *xiēyǔcí* 歇语辞 (final particles). It is surprising that the Chinese term suggested to him by his Chinese informants for the category of pronouns is *chènyǔcí*. These particle distinctions are certainly taken from those made by Wang Mingchang (1694: 162 ff.) in his 辩字诀 *Biàn zì jué*. We thank a reviewer for bringing this to our attention.

and Indo-European vocabulary. In his *A Grammar of Colloquial Chinese as exhibited in the Shanghai Dialect* (1853, 1868), Edkins discusses, in more depth, Bi Huazhen's (ca. 1840) *Yǎnxù cǎotáng bǐjì* which treats all words except substantives as *xū zì*.[6] These *xū zì* are then divided into four classes (Edkins 1868: pp. 58-59): adjectives or *dāi xū zì* 呆虛字; verbs or *huó xū zì* 活虛字; *kǒuqì yǔzhù xūzì* 口气语助虛字; and *kōnghuó xūzì* 空活虛字, adding that "the word *kōng* is prefixed to distinguish these particles from verbs". He does not give any English translation for these last two classes, but he does provide many examples taken from Bi Huazhen's treatise:

> "*Kǒuqì yǔzhù xūzì* 口气语助虛字: Under this head he gives the following examples: *yān* 焉, *hū* 乎, *zāi* 哉, *yě* 也 (interrogative and other finals); *cǐ* 此 'this', *suǒ* 所 'which', *qí* 其 'he', *zhī* 之 'of' (pronouns and the sign of the possessive); *shèn* 甚 'very', *kě* 可 'can', *zuì* 最, *wéi* 为 'be' (adverbs & auxiliary verbs).
> *Kōnghuó xūzì* 空活虛字: The examples he provides are: *suī* 虽 'although', *rú* 如 'like', *dàn* 但 'but', *ruò* 若 'as', *ér* 而 'further', *nǎi* 乃 'then' (conjunctions); *fēi* 非 'it is not', *hé* 何 'what?', *bù* 不 'not', *qǐ* 岂 'how? (negative and interrogative adverbs)'". (pp. 58-59)

Moreover, unlike Bazin, Edkins noted that Bi Huazhen was also interested, apart from parts of speech, in the construction of sentences, which undoubtedly prompted him to open chapters on syntax in his own works.

However, Edkins praised Bi Huazhen more for his intelligence in parts of the speech:

> "While grammar is a science still unknown to the Chinese, it is a mark of the intelligence of our author that he has approached so nearly, as the preceding article shows, to a western classification, and that he has defined[,] with precision, all the principal parts of speech". (p. 59)

In another work devoted to the Standard Mandarin of his time, *A Grammar of the Chinese Colloquial language commonly called the Mandarin Dialect* (1864), influenced by the work that Julien was undertaking (and that was published later in 1869-1870), Edkins recalls in Chapter 3, "Division of words into parts of speech" (pp. 105-107), that the traditional division between *shí zì* and *xū zì*, which he translates as 'full characters' and 'empty characters, particles', is efficient, particularly for pedagogical reasons. He adds:

6　The dates for Bi Huazhen are unknown, but we know that he obtained his provincial examination in 1807.

"Words may also be viewed as expressive of actions (verbs) and things (nouns).
These two kinds of words are *huó zì* (living characters) and *sǐ zì* (dead characters).
The importance of this distinction in Chinese school instruction arises
principally from the very frequent interchange of the verb and the noun".

Moreover, he cites several examples of Chinese nouns that can be used as verbs,
depending on the context.

He then analyses the nouns in detail in the second part of his work (Chapter 4,
pp. 107-127), as well as the classifiers that he calls 'numeral particles' in Chapter 5
(pp. 127-143), adjectives and all comparative constructions in Chapter 6 (pp. 143-
157), pronouns (personal, reflexive, demonstrative, and interrogative) in Chapter 7
(pp. 157-172), verbs and types of sentences in Chapter 8 (pp. 172-196),
prepositions and postpositions in Chapter 9 (pp. 197-200), adverbs in Chapter 10
(pp. 201-214), conjunctions in Chapter 11 (pp. 214-216), and miscellaneous
particles and interjections in Chapter 12 (pp. 217-218). The rest of the work, or the
third part, is devoted to syntax (pp. 218-266). He takes up the parts of the speech
he had detailed in the second part. No new allusion is made to the *Yǎnxù cǎotáng
bǐjì*, but there is no doubt that this book was an important source of inspiration for
the work by Edkins on the Standard Mandarin grammar of that time.

3. The *Yǎnxù cǎotáng bǐjì* 衍绪草堂笔记 (*Notes on the abundant heritage of the thatched cottage*)

3.1 The manuscript

As Uchida (2017, chapter 6, pp. 95-104) points out, the first study to have
mentioned this work by Bi Huazhen is He Qunxiong 何群雄 (2000), which also
assumes that it was a friend of Bi Huazhen named Li Shanlan 李善兰 who could
have recommended the *Yǎnxù cǎotáng bǐjì* to Edkins (pp. 131-136).[7] The
manuscript, however, was inaccessible until Uchida found a copy at the National
Library of Australia, under a different name: *Lùnwén qiǎnshuō* 论文浅说 '*Short
Treaty (for Writing) Essays*', called *Simple Chinese Grammar* by Uchida. These *Notes
on the abundant heritage of the thatched cottage*, written in Classical Chinese and devoted
to Classical Chinese, consist of 102 pages of text.[8] It is divided into four parts:

---

7   Li Shanlan (1810-1882) was a Chinese mathematician who collaborated with Alexander Wylie,
     Joseph Edkins, and others to translate many Western mathematical works into Chinese.

8   The number of pages and the numbering of the pages, which follows, refers to the only text
     currently available, at the National University of Australia. It can be consulted by clicking on
     the link that we added in the list of references under the entry Bi Huazhen. We have only
     renumbered the number of the pages, which appears in the manuscript that have combined
     the two pages, which are side by side.

Lùnwén qiǎnshuō (16 pages of 9 lines with 25 characters per line), *Lùnwén xùshuō* 论文续说 *'Treaty (for Writing) Essays, Continued'* (38 pages), *Yúlùn sìzé* 余论四则 *'Four additional items discussed'* (8 pages), and *Sìyán jùgé* 四言句格 *'Four chunk Format'* (40 pages).⁹ As noted by Hai Xiaofang (2014: 47), the fourth part is independent from the first three, which are devoted to the parts of speech, and concerns quadrisyllabic expressions. Like other previous works devoted to empty particles of the Classical Chinese language, the author also recognizes that his treatise aims to help apprentice-scholars to write well. Nothing surprising about that. As Bazin (1856: xxvi) had already noted, "In the Chinese system, grammar merged with the rhetoric of which it is the foundation".

3.2 The parts of speech identified in the Notes

Bi Huazhen (ca. 1840) takes up the traditional division between 'full characters' (*shí zì*) and 'empty characters' (*xū zì*), and, as Bazin and Edkins already noted, he then divided the 'empty characters' category into four sub-categories. This makes five independent parts of speech, four of which consist of function words. Only one of them consists of content words, or full lexical items. He wrote:

或问作文如何是法，余曰只一实字四虚字¹⁰ "If I am asked how to write well, I say that there is only one *shí zì* and four *xū zì*". (p. 1)

Bi Huazhen also immediately speaks of *bīn-zhǔ liǎng zì* 宾主两字 'two characters *bīn* and *zhǔ*' which are not parts of speech, but which conveniently resemble the functions of today's *zhǔyǔ* 主语 ('subject') and *bīnyǔ* 宾语 ('object'/'complement') (p. 1). He especially states that in the sentence *wén chuán shì* 文传世 [text - transmit - generation] (*The text has been transmitted through several generations*), *wén is a* zhǔ *character,* shì *is a* bīn *character, and the character* chuán *links the two (p. 5).*¹¹

---

9   Uchida's translations are *'More on Chinese Grammar'* for *Lùnwén xùshuō, 'Four additional Essays'* for *Yúlùn sìzé, 'Four-character-meter'* for *Sìyán jùgé.*
10   The punctuation is ours.
11   The original Chinese sentence is (p, 5): 文传世，文为主字，世为宾字，而以传字联缀上下也. Bazin (1856: xxvi) has another interpretation of the sentence, which is also possible, as he translates *wén* by 'book', *chuán* by 'interpret' and *shì* by 'world': "Les livres instruisent le monde (Books interpret the world)".

3.2.1 *Full words (Shí zì) or substantives*[12]

Bi Huazhen then divides the full words - which roughly correspond to the nouns (he says that "they cannot express actions") - into *zǐ zì* 子字 'child word' and *mǔ zì* 母字 'mother word', with the *zǐ zì* being in turn subdivided into *shízài zǐ zì* 实在子字 'concrete child words' and *gōnggòng zǐ zì* 公共子字 'common child words'.[13] He wrote:

> 实字有子母……如天有体，地有形势，人有性情容貌，物有质，事有原流。天、地、人、物、事为母字，体、质、形势、性情、容貌、原流 为子字。有实在子字，有公共子字……公共子字最多。
>
> "Full words are divided into 'child words' and 'mother words' … for instance Heaven has *tǐ* 体 'substance', Earth has *xíngshì* 形势 'form', Human beings have *xìngqíng* 性情 'temperament' and *róngmào* 容貌 appearances, Objects have *zhì* 质 'substance', Events have *yuán* 原 'origin' and *liú* 流 'development'. [All these words] are 'mother words'. Substance, Form, Temperament, Appearance, Origin, Development are 'child words'. There are 'concrete child words' and 'common child words' … [that are] the most numerous". (pp. 18-19)

This organization and description are quite complicated, to say the least, and it is easy to understand that Edkins, and Uchida after him, took the decision to use the terms 'substantive' for *mǔ zì* and 'attribute' for *zǐ zì*. We know that 'substantives' refer to the class of nouns (traditionally defined as 'substances', i.e., names of persons, places, things, etc.), but also to those items which function as nouns, as Bi Huazhen himself foresees. Attributes or attributives refer to the role of adjectives and nouns when they occur as modifiers of the head of a noun phrase.[14] See Figure 1.

---

12 The terms 'full characters' and 'empty characters' should be understood as 'full words' and 'empty words.' We are also using the term 'substantive' to refer to the class of nouns (traditionally defined as 'substances', i.e., names of persons, places, things, etc.), but also to those items which function as nouns, such as adjectives or pronouns, as Bi Huazhen himself foresees. See Crystal (2009: 463).

13 Uchida (2017: 101) calls the *zǐ zì* 子字 'attributes' and the *mǔ zì* 母字 'substantives'; the *shízài zǐ zì* 实在子字 'concrete attributes' and the *gōnggòng zǐ* 公共子字 'common attributes'. Edkins (1853/1868: 66) translations are: 'son characters' ("special son characters' and 'universal son characters') and 'mother characters', but he also uses the terms 'substantive' for *mǔ zì* and 'attribute' for *zǐ zì*.

14 See Crystal (2009: 43, 463).

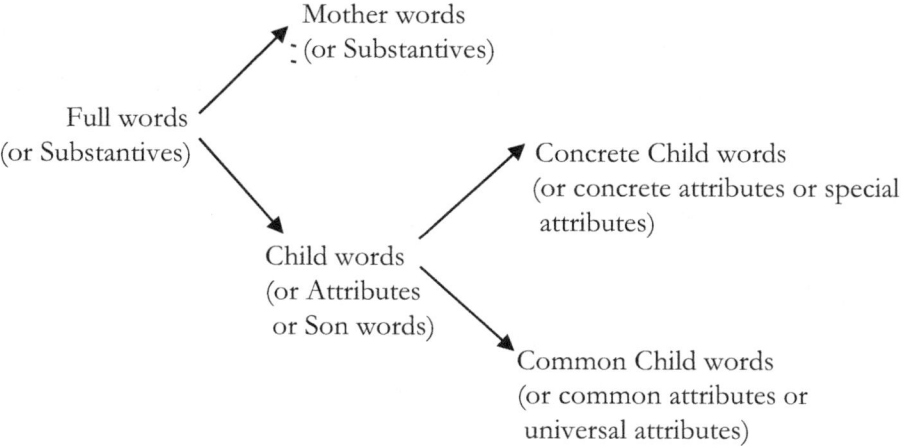

Figure 1: Division of Full words

……如人之五官，鸟兽之翎毛，花木之枝叶，此实在子字……一切
声音、色彩、气味皆是子字。

"For instance, the five senses of human beings, the feathers and fur of birds
and beasts, the branches and the leaves of flowers and plants, are all 'concrete
child words' … All sounds, colors, odors are 'common child words'" (p. 18).

Later, in the second part of his work, Bi Huazhen proposes to divide the *shí zì*
into fourteen semantic fields, out of which ten are devoted to concrete nouns
(see (i) below), and four devoted to abstract nouns (ii) which he calls *húnpò shí zì*
魂魄实字 (soul nouns):

(i) *tiāndì* 天地 'heaven and earth', *qúnshēng* 群生 'living beings', *wànwù* 万物
'all things on earth', *cǎoběn* 草木 'herbaceous', *niǎoshòu* 鸟兽 'birds and beasts',
chūnrì 春日 'springtime', *yīfù* 衣服 'clothes', *jiǔlǐ* 酒醴 'wine and sweet spirits',
lóugé 楼阁 'buildings', *bǎojìng* 宝镜 'treasure mirrors'
(ii) *zāojì* 遭际 'circumstances', *jīzhào* 机兆 'aura, omen', *duānní* 端倪 'inkling',
qínghuái 情怀 'feelings'.[15] (p. 26)

However, it is indeed the category of *xū zì* which is the most interesting, and the
most original, in the treaty of Bi Huazhen. It is very different from previous
treaties on 'empty words', and it has not been taken up by Bazin and only very
briefly by Edkins.

---

15 It is difficult to admit that some of these terms correspond to genuine semantic fields.

3.2.2 *Empty words (xū zì)*

The empty words, or functional morphemes, are divided into four different types: *dāi xū zì* 呆虚字 corresponding to adjectives [- dynamic words], *huó xū zì* 活虚字 corresponding to verbs [+ dynamic words], *kǒuqì yǔzhù xū zì* 口气语助虚字 'emotive particles' and *kōnghuó xū zì* 空活虚字 'circumstantial particles' or 'adverbials', to use Edkins (1868: 58) and Uchida's (2017: 97) translations. Note that Uchida also calls them 'non-inflected particles'. See Figure 2.

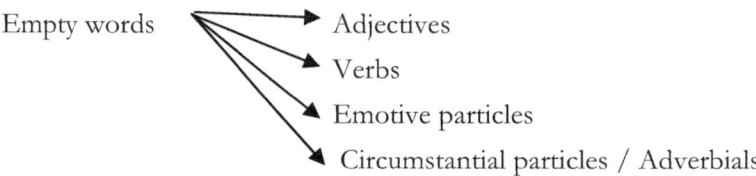

Figure 2: Division of Empty words

Regarding the *dāi xū zì* (that we will call today adjectives), Bi Huazhen's states that they are used to describe the state of things. Without adjectives, there would be no states of things. He gives the following definition:

> 呆虚字与实字相加以形容实字如何样，须形容得切，故实字不消做得，呆虚字要做。 "Adjectives are added to substantives (*shí zì*) in order to describe the way the noun is expressed, the description needs to be accurate, hence, full words (substantives) cannot do it, and adjectives have to do it." (p. 4)

He also introduced the contemporary notion of a 'phrase' when he adds that an adjective preceding a verb (*huó zì*) behaves like a single word.

As regards precisely this second category of empty words (*huó xū zì*), i.e., the verbs, they are characterized and defined by Bi Huazhen as follows:

> 活虚字之用，一以联缀上下……如云"文传世"，"文"为主字，"世"为宾字，而以"传"字联缀上下也。 一以写出人事，如云"作文""评文"之类，"作"字、"评"字皆人事也，无活虚字则宾主两字不能联贯，人事亦一毫写不出。活虚字最多习用者约两千上下……亦有两字拆不开者，如婆娑盘恒等双声字样，只作活虚字用。
>
> "The use of *huó xū zì* aims to link the preceding elements with the following ones … If we say *wén chuán shì* (the text has been transmitted through several generations), *wén (text)* is the subject, *shì (generation)* the complement and

chuán (transmit) connects the two. (If) we write down things about human activities such as *zuò wén* (to write a text) (or) *píng wén* (to criticize a text), the subject and the complement cannot be connected in the absence of the *huó zì* (and) the human activities cannot be written down. There are about no more than two thousand verbs commonly used … There are also some disyllabic words that cannot be separated, for instance *pósuō* (to dance), *pánhuán* (to linger in a place), etc.; they can be only used as verbs." (p. 5)

Bi Huazhen also develops the notion of action for these *huó xū zì*, which he describes as *dòng zì*, terminology that is also that adopted by the *Mǎ shì wén tōng*:

活虚字是动字……如云 "赏茶"，如云 "议事"，口必动也；如云 "携樽"，如云 "擎物"，手必动也；如云 "升阶"，如云 "践地"，足必动也；如云 "怀人" 如云 "治性"，心必动也。

"*Huó xū zì* are *dòng zì* (moving words or action words) … If we say, 'to taste tea', 'to discuss matters', the mouth certainly moves. If we say, 'to carry the barrel' 'to lift an object', the hands certainly move. If we say, 'to go up stairs', 'to tread the ground', the feet certainly move. If we say, 'to think about someone', 'to cultivate one's moral character', the mind certainly moves." (pp. 32-)

He also distinguishes several cases concerning the orientation taken by these action words. It is not at all easy to understand what he had in mind with these distinctions, as one can measure by reading the following:

人事须分内外，活虚要辨正借……如云"出门访友"，如云"持斧砍木"，此自内说出也。（斧木皆身外物）。有自外说入者，如云"宾从到门"，如云"人钦品学"，此自外说入也。有自内收入者，如云"受谏纳言"，如云"受恩承惠"，此自内收入也. 有自外勾出者，如云 "丝竹动情"，如云 "友朋劝驾"，此自外勾出也. 活虚字有正用者，如云 "射鸟" "钓鱼"，如云 "饮酒" "食肉"，此正用也. 如云 "射利钓名"，如云 "饮和" "食德"，此借用也。

"Human activities can be divided into internal and external; the verbs are used literally and metaphorically … For instance, in 'go out the gate and visit friends', 'carry an axe and chop wood', the verbs are 'verbs for externally directed action' (the axe and the wood are external objects').[16] There are

---

16 Uchida (2017: 103-104), from whom we borrowed a few translations above, but who did not translate everything, decided to render *zì nèi shuō chū* 自内说出 as "verbs for externally directed actions", *zì wài shuō rù* 自外说入 as "verbs for internally directed actions", *zì nèi shōu rù* 自内收入 as "verbs for internal actions", *zì wài gōu chū* 自外勾出 as "verbs for external actions".

'verbs for internally directed actions', for instance in 'the guest and the servant arrived at the gate' or in 'one admires conduct and learning (of an individual)'. There are 'verbs for internal actions', such as 'to accept advice' or 'to receive benefits and to accept favors'. There are 'verbs for external actions', such as 'strings and bamboos (of the musical instrument) stirred the emotions', and 'friends encourage you to do something'. Verbs are also used literally, as in 'to shoot birds', 'fishing', 'to drink alcohol', and 'to eat meat'. If one says, 'make money and false names' (using the two verbs *shè* 'to shoot' and *diào* 'to fish'), or 'enjoy harmony, kindness and beneficence' (with the verbs *yǐn* 'to drink' and *shí* 'to eat'), these are metaphorical uses". (p. 31)

There is no doubt that Bi Huazhen wanted to emphasize the logical relationships between the different elements of a sentence, and that he was well aware of the importance of semantics and that the grammar and structure of sentences are not totally independent. The differences between external (event-oriented) modifiers, and internal (participant-oriented) modifiers might be clear, but the system he tried to set up is still quite confusing and complicated.

The "emotive particles" *kǒuqì yǔzhù xū zì* 口气语助虚字 are defined as follows:

口气语助，不能划清，只作一类，如 "焉" "哉" "乎" "也"
"此" "其" "所" "以" 等类，凡数十字。
其文甚工，所作之文最工雅，可传后世。

"Emotive particles cannot be separated clearly, and they form together one group, such as the ten or so particles: *yān, zāi, hū, yě, cǐ, qí, suǒ, yǐ*, etc.
[Examples:] *qí wén shèn gōng* 'his text is extremely well-written' *suǒ zuò zhī wén zuì gōng yǎ* 'the writings he made are the best and the more elegant' *kě chuán hòu shì* 'can transmit to later generations'". (pp. 8-9)

For Bi Huazhen, the emotives are *shèn* 甚 'extremely' in the first example, *zuì* 最 'most' in the second example, and *kě* 可 'can' in the last one. Bi Huazhen adds:

无口气语助虚字则语皆拳局，说好说恶，总无分寸也。
"If there are no emotive particles (empty words), the discourse is rough and incomplete, good or bad are not distinguishable". (p. 13)

See section 2.2 for the list of these emotive particles taken from Bi Huazhen's treaty and given by Edkins.

We did not find better renditions, especially for the last two categories, that are rather unclear. However, we are not sure that it corresponds exactly with what Bi Huazhen had in mind.

The fourth and last category of these empty words comprises the *kōng huó xū zì* 空活虚字 (circumstantial particles or adverbials). Their difference from emotive particles is not easy to describe, and Bi Huazhen himself admits that the two categories could eventually become only one. He says:

> 与口气虚字略同，今欲逐层加入，故分此类，如"虽""但""如""若""非""不""而""乃""何""岂"等类，凡数十字。

"(These particles) are quite similar to the emotive particles, (but) now (that I) want to talk in more detail, I make a distinction for the ten or so following particles: *suī* 'although', *dàn* 'but', *rú* 'like', *ruò* 'if', *fēi* 'not be', *bù* 'not', *ér* 'and', *nǎi* 'then', *hé* 'what', *qǐ* 'how', etc.". (p. 9)

As we can see, these circumstantial particles are also interrogative pronouns like *hé*, adverbs like *bù* or *qǐ*, and conjunctions like *suī* or *ér*.

Bi Huazhen also makes a distinction between two types of sentences: *píng shí huó jù* 'concrete living sentences' and *kōng líng huó jù* 'abstract living sentences'. He writes:

> 是实有此人此文，故谓之平实活句。若空灵活句，则纯是我之议论，不指煞一人一事，以此为别。

"The implication is that there really is such a person in such and such circumstances. Hence, sentences with adverbials are called objective animated sentences *píng shí huó jù* 平实活句. Abstract animated sentences *kōng líng huó jù* 空灵活句 consist entirely of one's discussion. One is at a loss to specify who and what the sentence is about. These two types of sentences need to be distinguished".[17] (p.10)

In summary, the system set up by Bi Huazhen on the division between full words and empty words can be characterized as in Table 3.

---

17 The translation of this obscure passage has been borrowed from Uchida (2005: 100).

Full words (or Substantives)	Mother words (or Substantives)	
	Child words (or Attributes or Son words)	Concrete Child words (or concrete attributes or special attributes)
		Common Child words (or common attributes or universal attributes)
Empty words	Adjectives	
	Verbs	
	Emotive particles	
	Circumstantial particles or Adverbials	

Figure 3: Division of Full words and Empty words

3.3 Issues on syntax

It is in this area, that of syntax, that Bi Huazhen's treatise is undoubtedly more innovative than the old treatises on particles. As the few researchers who have had access to the Bi Huazhen treatise (Edkins 1864, Uchida 2017, Hai Xiaofang 2014) have suggested before us, Bi Huazhen has not only revisited the traditional division between *shí* and *xū* and its contribution is not limited to a study on parts of speech. He was also certainly interested in issues on syntax and on the syntactic functions of these full words and empty words, as mentioned above with the distinction he made between *zhǔ* (subject) and *bīn* (object / complement).

This distinction between *zhǔ* and *bīn*, however, is different from what is usually made today with our notions of 'subject' and 'object'. It is done primarily for stylistic reasons. For Bi Huazhen, it is always a question of giving advice on how to write perfectly, to "make the sequence of the constituents of the sentence fluid" (*chàng jù fǎ* 畅句法) as he points out (p. 13).

Bi Huazhen cites several examples where these words *bīn* are post-verbal and therefore in object position, such as *hòu shì* 后世 in *wén chuán hòu shì* 文传后世 'the text is handed down to the descendants', *shì* 世 in *wénzhāng chuán shì* 文章传世 'the writing has been transmitted through several generations, and *rén* 人 in *wén bǐ jīng rén* 文笔惊人 'the writing (style) amazed people' (pp. 6-7). But he also cites examples where the words *bīn* are pre-verbal like *cháo xī* 朝夕 (day and night) in *cháo xī zuò wén* 朝夕作文 'to write day and night' or *bīngxuě* 冰雪 (cleverly) in *bīngxuě chéng wén* 冰雪成文 'compose a text intelligently'. In these last two examples, the word *bīn* is no longer an object or a complement, but an adverbial. The fact remains that *zhǔ* and *bīn* are notions of syntactic functions, which are much more developed than those one could find sketched in in earlier treatises by Yuan Renlin (1710) or Liu Qi (1711).

As an expression of interest in syntactic problems, we can also cite the long-detailed analyses on negation markers in classical Chinese: *bù* 不, *wèi* 未, *fēi* 非, *wú* 无, and *mò* 莫. The meaning of the negative sentences in which they are used are not always the simple counterpart of the affirmative sentences. Their meaning often varies depending on the semantic nature of the verbs that are denied.

Bi Huazhen, finally, also attached great importance in his treatise to the types of sentences. He distinguishes three types of sentences (pp. 6-10): (i) *dāi jù* 呆句 'attributive', composed of nominatives (*shí zì* 实字), adjectives (*dāi xū zì* 呆虚字) or verbs (*huó xū zì* 活虚字) subdivided into 'single attributives' (a subject followed by an adjective predicate) and 'double attributives' (an adverbial + a verb/predicate + an object'); (ii) *dāi zhōng dài huó jù* 呆中带活句 'verbal attributives' composed of verbs and emotional particles; and (iii) *huó jù* 活句 'adverbial attributives' involving *píng shí huó jù* 平实活句 'objective animated sentences' and *kōng líng huó jù* 空灵活句 'abstract animated sentences'.

For each of these types, he provides sample sentences, such as *bǐ jī qīng lì* 笔机清利 'the inspiration is sharp' for (i), but it is almost impossible to really understand the rationale for this division. However, Hai Xiaofang (2014: 69) considers that Bi Huazhen's *dāi jù* are close to descriptive/declarative sentences, *huó jù* to discursive sentences, and *dāi zhōng dài huó jù* a mixture of both. This interpretation would undoubtedly need to be further argued.

3.4 The Notes and the *Mǎ shì wén tōng*

Hai Xiaofang and Uchida consider the Bi Huazhen manuscript to be a real grammatical treatise prior to the *Mǎ shì wén tōng*. Uchida even goes so far as to say that "surprisingly, even fifty years prior to the appearance of *Ma's guide to the Written Language (Mǎ shì wén tōng)*, the Chinese scholar Bi Huazhen wrote an outstanding treatise on grammar" (p. 104). This view is certainly excessive. The *Mǎ shì wén tōng* is undoubtedly much more advanced. The grammatical analyses are indeed more systematic, more consistent, and undoubtedly closer to Western grammatical treatises.

Was Ma Jianzhong aware of this Bi Huazhen treaty? It might sound weird, since Edkins obviously had a copy of it, but it looks like he was not, as Ma Jianzhong would probably not have hesitated to take whole paragraphs as they were, as he did with the work of Yuan Renlin (1710).

If any proof were necessary to show that Ma Jianzhong profited from the work of Yuan Renlin, it is sufficient to compare the following few passages, extracts from Yuan Renlin's *Xū zì shuō* (XZS) and recopied almost *ad verbatim* in the *Mǎ shì wén tōng* (MSWT), as has already been highlighted by Peyraube (2001b) and Chappell & Peyraube (2014):

XZS, p. 117: '(则) 字（即）字，乃直承顺接之辞，犹俗云（就）也， 与上影响相随，口吻甚紧 *zé zì jí zì, nǎi zhíchéng shùnjiē zhi cí, yóu sú yún jiù yě, yǔ shàng yǐngxiǎng xiāngsuí, kǒuwén shèn jǐn* "The characters *zé* and *jí* are words with the function of smooth coordination, and are similar to the vernacular *jiù*, in following the preceding context; the tone resembles it very closely".

MSWT, p. 495:（则）字乃直承顺接之辞，与上文影响相随，口吻甚紧 *zé zì nǎi zhíchéng shùnjiē zhi cí, yǔ shàngwén yǐngxiǎng xiāngsuí, kǒuwén shèn jǐn* "The character *zé* is a word with the function of smooth coordination, in following the preceding context; the tone resembles it very closely)".

XZS, p. 19:（第）字(但）字(独）字(特）字之声，皆属轻转，不甚与前文 批驳，只从言下单抽一处，轻轻那转，犹言别无可说，但只有一件 如此也 *dì zì dàn zì dú zì tè zì zhi shēng, jiē shǔ qīngzhuǎn, búshèn yǔ qiánwén pībó, zhǐ cóng yánxià dān chōu yíchù, qīngqīng nà zhuǎn, yóu yán bié wú kě shuō, dàn zhǐ yǒu yíjiàn rúcǐ yě.* "The tone of the words, *dì, dàn, dú,* and *tè* are all slightly adversative but do not contradict the preceding text to any great extent. They only focus on one feature in the actual text, making a slight shift, but just one of this sort, since there is no disagreement with the other points".

MSWT, pp. 523-524: '(第)（但)（独)（特)（惟)五字，皆转语辞……皆承 上文，不相批驳，只从言下单抽一端轻轻掉转。犹云则别无可说， 只有一件如此云云 *dì dàn dú tè wéi wǔ zì, jiē zhuǎnyǔ cí ... jiē chéng shàngwén, bù xiāng pībó, zhǐ cóng yánxià dān chōu yí duān qīngqīng diàozhuǎn, yóu yún zé bié wú kě shuō, zhǐ yǒu yíjiàn rúcǐ yún yún.* "These five words *dì, dàn, dú, tè,* and *wéi* are all conjunctions and continue the preceding text without any disagreement. They only focus on one feature in the actual text, making a slight shift, and just one of this sort, since there is no disagreement with the other points)".

However, we do not find anything of the sort (what must be called today plagiarism today) when we compare the *Yǎnxù cǎotáng bǐjì* with the *Mǎ shì wén tōng*.

Moreover, when we compare the very modern system, for the time, which Ma Jianzhong developed, with the certainly original, but much more opaque, formulations of Bi Huazhen, we can conclude that if Ma Jianzhong (MJZ) was aware of the Bi Huazhen's (BHZ) notes, he completely ignored them.[18] See Figure 4 for a comparison of MJZ and BHZ terminologies.

	MJZ	BHZ
Substantives (Full words)	*Míngzì* 名字	*Shí zì* 实字 (Full words) Child words *zǐ zì* 子字 (concrete & common) Mother words *mǔ zì* 母字
Pronouns (Full words)	*Dàizì* 代字	*kǒuqì yǔzhù xū zì* 口气语助虚字
Verbs (Full words)	*Dòngzì* 动字	*huó xū zì* 活虚字 (Empty word)
Adjectives (Full words)	*Jìngzì* 静字	*dāi xū zì* 呆虚字 (Empty word)
Adverbs (Full words)	*Zhuāngzì* 庄字	*kǒuqì yǔzhù xū zì* 口气语助虚字 & *kōnghuó xū zì* 空活虚字
Prepositions (Empty words)	*Jièzì* 介字	
Conjunctions (Empty words)	*Liánzì* 连字	*kōnghuó xū zì* 空活虚字
Particles (Empty words)	*Zhùzì* 助字	*kǒuqì yǔzhù xū zì* 口气语助虚字 & *kōnghuó xū zì* 空活虚字
Interjections (Empty words)	*Tànzì* 叹字	

Figure 4: Comparative analysis of MJZ and BHZ terminologies

At this point we have to remember that the *Mǎ shì wén tōng* is divided into three fundamental parts: parts of speech (grammatical categories, labelled *zì* 字), syntactic functions (called *cí* 词) and positions or cases (called *cí* 辞), with this final part being very original, obviously inspired by Western grammars. Nothing of the sort can be found in the manuscript of Bi Huazhen. Another original feature of the *Mǎ shì wén tōng*, which is also ignored in the *Yǎnxù cǎotáng bǐjì* is the distinction between *jù* 句 and *dòu* 读, a distinction which is not always very clear, but corresponds in many cases to the modern distinction between sentences (*jùzǐ* 句子) and clauses/propositions (*fēnjù* 分句).

Did Bi Huazhen know of any grammatical treatises written by Westerners on languages other than Chinese, like Ma Jianzhong who later admitted having been inspired and influenced by Western grammars? It is not easy to answer this question, but it is unlikely. Hai Xiaofang (2014: 45) asserts however that Edkins had suggested that Bi Huazhen's *Notes on the abundant heritage of the thatched collage* were influenced by Abel-Rémusat (1822). If we again compare the *Yǎnxù cǎotáng bǐjì* with the Abel-Rémusat's *Élémens de la grammaire chinoise*, we could not draw any

---

18 For a detailed examination of the terms used in *Mǎ shì wén tōng*, and a comparison with Arnauld & Lancelot's *Grammar of Port-Royal* (1660), see Peyraube (2001a).

conclusion that the *Yǎnxù* is indebted to the *Élémens*, even if only episodically.

If we take up again the classification of ancient works suggested by He Jiuying (1985) between rhetorical / stylistic treatises and philological treatises closer to linguistics, there is no doubt that Bi Huazhen's treatise is rhetorical / stylistic in nature, while the works of Abel-Rémusat and of Ma Jianzhong are grammars that claim to be such, even if the *Mǎ shì wén tōng*, obviously more philological than rhetorical, has nevertheless kept some stylistic ingredients.

4. Conclusion

Bi Huazhen's *Notes on the abundant heritage of the thatched cottage* is certainly a treatise much more developed than the previous works, whether it be Lu Yiwei (1311), Yuan Renlin (1710), Liu Qi (1711), Wang Yinzhi (1798), or the even later Yu Yue (contemporary of Ma Jianzhong), from the point of view of the classification of parts of speech within the traditional division between 'full words' and 'empty words'. It is also an original treatise in that it contains purely syntactic analyses, with detailed accounts of the sentence structure and its various components. However, these analyses are far from being clear and consistent.

We can understand that these *Notes on the abundant heritage of the thatched cottage* may have slightly influenced some Western grammarians who became interested in the Chinese language at the end of the 19th century, but this influence, if any, has been very limited.

In any case, we conclude that this work of Bi Huazhen cannot be considered as the first authentically grammatical treatise written by a Chinese researcher, which would have preceded the *Mǎ shì wén tōng* by almost half a century.

The *Mǎ shì wén tōng* remains the first successful attempt at a proper grammatical analysis of Classical Chinese, which later influenced most of the grammars of the Chinese language, Classical or Modern, of the 20th century. As Mair (1997) quite rightly put it once, Ma Jianzhong's book is often quite impenetrable and incomprehensible, and it would be a nightmare to have it translated into English or another Western language. Certainly, but the internal consistency of the *Mǎ shì wén tōng* is indisputable. Mair's judgment could indeed be more appropriate if applied to the *Yǎnxù cǎotáng bǐjì*.

References

1. Primary Sources

Abel-Rémusat, Jean-Pierre. 1822. *Élémens de la grammaire chinoise ou principes généraux du kou-wen ou style antique et du kouan-hoa, c'est-à-dire de la langue commune généralement usitée dans l'Empire chinois.* Reedition of the 1857 version, Buc (France): Ala production, 1987. Reedition of the 1857 version.

Arnauld, Antoine and Claude Lancelot. 1660. *Grammaire Générale et raisonnée contenant les fondements de l'art de parler, expliqués de manière claire et naturelle, les raisons de ce qui est commun à toutes les langues, et des principales différences qui s'y rencontrent.* Paris : Allia, 1997.

Bazin, Antoine. 1845. *Mémoire sur les principes généraux du chinois vulgaire.* Paris : Imprimerie royale.

Bazin, Antoine. 1856. *Grammaire mandarine ou principes généraux de la langue parlée.* Paris : Imprimerie impériale.

Bi Huazhen 华华珍. ca. 1840. *Yǎnxù cǎotáng bǐjì* 衍绪草堂笔记 (*Notes on the abundant heritage of the thatched cottage*). Available at http://nla.gov.au/nla.gen-un1908951.

Edkins, Joseph. 1853 *A grammar of colloquial Chinese as exhibited in the Shanghai dialect. 2nd ed.,* Shanghai: Presbyterian mission press, 1868.

Edkins, Joseph. 1857. *A Grammar of the Chinese Colloquial Language Commonly Called the Mandarin Dialect. 2nd ed.,* Shanghai: Presbyterian Mission Press. 2nd edition 1864.

Edkins, Joseph. 1871. *China's place in philology: an attempt to show that the languages of Europe and Asia have a common origin.* London: Trübner & Co.

Gabelentz, Georg von der. 1881. *Chinesiche Grammatik mit Ausschluß des niederen Stiles und der heutigen Umgangssprache.* Leipzig: Weigel.

Julien, Stanislas. 1869–70. *Syntaxe nouvelle de la langue chinoise fondée sur la position des mots, suivie de deux traités sur les particules et les principaux termes de grammaire, d'une table des idiotismes, de fables, de légendes et d'apologues, traduits mot à mot par Stanislas Julien.* Paris : Imprimerie nationale.

Liu Qi 刘淇. 1711. *Zhùzì biànluè* 助字辨略 (*Compendium of grammatical particles*). Beijing: Zhonghua shuju, 1954.

Lu Yiwei 卢以纬. 1311. *Yǔzhù* 语助 (*Grammatical particles*). Beijing: Zhonghua shuju, 1988.

Ma Jianzhong 马建忠. 1898. *Mǎ shì wén tōng* 马氏文通 (*Basic principles for writing clearly and coherently by Mister Ma*). Reedition, Beijing: Zhonghua shuju, 1954. In Classical Chinese.

Prémare, Joseph Henri de. 1728. *Notitiae Linguae Sinicae.* Malacca: Cura Academia Anglo-Sinensis, 1831.

Wang Mingchang 王鸣昌. 1694. *Biàn zì jué* 辩字诀 (*Debate on characters formula*). In Wang Kezhong 王克仲 (ed.) *Zhu yu ci ji zhu* 助语辞集注 (*Collection and notes on particles*). Beijing: Zhonghua shuju, 1988.

Wang Yinzhi 王引之. 1798. *Jīngzhuàn shìcí* 经传释词 (*Explanation of particles in the Classics and the Commentaries*). Changsha: Yuelu shushe, 1984.

Yu Yue 俞樾. No date. *Gǔshū yíyì jǔlì* 古书疑义举例 (*Examples of disputable problems from the classics*). Beijing: Zhonghua Shuju, 1983.

Yuan Renlin 袁仁林. 1710. *Xū zì shuō* 虚字说 (*Treatise on empty words*). Beijing: Zhonghua shuju, 1989.

2. General References

Casacchia, Giorgio & Mariarosaria Gianninoto. 2012. *Storia della linguistica cinese*. Venezia: Libreri Editirice Cafoscarina.

Chappell, Hilary & Alain Peyraube. 2014. The History of Chinese Grammars in Chinese and Western Scholarly Traditions. *Language and History vol.* 57, no. 2, pp. 113-142.

Chen Guohua 陈国华. 1997. Pǔbiàn wéilǐ yǔfǎ yǔ *Mǎ shì wén tōng* 普遍唯理语法与马氏文通 (General and reasoned grammar and the *Mǎ shì wén tōng*). *Guowai yuyanxue* vol. 3, pp. 1-11.

Crystal, David. 2009. *A Dictionary of Linguistics and Phonetics*. 6th ed., Oxford: Blackwell.

Gao Mingkai 高明凯. 1953. *Guānyú hànyǔ de cílèi fēnbié* 关于汉语的词类分别 [On the division of parts of speech in Chinese]. *Zhongguo yuwen vol.* 10, pp. 13-16.

Gianninoto, Mariarosaria. 2022. Linguistic variation in Late Qing Western sources: an analysis of Edkin's grammar of Shanghainese. N. McLelland *et al.* (eds.) *Language standards, norms and variation in Asia*. Multilingual matters, pp. 40-55.

Hai Xiaofang 海晓芳. 2014. *Wénfǎ cǎochuàngqī zhōngguórén de hànyǔ yánjiū* 文法草创期中国人的汉语研究 (*Studies in the period of creation of Chinese grammars by Chinese scholars*). Beijing: The Commercial Press.

He Jiuying 何九盈. 1985. *Zhōngguó gǔdài yǔyánxué shǐ* 中国古代语言学史 (*History of linguistics in Ancient China*). Henan: Henan renmin chubanshe.

He Qunxiong 何群雄. 2000. *Chūgokugo bunpōgaku kotohajime* (*The Beginnings of the Study of Chinese Grammar*). Tokyo: Sangensha.

Lü Shuxiang 吕叔湘 and Wang Haifen 王海芬. 1986. Mǎ shì wén tōng *dúběn* 马氏文通 读本 (*Mǎ shì wén tōng reader*). Shanghai: Jiaoyu chubanshe.

Mair, Victor H. 1997. Ma Jianzhong and the Invention of Chinese Grammar. C. Sun (ed.), *Studies on the History of Chinese Syntax*. Berkeley: Journal of Chinese Linguistics - Monograph Series, no. 10, pp. 5–26.

Peyraube, Alain 贝罗贝. 1998. Ershí shìjì yǐqián ōuzhōu hà yǔ yǔfǎxué yánjiū zhuàngkuàng 二十世纪以前欧洲汉语语法学研究状况 (Studies in Chinese grammar in Europe before the 20th century). *Zhongguo yuwen* vol. 5, pp. 346-352.

Peyraube, Alain. 1999. Sur les Sources du *Mǎ shì wén tōng*. *Histoire, Epistémologie, Langage* vol. 21, no. II, pp. 65-78.

Peyraube, Alain. 2001a. Some Reflections on the Sources of the *Mǎ shì wén tōng*. In Michael Lackner, Iwo Amelung and Joachim Kurtz (eds.), *New Terms for New Ideas – Western Knowledge & Lexical Change in Late Imperial China*, pp. 341-356. Leiden: Brill.

Peyraube, Alain 贝罗贝 2001b. Qīngdài *Mǎ shì wén tōng* yǐqián de yǔfǎ zhīshí 清代马氏文通以前的语法知识 (The grammatical knowledge in the Qing dynasty before the

Mǎ shì wén tōng). In Redouane Djamouri (ed.), *Collected Essays in Ancient Chinese Grammar, pp. 1-8.* Paris: EHESS.

Uchida, Keiichi 内田庆市. 2005. *Mǎ shì wén tōng* yǐqián Zhōngguórén de yǔfǎ yánjiū – guānyú Bì Huázhēn de *Yǎnxù cǎotáng bǐjì de pǐncí fēnlèi fǎ* 马氏文通以前中国人的语法研究－关于毕华珍《衍续草堂笔记》的品词分类法 (*Research on Grammar by Chinese scholars before the* Mǎ shì wén tōng – *on the classification of parts of speech in Bi Huazhen's* Notes on the abundant heritage of the thatched cottage). *Minutes of Chinese Literature Society of Kansai University vol.* 26.

Uchida, Keiichi 内田庆市. 2011. Hànyǔ yǔfǎ yánjiū zhōng de cílèi huáfèn jí shùyǔ yǎnbiàn wèntí 汉语语法研究中的词类划分及术语演变问题 (Word class division and terminological evolution in the study of Chinese grammar). *Journal of East Asian Cultural Interaction Studies vol.* 4, pp. 309-325 (Kansai University Institutional Repository).

Uchida, Keiichi. 2017. *A Study of Cultural Interaction and Linguistic Contact –Approaching Chinese Linguistics from the Periphery.* Göttingen: V&R Unipress.

Chapter 6

Cultural Interaction Studies and Linguistic Research

Keiichi Uchida
(Kansai University, Japan)[1]

Abstract

What are "Cultural Interaction Studies"? At the present time, the author still has no clear answer to that question. For this reason, we aim to categorize "Cultural Interaction Studies" as an entirely new field of study that we are pursuing at the moment.

Below, the author would like to shortly introduce the fundamental concepts of Cultural Interaction Studies:

In the past, when conducting research on cultural interaction, for instance, the history of cultural interaction between China and Japan, in most cases we took the two countries as basic units. Focusing on the division of research areas and branches, we carried out individual analyses and investigations from the particular perspective of scientific fields such as linguistics, thought, ethnography, religion, literature, and history. However, this method is not able to yield the complete picture of cultural interaction. Therefore, the concept of "Cultural Interaction Studies" which I advocate for in this article, aims to replace the former practice to take the country, the nation, as well as the individual scientific fields as basic units. Instead, it takes the complex of East Asian culture as a whole, and carries out comprehensive and systematic analyses on its inherent processes of cultural development, transmission, contact, and transformation. This is the basic concept of Cultural Interaction Studies which I am going to argue for in this article.

The article takes the perspective of linguistics (Chinese linguistics) as a point of departure and analyzes as well as examines the relation between the "periphery" and the "center". Furthermore, we explore the possibility and effectiveness of the "approaching the center from the core" approach for Chinese linguistic research by analyzing the connection between concepts such as "individual" and "general", "special", and "universal". In addition, we conduct further investigation of its peripheral materials.

---

1 English translation: Lukas Betz; Classical Chinese examples: Barbara Meisterernst.

1. The vehicles of cultural interaction: objects, humans, and language

When we talk about cultural interaction or cultural exchange, we can only concretely think of first, the Buddhist scriptures that entered China via the Silk Road, and second, the Western knowledge that entered China together with Christianity after the 16th century. As vehicles of cultural interaction, the author assumes that we can single out "objects", "humans", and "language".

One obvious example for cultural interaction via the transmitter "object" are the scriptures and goods that came from the Western Territories via the silk road:

葡萄：＂大宛在匈奴西南，在漢正西，在漢可萬裡，有葡萄酒，多善馬。＂（『史記』）
＂張騫使西域，得其種而還，中國始有。＂（『通志略』）
Grape: "Dayuan is in the south-west of the Xiong-nu territory, it is immediately
           to the west of the Han empire, around 10,000 li away from Han; they
           have grape wine and many good horses." (*Shiji* 1st c. BCE)
           "When Zhang Qian was sent to the Western Regions he obtained their
           crops and brought them back, and [so] Zhongguo started to have them."
           (*Tongzhi lüe* 12th c. CE)

安石榴：＂張騫使西域，得安石國榴種以歸，故名安石榴。＂（『博物志』）
Pomegranate: "When Zhang Qian was sent to the Western Regions, he obtained
               pomegranates from the Anshi country and brought them back,
               therefore one calls them An pomegranates." (*Bowuzhi* 3rd c. CE)

獅子：＂烏戈有桃拔、師子、犀牛。＂（『漢書』）
Lion: "In Wuge (name of a state south of the ancient state Shǔ 蜀) there are
           hornless deers, lions and rhinoceroses." (*Hanshu* 2nd c. CE)

酥：＂蘇，酪也＂（『玉篇』）＂酥，酪屬，牛羊乳為之＂（『韻會』）
Yogurt: "sū: sū 'flaky paste', is lào/luò (Pulleyblank 1991) 'fermented milk,
        yoghurt. (*Yupian* 6th c. CE) sū, belongs to fermented milk, yoghurt, the
        teats of cows and sheep produce it." (*Yunhui* 13th c. CE)"

Furthermore, an additional example are the goods that entered China through the missionaries as vehicles, during the second wave of Western knowledge spreading to the East. Objects such as images and statues of God, portraits of Maria, bibles, crucifixes, clocks, world maps, and pianos, all entered China during the time the missionary Matteo Ricci 利瑪竇 (1552 – 1610) was spreading the gospel in China.

> 萬曆二十八年。瑪竇偕龐迪我等八人。齎貢物。詣燕京進⋯⋯謹以原攜本國土物，所有天主圖像一幅，天主母圖像二幅，天主經一本，珍珠鑲嵌十字架一座，報時自鳴鐘二架，萬國圖誌一冊，西琴一張等物，敬獻御前。此雖不足為珍，然自極西貢至，差覺異耳，且稍寓野人芹曝之私。（黃柏祿『正教奉褒』）

"In the 28th year of Wanli, Matteo Ricci was accompanied by eight missionaries, among them Diego de Pantoja. They entered Yanjing to give gifts. ... and respectfully offered before the emperor a picture of Christ, two portraits of the Mother of God, one bible, a crucifix with pearl inlets, two clocks, one world map, and one piano, all things they had attentively brought along from their home countries. Although this was not precious enough, it nevertheless arrived as a tribute from the far West and was appreciated by its difference, and it comforts my private wish as a most humble person to present this humble gift to my ruler." (Huang 1894)

Other goods such as the prism and Western books (such as Aesop's fables or the Bible) were also brought into China.

> 他在南昌也和在肇慶時一樣，把西洋的奇珍物品陳列出來，供人參觀。還屢次把這些東西借給幾個重要人物拿回去仔細賞鑒，比方那人稱寶石的三稜玻璃，那畫得極精美的聖母抱耶穌油畫像，封面裝釘有花紋邊上鍍金的西洋書籍，這就叫他們知道我們西洋地方也講文理，因為他們心目中以為我們沒有讀他們的書，卻能做一個有學問的人，這是一件極難相信的事。
> （斐化行『利瑪竇司鐸和當代中國社會』商務印書館、1937: p. 208）

"In Nanchang, he proceeded the same as he did in Zhaoqing. He displayed Western rarities and let the people observe them. Often, he also lent these objects to a few important persons in order to let them carefully appreciate them. Among these objects were what people called triangular glass, the finest and most beautiful oil painting of the Holy Mother holding Jesus in her arms, and Western books with flower patterns on their cover and their spine coated in gold. He did this to let them know that we westerners also knew about literature and science. Because they couldn't believe that without having read their books, we were nevertheless men of knowledge."
(Bernard-Maitre 1937)

Especially worth mentioning is the following intriguing record regarding holy paintings:

> 當皇帝看到耶穌受難十字架時，他驚奇地站在那裡高聲說道：“這才是活神仙。”儘管這是中國人地一句陳詞老調，他卻無意之中說出了真相。這個名詞在中國至今仍用於耶穌受難十字架，而從那時起，神父們就被稱為給皇帝帶來了活神仙地人。皇帝似乎從驚奇變得害怕看見這些雕像，他不敢和這些雕像目光相對，便把聖母像送給了他的母親。而她是篤奉她那沒有生命的佛像的，看到活生生的神的形象也感到不安。她害怕這些雕像的逼真的神態，於是下令把它們放到她的庫藏裡，在那裡太監們偶爾給一些官員們觀看一下。
> （『利瑪竇劄記』p. 402）

"When the emperor saw the suffering Jesus at the cross, he was standing there in amazement and cried out loud: "This is indeed a living immortal." Although this was a common Chinese platitude, he unintentionally spoke out the truth. Until the present, this term is used in China to refer to the suffering Jesus at the cross and from this time on, the missionaries were called the men that brought the Living Immortal to the emperor. Apparently, the amazement of the emperor turned into fear when he saw these sculptures. He didn't dare look them in their eyes. Therefore, he gave the statue of Mary to his mother. But since she was praying to her lifeless Buddha statues, seeing the statue of the living god made her feel uneasy as well. She feared the realistic expression of these sculptures. Therefore, she commanded that they be put into her storage room. From time to time, the eunuchs allowed some officials to take a look at them."
(Ricci 1615: p. 402)

From the record described above we can understand clearly that the Shenzong emperor as well as the empress dowager Cixi who saw the suffering Jesus at the cross with their own eyes, in fear of the lifelike expression of the sculptures, hid them in their storage rooms where the daylight would not reach them anymore. The hidden mystery of the holy statues and paintings, that caused the continuous amazement of the emperor, lies in the difference of the composition of Western art and Chinese traditional *Ao tuhua* (two-dimensional painting).

> 利瑪竇西洋歐羅巴國人也。面皙，虯鬚，深目而睛黃如貓，通中國語，來南京居正陽門西營中。自言其國以崇奉天主為道，天主者，制匠天地萬物者也。所畫天主，乃一小兒，一婦人抱之，曰天母。畫以銅板為幀，而塗五采於上，其貌如生，身與臂手儼然隱起幀上，

臉之凹凸處，正視與生人不殊。人間畫何以致詞，答曰：中國畫但
畫陽，不畫陰，故看之人面軀正平，無凹凸相。吾國畫兼陰與陽寫
之，故面有高下，而手臂皆輪圓耳。凡人之面，正迎陽，則皆明而
白，若側立，則向明一邊者白，其不向明一邊者，眼耳鼻口凸處皆
有暗相。吾國之寫像者解此法，用之故能使畫像與生人亡異也。
（顧起元『客座贅語』(1617 年序)卷六）

"Matteo Ricci is a Westerner from the European continent. His face is white,
his beard is coiled, his eyes are deep set and yellow like the eyes of a cat. He
speaks Chinese, came to Nanjing and lives in the West Camp of the Xiyang
Gate. He says that his home country worships (the Christian) God. God is
the creator of heaven, earth, and all living beings." God is depicted as a little
child that is carried by a woman, who is called the Mother of God. As for the
image, it is engraved in bronze and it is painted in diverse colors. Its appearance resembles living beings, the body and the arms arise in a dignified manner from the background of the bronze engraving. The concave and convex
parts of the face look exactly like those of a living human. When people ask
how to describe the painting, he answers: Chinese painters do only paint the
light parts but not the one in the shade, therefore the face and the body appear
to be flat and not three dimensional. The painters of my country do paint the
light as well as the parts in the shade, therefore there are differences in height
in the surface, and the arms are all round. If one directly faces the light, the
whole face is bright. But if one has the light to one side, the side which faces
the light is bright, but as for the side that is averted to the light, the protruding
parts of the eye, ear, nose and mouth are all dark. The artists of my country
are all acquainted with this technique, and using it ensures that the image appears to be no different from a living human. (Gu Qiyuan 1617)

Among the three vehicles "object", "human", and "language," I believe that "language" is the most important one. In the process of interaction between different
cultures, the transmission of new objects is always accompanied by the derivation
of a corresponding "language". Like Xunzi 荀子 and Mozi 墨子 said, the actual
value of language lies in its purpose to differentiate.

名也者，所以其累實也。（荀子，正名）
"Regarding names, they are by which one defines and binds realities." (Xunzi,
Rectifying Names)

以名舉實，以辭抒意。（墨子，小取）
"With names one points to/raises realities, with phrases one expresses meaning." (Mozi, *Xiaoqu*)

For example, if one tries to use a different language to explain the object "A", then, at the same time, there has to exist a corresponding word "A" within the commonly used language of the local speech community. This exactly is the quintessence of translation.

2. What is translation?

When we normally try to find a definition for "translation", in a broader sense, we explain it as converting the language that one uses into another language.

For example, the corresponding term for "God" (in Chinese) is 神 *shén*, the corresponding term for "dog" is 狗 *gǒu*. As soon as the correspondence between "dog" = 犬 *inu* (Japanese) = 狗 *gǒu* (Chinese) is established, we can say that the phonetic and morphological forms of these three terms are in a state of equivalence. However, the problem which appears with the notion of correspondence described above is: what, after all, is the meaning of "equivalence"?

The question of what "translation" is that the author just raised, is actually closely connected to the questions of what "language" is and what the concept of "language view" is.

Regarding the question of what "language" is, in ancient as well as modern times, in China as well as in the West, we find plenty of similar answers. The broader definition goes as described below:

語言是人類最重要的交際工具，人們利用語言進行交際，交流思想，
達到互相瞭解。
（《語言漫語》於根元等編，上海教育出版社，1981: 35）
"Language is the most important tool of humanity for interaction. Humans use language to carry out interaction, exchange thoughts, and arrive at mutual understanding." (Yu 1981: p. 35)

Certainly, this definition is but one of the multiple ideas about the concept of language. The author does not agree with the above stated notion of "language as a tool".

The concept of language that the author wants to elaborate on here, follows below. First of all, "language" is one way of human self-expression. Without a doubt, language is by far not exclusive in this respect. Other means of self-expression include painting, film, photography, as well as music. "Language" constitutes only a small share among them.

When we talk about the ways of expressing the human mind, the so-called "human" must necessarily contain an opposite in speech, in writing, and in expressing. Also, as for the expression methods painting, film, and language, there have to exist similarities as well as differences. Let us now try to think about the pictures below (Miura 1976).

By observing the two pictures A and B in Figure 1, we naturally would say that both of them consist of the three elements "child", "desk", and "book". But there exists another very important aspect regarding these two pictures, namely the drawer's differentiation in terms of the direction of the line of sight (視線所及) and "perspective". This exactly illustrates an important feature of drawing: the fate of the painter that something not intended to be expressed will nevertheless manifest itself in the painting. Furthermore, the notions of "position" and "perspective" mentioned by the author are precisely the basic concepts of "subjective expression". In opposition to the drawer's "subjective expression", the "child", the "desk", as well as the "book" stand for "objective expression". The same principles can, for instance, be found in the news reports about the Iraq War. The content as well as the conclusions of the news reports were fundamentally different, depending on whether reported from the perspective of the American government, or from the perspective of the Iraqi government. No wonder that there exists the saying that "portraying the truth" 写真 *shashin (Japanese for 'photograph')* is equal to "portraying one's emotions" 写心 *shashin* (in Japanese, the Kanji for `truth' 真, as well as the Kanji for `heart' 心, are both pronounced *shin*).

(A)   **(B)**

Figure 1: Perspective and line of sight

On the other hand, if we try to find an explanation from the perspective of language, we observe that different word categories cause semantic differences. Chinese traditional thinking captured this difference by the partition of "function words" 虛詞 *xūcí* and "content words" 實詞 *shící*.

(1)

他	明天	來。
tā	míngtiān	lái.
3SG	tomorrow	come

"He will come tomorrow."   = objective expression

(2)

他	明天	也許	來。
tā	míngtiān	yěxǔ	lái.
3SG	tomorrow	maybe	come

"He might come tomorrow."   = 也許 *yěxǔ* is a subjective expression

However, no matter if we talk about painting or language, both are built via the process of "from object to perception to expression". It is obvious that Stalin's most characteristic theory of treating language as a tool, found in his theoretical works on translation, is diametrically opposed to the view on the concept of language which the author here advocates. From the perspective of the "language as a tool" theory, humans are not doing more than using the tool "language", which they take out of the toolbox that is a dictionary. Maybe this metaphor is not quite accurate, since a dictionary does not even include a tool such as language in the first place. What we find in a dictionary is the vocabulary. The vocabulary contains the basic perception of a foreign language as well as its speakers. This kind of understanding constitutes an abstract concept. Like grammar, common and universal conceptions, it constitutes the norm of the masses of the common people. Language, however, is not part of these social norms. A simple example would be, that if I utter the word "dog", then the image of the "dog" that comes into my mind is probably different from the image that comes into the mind of somebody else uttering "dog".

As a matter of fact, the discussion above reflects the author's own understanding of the concept of language. From the perspective of this understanding of language, the imagery of a language does always contain and reflect the history, thought, as well as the way of thinking of its speakers. Therefore, translation is not merely the process of converting phrases and words.

If the equation of "dog = 犬 *inu* = 狗 *gǒu*" can be established, then the focus of this equivalence does not lie on whether the pronunciation or the characters of these words are the same, but it manifests itself on the value, the significance, the foresight, and concepts similar to those. This abstract concept exists within the way of thinking and the culture of the speech community.

The consequence is that translation does not just concern language, but also acculturation and cultural integration.

3. "Present here but missing there, present there but missing here"

Below, there are listed a few examples of translation experiences, where words or expressions of one language do not exist in another language and the other way round:

Japanese:
(3)

白線	の	内側	で	お待ち	下さい
Hakusen	no	uchigawa	de	omachi	kudasai
white.line	GEN	inside	LOC	wait	Please

Chinese:

請	在	白線	外邊	等候
qǐng	zài	báixiàn	wàibian	děnghòu
please	LOC	white.line	outside	wait

"Please wait behind the white line."

(4)
Japanese:

昨晚	は	何時	まで	起きていました	か
sakuban	wa	nanji	made	oki-teimashi-ta	ka
Last.night	TOP	what.time	until	stay.up-PROG.FOR-PST	Q

"Until when were you up last night?"

Chinese:

昨天	晚上	幾點	睡覺
zuótiān	wǎnshàng	jǐdiǎn	shuìjiào
yesterday	evening	what.time	sleep

"When did you go to bed last night?"

(5)
Japanese:

郵便局	は	何時	まで	開いています	か
yūbinkyoku	wa	nanji	made	ai-teimasu	ka
post office	TOP	what.time	until	be.open-PROG.FOR	Q

Chinese:

郵局	幾點	關門	（開	到	幾點）
Yóujú	jǐ diǎn	guānmén	kāi	dào	jǐ diǎn
post office	what time	close	open	until	what time

"What time does the post office close? (Until what time is it open?)"

(6)
Train announcement of Shinkansen N700 "Nozomi":
English:
Wireless internet connection service will not be available after leaving Shin-Osaka.

Chinese:

無線網路	的	免費服務	只	能	使用	到	新大阪站
wúxiàn wǎnglù	de	miǎnfèi fúwù	zhǐ	néng	shǐyòng	dào	Xīn Dàbǎn
Wifi	DE	free service	only	can	use	until	Shin-Osaka

There are many more illustrative examples:
The often heard phrase "下午好" *Xiàwǔ hǎo* (literally: "Good Afternoon") in Starbucks cafes in China is a translation of the English phrase "Good afternoon!". But actually, this translation, which causes a slight discomfort to the hearer's ear, is based on a misunderstanding of the phrase "Good afternoon". That is to say, the English expression "Good afternoon" is also often used before noon. In

English, greeting phrases express a "future-oriented wish" (Japanese: "将来希求型"). In Japanese as well as Chinese, on the contrary, greeting phrases express "present confirmation" (Japanese: "現在確認型"). What can be easily seen here, is that the language user made a mistake in terms of the understanding of greeting expressions.

There can also be made interesting observations in terms of expressing cardinal directions as well as "right" and "left":

(7)

北	西	風 (Japanese)	-	西	北	風 (Chinese)
hoku	sei	Fū		xī	běi	fēng
north	west	wind		west	north	wind

"Northwest wind"

(8)

ノース	ウェスト	航空 (Japanese)	-	西	北	航空公司 (Chinese)
nōsu	uesuto	Kōkū		xī	běi	hángkōng gōngsī
North	west	Airline		west	north	Airline

"Northwest Airlines"

But Japanese also possesses technical terms such as "西南之役"*Seinan no eki* (Satsuma Rebellion), "東南亞"*Tōnan'a* (Southeast Asia), and "東北地方"*Tōhoku Chihō* (Tōhoku).

As for expressing left and right, the Chinese expression 左青龍右白虎 *zuǒ qīnglóng yòu báihǔ* (The Azure Dragon to the left, the White Tiger to the right), with the four cardinal directions being represented by the Black Tortoise of the North (玄武 *Xuánwǔ*), the Vermilion Bird of the South (朱雀 *Zhūquè*), the Azure Dragon of the East (青龍 *Qīnglóng*), and the White Tiger of the West (白虎 *Báihǔ*), can only be understood if one knows that the Chinese concept of the North is equal to 坐北朝南 *zuò běi cháo nán* (sitting in the North and facing the South).

There is yet another similar example:

他們把筆劃，或整個有意義的字組合在一起，用這個法子創造新的不同的

字，賦予另外涵義。例如，用一表示單一，加上一豎成為"十"，即
10，在下
面加一橫成"土"，意思是土地。上面加一橫成"王"，意為國王，在
它左上
側，頭兩橫之間加一撇成"玉"，意為寶石，再加一些筆劃便成珠。
（曾德昭 《大中國志》 ）

"They combine single strokes or whole characters, and by this method create
new different characters with different meanings. For example, the character
一 *yī* expresses "one, single". If one adds a vertical stroke, the result is the
character 十 *shí* , which means "ten". Now, if one adds a horizontal stroke
below, one gets the character 土 *tǔ*, with the meaning of "earth, land". After
adding another horizontal stroke above, the resulting character is 王 *wáng* ,
which means "king". If one adds a left falling stroke between the first two
horizontal strokes on the left, one gets the character 玉 *yù*, which means
"jade". and if one adds a few other strokes then we get the character 珠 *zhū*
"pearl"." (Semedo 1655)

4. Robert Thom's view on translation

Below, there are listed the initial lines of a couple of texts:

盤古初，鳥獸皆能言，一日豺與羊同澗飲水……
"When Pwan koo first began, all the birds and beasts could speak. One day, a
wolf with a sheep at the same stream was drinking water…"

山海經載，獅子與人熊同爭一小羊，……
"In the chronicle of the Hills and Seas it is written, that a lion with a bear were
once contending together for a lamb…"

禹疏九河之時，凡鳥獸魚鱉紛紛逃匿，適兔與龜同行，……
"When the Great Emperor Yu drained off the waters of the Deluge in nine
streams, all the birds, beasts, fishes, and tortoises ran away in crowds helter-
skelter and hid themselves: – and it so happened that the Hare and the Tortoise
traveled in company, …"

神農間有豺食物，
"In the time of the Divine Husbandman (Shinnung) was there a wolf who, from
eating something or other, …"

羅浮山下蘭若幽棲小犬守於門外，
"At the bottom of the Lo-fow mountain, and in a retired temple's secluded spot, a little dog was keeping watch outside the door, …"

齊人有一妻一妾而處室者，其妻老而妾少，
"A Simpleton had a Wife and a Concubine; and regarding those who inhabited his mansion, the Wife was old, the Concubine was young, …"

峨眉山下有故園，中有花匠種植樹木調理花草，甚屬整齊，……
"At the bottom of the Go-me mountain was an ancient garden, within which lived a Gardener, who planted and reared all kinds of trees and shrubs, and who prepared and looked after all kinds of flowers and herbage. Everything was most properly arranged, …"

虞舜間天下太平，春間花木茂盛，人熊遊於郊外，……
"During the reigns of Yu and Shun there was perfect peace in the Empire. And in spring-time the flowers and trees displayed an exuberant foliage. (Under these circumstances) a Bear went to take a ramble outside the city, …"

無稽村外有兩雄雞相鬥，
"On the outskirts of a certain hamlet which shall be nameless, two Cocks were fighting together,"

摩星嶺上有古樹，其頂則為鷹巢，……
"On the summit of the ridge of the Mo-sing mountains was an old tree, the top of which was crowned with an Eagle's nest, …"

靈臺上馬鹿同遊，……
"Upon Lingtae (spiritual terrace), a Horse and Stag used to roam together, …"

昔大禹治水，泗淮騰湧，……
"A long time ago, when the Great Emperor Yu was draining off the waters, & the rivers Sze & Hwae were boiling and bubbling (like two cataracts), …"

大禹末治水之先，飛禽走獸兩不相合，……
"Before the Great Emperor Yu had drained off the Waters of the Deluge, the Birds of the air, and Beasts of the field, were not on good terms with each other, …"

Below, there are a few passages taken from Aesop's well-known fables.

愚夫癡愛
昔有愚夫家畜一貓，視如珍寶，常祝於月裡嫦娥曰，安得嫦娥將我
家貓兒換去
形骸，變一美人，是餘之所願也。由是夜夜祈禱，嫦娥感其痴誠，
姑將其貓暫
變美人。愚夫見之，喜可知也。於是寵幸如夫妻焉，一夜同臥帳中，
嫦娥以鼠
放入房內，美人聞鼠氣，疾起而擒之。嫦娥責之曰，吾既托爾為人，
自當遵行
人事，何以復行獸性。遂復仍變為貓。如世人貪狡之徒，雖別暫行
正道，一時
財帛觸目，自然露出真形。俗云，青山易改，品性難移，正此謂也。

The Foolish Swain and his Cat

In olden times lived a Foolish fellow, who had brought up a Cat in his house, which he looked upon as a pearl above all price. He was constantly praying to Chang-go the nymph of the moon, (i.e. the Chinese Diana) saying, "oh! How shall I get Chang-go, to take this domestic Cat of mine; and divesting her of her outward form, change her into a fair virgin! Such indeed is my ardent prayer!" Thus it was that he prayed night after night: – and at last Chang-go, touched by the foolish sincerity of his love, compassionately took the Cat, and transformed her for the time-being into a beauteous maiden! The besotted admirer seeing her, his joy may be well supposed! And in short they straightway loved each other fondly as Husband and Wife! One night while sleeping with the curtains, Chang-go (on purpose to try her), let a Mouse into the room where they slept; no sooner did the beauteous bride perceive the scent of the Mouse, than she arose and caught it! Chang-go immediately railed at her, saying, "when I granted you to become a human-being, you ought submissively to have acted like others of mankind! How then is this, that you again give signs of your brutish nature?" and thereupon she changed her into a cat as she had been before! Thus it is among the men of this world! There is a class of greedy tricky rascals, who altho' they may walk straight-forward for the moment, yet where riches in any shape come before their eyes, then do they in very deed discover their real characters! The proverb saith, "the green hills may easily change, but it is difficult to alter the natural disposition!" (anglicè, what is bred in the bone, comes out in the flesh) which is just the moral of what we have been saying! (Mun and Thom 1840)

車夫求佛

一日車夫將車輪陷於小坑、不能起、車夫求救於阿彌陀佛、佛果降臨問曰、你

有何事相求、夫曰、我車落坑求佛力援救、佛曰、汝當肩扛其車、而鞭其馬、

自然騰出此坑、若汝垂手而待、我亦無能為矣、汝世人急時求佛、亦當先盡其

力乃可、任爾誦佛萬聲、不如自行勉力。

The Waggoner and Hercules

One day a Waggoner was so unfortunate, as to have the wheel of his waggon sink into a rut or hole, when he could not get it out again; and so he began to implore assistance from O.mē.to Fō (alias Amida Budh.). Fō (it is said) in very deed descended (from the sky), and asked him, saying, "what is the matter that you are thus begging me to assist you?". The Waggoner said, "the wheel of my waggon has got into a hole, and therefore I implore the power of the great god Fō, to pull it out for me again!" Fō replied, "you ought to put your shoulder against the waggon, and flog your horses soundly; and then you will quickly start it out of this hole: – but if you hang down your hands and wait, I really have no power to do anything for you!" Thus it is with the men of this world! In times of difficulty and danger they call on Fō, when they ought in the first instance to exert their strength to the uttermost; for granting you to call on the name of Fō ten thousand times, it is not nearly so efficacious, as the simple putting forth of your own exertions. (Mun and Thom 1840)

The passages above from Aesop's fables were all translated by Robert Thom (羅伯聃 *Luó Bódān*, 1807 – 1846). Thom's view on translation can be best summarized as "Aesop's fables in a Western body wearing a Chinese suit" and "設身處地為對方著想", meaning "put myself on the other side".[2]

This view on translation coincides with the concept of "adaptationism" (適應主義) of the Presbyterian missionary Robert Morrison's (馬禮遜 Mǎ Lǐxùn 1782 -1834). The picture of Christ in Figure 2 is a classic example of the Jesuits' adaptationism, and from the preface of the dictionary that Robert Morrison compiled, we can also get an idea of the meaning of adaptationism.

---

2   For a more detailed discussion see Uchida (2001).

Figure 2: Jesuit adaptationism

"The Student must not expect from this Work, the precise words to be employed in translation, but so much of the meaning of a word, as will furnish him with a clue to select a proper phrase. Nor must the Poetical meaning of words be expected to be given with precision; nor the whole of the figurative meaning; nor the Classical allusions on occasions. These require more associated efforts, more diversity of talent, and of pursuit, than have yet been applied by Europeans to the Chinese Language."

"[…] cannot learn Chinese from a Dictionary, which contains only a definition of single word-, and of detached sentences." (Morrison 1815)

5.1 The Validity of Peripheral Material

5.1.1 European Studies of Chinese

In China, the establishment of the scientific field that is called "Linguistics" is quite a recent development. But that does not mean that the people of Ancient China did not explore the question of what "language" is. Actually, from the earliest times onward, the Chinese were engaging in trying to find an answer to that question. For example, in the chapter "Rectifying Names", Xúnzi 荀子 (c.

310 – c. 235 BC) discusses matters such as "the purpose of language", "the normative aspect of language", or "the relation between the development of human cognition and words", as illustrated below:

The purpose of language is to differentiate between objects and to express one's thoughts:

異形離心交喻，異物名實玄紐，貴賤不明，同異不別，如是則志必有不喻之患，而事必有困廢之禍，故知者為之分別制名，以指實，上以明貴賤，下以辨同異，貴賤明，同異別，如是則志無不喻之患，事無困廢之禍，此所爲有名也。

"Different shapes and separate minds [maybe 'concepts in the mind'] explain each other; for unusual things, names and realities are hidden and entangled, the worthy and the unworthy are not clarified, same and different are not distinguished. If this is the case, then intentions necessarily have the annoyance of not being explained and affairs necessarily have the misfortune of being in straits and abandoned. Therefore, someone who knows thus separates and distinguishes and determines the names in order to refer to the realities. On the one hand, one thus clarifies the worthy and the unworthy, on the other, one thus distinguishes the same and different, and the worthy and the unworthy are clarified, the same and different are distinguished. If this is the case, then intentions do not have the annoyance of not being explained and the affairs do not have the misfortune of being in straits and abandoned; this is why they have names."[3]

名也者，所以期累實也。
"Regarding names, they are by which one defines and binds realities." (Xunzi, *Rectifying Names*)
彼名辭也者，志義之使也。
"Those names and expressions are the ambassadors of intention and right sense."

名無固宜，約之以命，約定俗成，謂之宜，異於約，則謂之不宜，名無固實，約之以命實，約定俗成，謂之實名。
"Names do not have a determined appropriate correspondence; one conventionalizes them by establishing a name. When the convention is established, the cus-

---

3   ＜語言的社會規範性＝物件物與語言之間沒有直接的關係＝約定俗成＞ Thwaits: The normative aspect of language, or the lack of a direct connection between words and their denotations.

tom is perfected, and one calls it appropriate correspondence. If they are different from convention, then they are named inappropriate correspondences. If the names do not have a fixed actuality/reality and one conventionalizes them in naming the actuality, and when the convention is established and the custom is perfected, one calls it a real name."[4]

單足以喻單則單，單不足以喻則兼。
"If a single [reference] suffices to explain a single referent, then it is single; if a single [reference] does not suffice to explain, then it is multiple."

單與兼，無所相避，則共。
"If single and multiple do not evade each other, then it is common."

萬物雖眾，有時而欲徧（無）舉，故謂之物，物也者大共名也。推而共之，共則有共，至於無共，然後止。有時而欲徧舉之，故謂之鳥獸，鳥獸也者大別名也。推而別之，別則有別，至於無別，然後止。
"Although things are innumerable, there are times when we wish to speak of them all in a general way, so we call them 'things'. 'Things' is the most general term. We press on and generalize, we generalize and generalize still more, until there is nothing more general. Only then we stop. There are times when we wish to speak of one aspect, so we say 'birds and beasts'. 'Birds and beasts' is a great classifying term. We press on and classify. We classify and classify still more, until there is no more classification to be made, and then we stop."

In addition to Xúnzi, other thinkers such as Mòzi 墨子 (c. 470 – c. 391 BC) or Gongsun Long 公孫龍 (c. 325–250 BC) also formulated insightful ideas about language. But as for the scientific field of linguistics or the study of grammar, one had to wait until the end of the Qing Dynasty, when Ma Jianzhong 馬建忠 (1845 - 1900) in 1898 published his *Mashi wentong* (馬氏文通 *Mǎshì Wéntōng*), which constituted the first piece of systematic linguistic research. All previous studies on grammar were merely appendages of the study of the classics (經學 *Jīngxué*) in which the main focus was placed on the explanations of words and function words 助字 *zhùzì*, which appeared in the form of annotations on the classics (訓詁學 *Xùngǔxué*).

---

4 ＜人的認識發展過程（具體方向與抽象方向）與詞的關係＝"單名""兼名""共名""別名"等＞ The developing process of human cognition (concrete direction and abstract direction) and the relation of words, …

In comparison, in Europe, the scientific discipline of linguistics had already been established in Ancient Greek as well as the Roman Empire. In the 16th century, the study of the Chinese language, which was based on the tradition of linguistics and mainly carried out by missionaries, had already been developed. These missionaries possessed great linguistic analytical skills and accurately described many important characteristics of the Chinese language (e.g. monosyllabism, the relation between initial and final, the dominant position of vowels, the shifting of parts of speech, the existence of classifiers, the concrete meaning of verbs, the difference between Mandarin and the "dialects", and the difference between the written and vernacular language). Already before the middle of the 18th century, there had been published a decent amount of work on research of Chinese.

5.2. *The validity of European studies on Chinese*

Can the material of European research on Chinese be helpful for Chinese linguistic research? If it turns out to be helpful, then for what reasons?

The reasons for the value of the European research for Chinese linguistics can be summarized by the following points:

(1) Linguistics or the study of grammar was already established in Europe quite early.

(2) Since these Europeans were non-native speakers of Chinese, by comparing their own mother tongue with the Chinese language, they were able to notice phenomena which a Chinese native speaker may have taken for granted, and they were able to objectively describe their characteristics.

(3) They employed a phonetic script, by using the Latin alphabet to transcribe Chinese characters. This method allowed them to record the Chinese phonology of that time in a more scientific way (in comparison with the Chinese traditional "Fanqie"-method 反切 *Fǎnqiè*).

(4) Since they were missionaries, and the range of their missionary activities was rather large, they were able to learn the differences between "Mandarin" and the locally spoken "dialects". Their exposure to locally spoken dialects was also due to the fact that they were, for the most part, confined to the few open cities along the coast, in many of which Mandarin was not spoken.

The arguments listed above can be summarized by the Chinese phrase 旁觀者清 *pángguānzhě qīng*, "the spectator sees most clearly".

In Japan, scholars such as Kōsaka Jun'ichi 香阪順一 (1915 - 2003), Ōta Tatsuo 太田辰夫 (1916 - 1999), Yoshio Ogaeri 魚返善雄 (1910 - 1966), and

Ozaki Minoru 尾崎實 (1937-2003) started from the 1950s on to repeatedly emphasize the usefulness of the European research material. For example, Ōta explained the characteristics of the Beijing dialect and the Southern dialects based on the two, or even three line glosses in "A course of Mandarin lessons, based on idiom" 官話類編 by Calvin Wilson Mateer 狄考文 (1836 - 1908), as well as the "Jiujiang Book Club's *Guide to Mandarin*" 官話指南 (Ota 1950, 1964, 1965). Kōsaka Jun'ichi and Ozaki Minoru used the notes found in Mateer (1892), Wade (1867), and Wieger (1895) to explicate the characteristics of pre-modern Chinese. Yoshio Ogaeri also started quite early on to take the research on Chinese by European and American missionaries into consideration. He not only reprinted the "Amplified Instructions on the Sacred Edict" 聖諭廣訓, one of the "must-reads" for any European who wanted to study Mandarin, but also made use of peripheral material such as the Ryukyuan Mandarin textbooks.

In China, however, besides Luo Changpei 羅常培 (1899 - 1958), who used the work of early-period missionaries such as Nicolas Trigault 金尼閣 (1577 - 1628) to carry out phonological research (Luo 1930), there are still only a few researchers who take the European work on Chinese into consideration. Nevertheless, research in this field has been rapidly increasing recently, mainly advocated by the Research Center for Overseas Chinese Studies at the Beijing Foreign Language University. The same trend can be observed in Europe. In the future, research based on the European material will gain acceptance worldwide.

5.3 The concrete content of peripheral material

The peripheral material of Chinese linguistic research is not limited to European studies but does also include materials such as those listed below:

(1) Korean material: "Nogeoldae" 老乞大, "Bak Tongsa" 朴通事, "An Introduction to Chinese Pronunciation" 華音啟蒙

(2) Thwaits: Mongolian-Mandarin and Manchu-Mandarin materials: so-called "matching" 合璧 materials, such as *The Essentials of Manchu* 清文指要

(3) Ryukyuan Mandarin textbooks: "Bai Shiyun's Mandarin" 白姓官話

(4) Thwaits: Chinese conversational materials, including interpretation textbooks, such as "Essentials of Chinese Conversation", Tanghua materials 唐話纂要, and castaway materials

(5) Textbooks edited by Japanese scholars: "Mandarin Primer" 官話指南

(6) Vietnamese materials: Vietnamese vernacular characters 字喃 and Chinese loanwords mainly from the Ming and Qing periods

In addition, materials such as travel reports (especially the reports collected in the "*Going out into the world* book series" 走向世界叢書), Chinese dictionaries, as well as Chinese bible translations are all important for the research on vocabulary.

Furthermore, the concept of the "periphery of the Chinese language" can also be thought of in terms of an Inner-Chinese center and periphery. If we shift our attention to the inner parts of Chinese, the relationship between standard language *yayan* 雅言 and dialect *fangyan* 方言, official Mandarin *guanhua* 官話 and rural vernacular *xianghua* 鄉話, Standard Mandarin *Putonghua* 普通話 and the Chinese dialects *fangyan* 方言, Written Chinese *shumianyu* 書面語 and Vernacular Chinese *kouyu* 口語, as well as the Classic Language *gudianyu* 古典語 and the Modern Language *xiandaiyu* 現代語 inevitably catches the eye.

6. Periphery and center

6.1. The periphery and the center within linguistic research - the relationship between "individual" and "general" or "special" and "universal"

Within linguistics, the relationship between periphery and center is interlinked with the relationship between the concepts of "individual" and "general" or "special" and "universal". In a nutshell, they do not contradict each other, but rather complement each other. They do not stand in a relationship of "either – or" but "as well as".

However, many linguists, for example scholars who work on individual languages (e.g. Chinese, Japanese, English), limit themselves to the research on their particular language. General linguists, on the other hand, partly believe that general linguistics is determinative of linguistic theory and capable of solving any problem for any language.

Regarding the concepts of "individual" and "general" as well as "special" and "universal" within linguistics, the Japanese scholar Tokieda Motoki 時枝誠記 (1900 - 1967) who was researching the Japanese language, had already written in the year 1941:

"We cannot assume that the research object of linguistics is a general language that remains after we get rid of any individual (natural) language (actually, such a thing does not exist). At the same time, we have to put Japanese linguistics into a general theoretical framework so that the research on Japanese will shed light on the essence of language." (Tokieda 1941, p. 4)

"But what after all is the essence of language? This should be the foremost research question of Japanese linguistics, and the ultimate goal of Japanese linguistics is, via the research of the particular phenomena of the Japanese

language, to get a grasp of the essence of language which lies hidden behind."
(Tokieda 1941, p. 4f.)

"Japanese linguistics, that is the mission of the scientific research of Japanese,
is to single out all of the linguistic phenomena (characteristics) found in the
Japanese language, to describe them, and find out the specific properties of
Japanese. At the same time, we should abstract a universal theory from the
many phenomena of Japanese that can be applied to all (natural) languages.
In that way, we can participate in the establishment of the scientific field of
linguistics and contribute to the consolidation of our view on the essence of
language."[5]

That is to say, research on an individual language should always, via the research of the characteristics of this particular language, try to understand all
of the essence of language that can be found behind. Certainly, there is no
doubt about Tokieda's view. But during the time of Tokieda, the two of them
(that is research on individual languages and general linguistics) existed as two
opposing frameworks, and general linguistics yielded the guiding principles
for individual linguistic research. This was the earlier established theoretical
framework.

"However, Japanese Linguistics sees modern linguistics as offering a general
basic theoretical framework, and is a scientific field which stands in opposition to Japanese linguistics. From the view of Japanese linguistics, (modern)
linguistics initially established a theoretical framework that acts as a guiding
principle. This is the commonly perceived relationship between Japanese linguistics and (modern/general) linguistics."

As for the reasons for the development of this relationship, Tokieda gives the
following explanation:

"When linguistics entered Japan, it established a very special relationship with
Japanese linguistics. This particular relationship can also be viewed as one of
the shared phenomena that occurred in every scientific discipline after the
Meiji Restoration which was accompanied by the introduction of Western
scholarly traditions in Japan. Before anyone could investigate on any matter,

---

5   The attitude of linguistic research 言語研究の態度 Gengo kenkyu no taido [The attitude of
    linguistic research], p. 3)

they were first of all taught the so-called scientific methodology, and consecutively had to conduct research according to this methodology. Japanese linguistics did not aim to contribute its individual research achievement to linguistics as a whole, but instead treated linguistics as the (theoretical) guidance on which it depended on." (Tokieda 1941: p. 5)

"I think the fact that we observed such a weird development within Japanese linguistics during the Meiji period can be traced back to two reasons. First, before the Meiji period, the standards of Japanese schooling were way behind when compared to the West. Although sufficient on a temporary basis, in the long term it was inevitable to adopt other theories in order to restore its condition. [...] That Japanese linguistics during the Meiji period was in search of their own place within Western linguistics couldn't be helped (after all)." (Tokieda 1941: pp. 6-7)

As a matter of fact, this was a natural consequence of Japan's modernization. For the sake of promoting modernization, Fukuzawa Yukichi 福沢諭吉 (1835 – 1901) advocated his theory of "De-Asianization" 脱亜論. Finding himself put in such an environment, Natsume Sōseki 夏目漱石 (1867 – 1916) concluded through the voice of the nameless man who sits next to Sanshirō on the train from his novel Sanshirō 三四郎 (Natsume 1909) that the modernization movement is condemned to fail. One could say that Tokieda's views are identical with those of the nameless man.

In a nutshell, Tokieda's conclusion on the relation between "special" and "universal" is as follows:

"People generally believe that the theory and methodology of (general) linguistics is universal, and in contrast to that, that the theory and methodology of Japanese linguistics is specific. This is but a very superficial view and an incorrect judgment. [...] Universality and specificity do not exist in opposition, but all specific phenomena always possess a universal character. This reasoning does not only apply to Japanese linguistics, but is true for any object. The research on specific phenomena in Japanese might also elucidate the universal shape of language." (Tokieda 1941: pp. 8-9)

Linguists, no matter if they research a particular language or within general linguistics, should all reflect on Tokieda's thoughts about the relationship between specificity and universality. Especially, many of the anglicists in Japan would be well-advised to do so. There are people [in linguistics] who blindly follow any trend. When structuralism was in vogue, they worked within the framework of structuralism. When structuralism was no longer the way to go, they adopted the framework of transformational grammar, and when this no longer worked out, they switched to case grammar. Nowadays, the newest trend is cognitive grammar. These people are only blindly relying on imitation, but do not search for the fundamental theory and principles. The author Edgar Allan Poe (1809 - 1849) wrote the following regarding this issue:

> "You will see at once that all argument upon this head should be urged, if at all, against the rule itself, and for this end we must examine the *rationale* of the rule." (Poe 1842)

The situation in China is more or less identical. After the Opium Wars (First Opium War (1839 - 1942), Second Opium War (1856 – 1860)), the Imperial Powers forcefully entered into China. China found itself in a backward state. Against this background, Ma Jianzhong 馬建忠 (1845 – 1900) had no other choice than to imitate the grammar of Latin to develop a systematic grammar for Chinese. However, later on, the majority of Chinese linguists held onto the practice to explain Chinese grammar through the framework of Western grammars (certainly, among scholars like Chen Wangdao 陳望道 (1891 - 1977) and Zhang Shilu 張世祿 (1902 - 1991) who belonged to the so-called "Haipai" 海派 circle, there had been people who proposed a native Chinese grammar). Reflection on the research methodology described above has just begun in recent years (e.g. Zhu Dexi 朱德熙 (1920 - 1992) or Shen Xiaolong 申小龍 (1952 -)).

But Tokieda's method also bears the risk of falling prey to narrow-minded nationalism. This is comparable to a lot of advocators of the old *kana*-orthography (*Kyū-Kanazukai* 旧仮名遣) who often also hold nationalist views. Although I am also an advocate of the former writing system, I am definitely not a nationalist. Everything has to be checked against whether it is scientific, and whether it is reasonable. This was also Tokieda's own view:

> "Therefore, the relationship between general linguistics and Japanese linguistics is not one in which the former acts as the guiding principle on which the latter relies. ... This does not imply that one should adopt a self-centered, narrow-minded point of view that rejects any deviating opinion, but aims for a realistic consideration of the future path that Japanese linguistics should take, and at the same time advocates for nurturing a scientific spirit that can serve as a foundation for Western linguistics."

The concepts discussed above of "individual" and "general", "special" and "universal", relate to each other as the concepts of "periphery" and "center" do. The author's belief is that the relationship between the latter is identical with the relationship between the former.

6.2. "Individual" is equal to "general", and "special" is equal to "universal" - The differentiation of function words and content words as an example

In the Indo-European languages, a regular sentence always contains a subject, and this subject normally is also the agent of an action. This observation supports the a priori assumption that a sentence consists of a subject and a predicate. Even Noam Chomsky, now praised as the "revolutionary of linguistics", started to analyze sentence structures based on the premise that S=NP+VP.

However, this is not completely true for Japanese and Chinese. As for Japanese, there has been put forward a theory to abandon the subject (主語廢止論), and as for Chinese, there exist sentences which cannot be explained with the "subject-predicate" framework of the Indo-European languages. For example:

(9)

前邊	來	了	一	個	人。
qiánbian	lái	le	yī	ge	rén.
the.front	come	LE	one	CL	human

"There came someone in the front."

(10)

臺	上	坐	著	主席團。
tái	shàng	zuò	zhe	zhǔxítuán.
stage	on/above	sit	ZHE	presidium

"The presidium is sitting on the stage."

(11)

玻璃	碎	了。
bōlí	suì	le
Glass	break	LE

"The glass is broken."

(12)

房子　　　燒　了。

fángzi　　　shāo　Le

apartment　burn　LE

"The apartment burnt down."

(13)

這裡　的　水　　可以　喝。

zhèlǐ　de　shuǐ　kěyǐ　hē

here　DE　water　can　drink

"The water here is drinkable."

(14)

這些　　給　你。

zhèxiē　gěi　nǐ

these　give　2SG

"I'll give you these."

(15)

下　雨　了。

xià　yǔ　le

down　rain　LE

"It's raining."

The sentence structures above include so-called existential sentences, natural passive sentences, and topicalized sentence structures. None of them can be subsumed under the Indo-European "subject – predicate" paradigm. Observing the contrast described above, the rule "Sentence = Subject + Predicate" rather belongs to the rule set of individual languages than being part of the essence of language or being a general property of language. Regarding this point, Tokieda writes as follows:

"(Linguistic) Phenomena that do not exist in Japanese, cannot be taken to be general properties of language. General language properties that do not exist in Japanese, if there are any, are also not more than characteristics of some individual language."

The differences between the Indo-European languages and Chinese or Japanese are not confined to the subject and the predicate, but also include the relationship between the verb and the object. In Indo-European languages, the relationship between verb and object can be compared to the relationship between an arrow and its target. In Chinese, however, the relationship between these two is much more complex. Comparable to the Indo-European view on sentences being constructed as "Sentence = Subject + Predicate", within the Chinese grammar tradition there exists the division of words into function words 虛詞 *xūcí* and content words 實詞 *shící*. According to this view, the concept of a sentence is explained as follows:

> 構文之道，不過實字虛字兩端，實字其體骨，而虛字其性情也.
> "To compose a text, one does not need more than content words and function words. The content words yield its body and the function words yield its character/soul." (Liu 1771)

> 構文之道，不外虛實兩字，實字其體骨，虛字其神情也。(《馬氏文通》例言)
> "To compose a text, one does not need more than content words and function words. The content words provide the body and the function words fill it with life." (*Mashi Wentong*, Introductory Remarks)

That is to say, the Chinese view was that a sentence is composed of function words and content words. This view was also held by the Edo period Sinologists Itō Tōgai 伊藤東涯 (1670 – 1736), Minagawa Kien 皆川淇園 (1735 – 1807), and Ogyū Sorai 荻生徂徠 (1666 – 1728), as well as the Japanese Linguists Suzuki Akira 鈴木朖 (1764 – 1834), and Fujitani Nariakira 富士谷成章 (1738 – 1779). Especially Suzuki Akira in his work "The Four Types of Words" 言語四種論, differentiated between the two categories of "words" 詞 (*shi*, which refer to objects) and "particles" テニヲハ (*teniwoha*, which add feelings to the words 心聲). The former, he further divided into "words of substance" 體之詞 (i.e. substantives), "words of shape" 形狀之詞 (i.e. adjectives), and "words of effect" 作用之詞 (i.e. verbs):

"Words can be divided into four categories. Of these four word categories, the first one is the set of terms for all existing objects, the "words of substance". They are also called "non-movables". The second category is called "particles." The third one is called "words of shape". And the last one is called "words of effect (of an action)". Together, the last two categories are called "words of usage", "movables". "words of inflection", or just "inflectables".
If we compare the three word categories with the "particles", they differ in that whereas the former all denote an entity, the "particles" do not. If we treat the former as words, then "particles" are sound. Whereas the former three denote objects, the "particles" give sound to the word; the words are like gems, particles are like strings. If words are like tools, particles are like the hand that uses this tool." (Suzuki 1824, p.8)

Suzuki Akira's word classification was based on the Chinese "function word – content word" distinction. Later, is was inherited in Tokieda Motoki's theory of words 詞辭論. Tokieda Motoki categorized words into two categories, *ci* 詞, for objective expressions, and *ci* 辭, for subjective expressions. He believed that the structure of a sentence was "詞包辭" [詞 wraps 辭]. Therefore, Tokieda did not think of "subject" and "predicate" as two complementary, opposing concepts, but actually he subsumed them both under his "objective expressions". What held these two together was Tokieda's *ci* 辭, viz. his "subjective expressions". This is precisely the view that language, like music and painting, is a means of expression which is built up through the process of "from object to perception to expression". This is founded on the view of language, that "語言就是主體性活動本身 [Using language is proactive]", and differs fundamentally from the structural linguistic view on language, as well as the "language as a tool"-theory, most prominently advocated by Joseph Stalin.

If we carefully look at the studies on Chinese carried out by the Europeans, we observe that they artfully assimilated the traditional Chinese "function word – content word" paradigm into their work.

The Europeans termed content words as "solid characters" (Prémare), "full characters" (Edkins), and termed function words as "vacant or empty characters" (Prémare), and "empty characters" (Edkins). Alternatively, they termed content words as either "living characters" (Prémare) or "living words" (Morrison), and function words as "dead characters" (Prémare) or "dead words" (Morrison).

Through this observation we can get an idea of how they integrated Chinese views and thoughts on matters into their own research. Edkins's explanation of function words ("In this sentence *tu* and *liau* mean nothing when viewed apart from context") does faithfully draw on the ancient Chinese concept of the function word. This is not only positive evidence for the fact that they meticulously studied the Chinese language, but furthermore, that they inherited the guiding principle of the Jesuit mission, namely their "adaptationism". It also reveals that they advocated a view on translation, pioneered by Morrison, that respects the local culture and tries to view the local culture from the perspective of the local people.

However, there appears to be more than one single reason that the Europeans adopted the "function word – content word"-paradigm that can be justifiably regarded as the traditional Chinese view on language. That is to say, they also possessed the "necessary condition" to adopt this concept, namely the European Port-Royal grammar (originally published in 1660 by Antoine Arnauld and Claude Lancelot).

The "Port-Royal grammar – General and Rational Grammar" (henceforth PR Grammar) was a highly praised 17th and 18th century Latin prescriptive grammar which greatly influenced the English grammar in the 18th and 19th centuries. The central statements of that grammar are listed below:[6]

"What the term 'grammar' refers to is the method/technique of speech. Speech is the result of a process that humans went through, that is the development to express one's thoughts through signs." (PR Grammar, p. 5)

"All philosophers agree that our mind has three functions. These are perception, judgment, and reasoning." (PR Grammar, p. 34)

"The third function is nothing else but an extension of the second function." (PR Grammar, p. 35)

"The reason to speak is to express judgments about the objects one perceives." (PR Grammar, p. 35)

"Judgments that we make about an object, such as the utterance "The earth is round." are called propositions. Every proposition necessarily consists of two terms. One of them is called the subject, which refers to the object that is judged upon. The other one is called the attribute which refers to the content of the judgment. Besides, there are other elements that connect these two terms.

---

6   Excerpts taken from the translated version by Minamitate (Lancelot and Arnauld 1972).

We can easily understand that the two terms strictly speaking are part of the first function of our mind. This is because they refer to the object that we perceive, the object that we think about. Furthermore, we can easily locate the connection between the terms in the range of the second function. One can say that this is an inherent function of our mind, it is our way of thinking." (PR Grammar, p. 35 – 36)

"From the description above, we arrive at the following conclusion: For the purpose of expressing the thoughts that the mind produces, humans need signs. At the same time, the most general distinction of words and phrases is that one category expresses the objects that are thought about, and one category that expresses the form and manner of our thinking." (PR Grammar, p. 36)

What we can observe from the passages above is that the authors of the Port-Royal Grammar, based on the assumption that the functions of the mind can be distinguished into two big categories (actually, there are three functions, but since the third function is merely an extension of the second function, the second and third function can be conflated), divided words and phrases into two categories. The first one contained expressions of objects that are thought about and the second one contained expressions of the form and manner of our way of thinking. The subject as well as the attribute of a sentence both belong into the first category. They both express objects that are perceived. The group of items that connects these two terms, the so-called "connectors", do actually subsume the entirety of what expresses the form and manner of our way of thinking. The objects that are thought about are equal to the "objective expressions" mentioned above, and the form and manner of our way of thinking equals the "subjective expressions" (words that express the intentions or emotions of the speaker). This shows that this kind of view on language is exactly the same as the Chinese "function word – content word" distinction, as well as Tokieda's theory of words. Therefore, this is an actual case that can be classified as being a "language universal", appearing to be both individual and general, and both special as well as universal.

Noam Chomsky reinterpreted the Port-Royal Grammar, viewing it as the earliest predecessor of his idea of a "deep structure". One of the most important reasons for Chomsky, the "father of modern linguistics", to develop his transformational grammar, was that structural linguistics, which only payed attention to the form of language, but not to its meaning or content, was not able to explain why there exist sentences that exhibit the exact same form, but possess two or more different meanings: i.e. the problem of (structural) ambiguity.

Let us take the phrase "a light house keeper" as an example. This phrase has two meanings. It can either refer to the keeper of a lighthouse, or it can refer to a housekeeper that does not weigh much. For this kind of ambiguous structures, Chomsky proposed that although their surface structure is identical, their deep structure is not. For the "lighthouse keeper" reading, the deep structure would be built up by first merging "light" and "house", and after that merging this constituent with "keeper". For the "housekeeper that doesn't weigh much" reading, the deep structure would in turn be constructed by first merging "house" and "keeper", and afterwards merging that constituent with "light". Chomsky argued that the problem of (structural) ambiguity could be solved by reading off the different deep structures.

However, where exactly should the "deep structure" be located? What we call language is actually nothing else but the already uttered "surface structure". Moreover, if we assume that expression through speech/language is built via the process of "from object to perception to expression", then it is impossible to separate "perception" from the "object" and treat it as an isolated object of study. And as for the phenomenon of "ambiguity", in an actual speech situation, or in the speaker's mind, there always exists only one meaning. The hearer has to rely on his experience. Taking the surface structure as the starting point, he has to think about the object in order to arrive at the speaker's perception. During this process, it sometimes happens that the hearer arrives at a different perception as intended by the speaker. This results in what is commonly called a "misunderstanding".

Chomsky's concept of a "deep structure" actually refers to a problem of "cognition" which operates on a more abstract level than language. If one separates cognition/perception from the object, and assumes a priori that it is able to create concrete sentences (i.e. surface structures), then this is the cause for the problem of "misunderstanding/misconception". This is what causes people to believe that the vocabulary stored in the dictionary constitutes the actual language. Or also, that people believe that the rule book of language (i.e. the grammar) which mediates through language is the actual language. As Tokieda aptly stated, the "vocabulary" which is stored in a dictionary consists of abstractions from concrete words. Like the illustration of a cherry blossom printed in a natural history book, which is nothing more but a concrete sample of an individual object, the vocabulary is also not concrete language (Tokieda 1941: p. 13). In other words, although we might both use the same word "dog", expressed in an actual linguistic context, our uttered "dogs" probably refer to two different animals.

In conclusion, the correct understanding of "ambiguity" (polysemy) in language might be as follows:

一詞有多義，是從詞的各種用法中總結出來的，到了具體語言環境
裡，到了一個句子裡，一般地說，一詞還是一義。

"The multiple meanings one word can have are the sum of the different usages this word can have. In a concrete linguistic context, that is in an uttered
sentence, normally one word has only one meaning." (Zhang 1980)

6.3. The task that lies ahead of "cultural interaction studies" – The "translation of culture"

In the course of "cultural interaction" or "foreign culture contact", it is natural
that there occurs exchange via "goods". But even more common is that "language" functions as the vehicle of exchange, and during this process the problem
of "translation" is ubiquitous. So, what does "translation" mean after all?

From the perspective of the phenomenon itself, we could certainly say that
translation refers to the process of substituting word 'a' of language 'A' with word
'b' of language 'B'.

However, since "language, like music and painting, is a way of human expression", and if we presume that language is built up through the process "from
object to perception to expression", then the human itself which is the foundation of linguistic expression becomes the most important condition which cannot
be omitted.

Additionally, language originally has no direct connection to the thing it refers
to, and the sensual perception in the process of interflow of language is something that is overlooked. The interflow of language is something that is in process
within the nature of foresight in language. This foresight aspect of language can
also be called the "common perception" of a speech community, or the "rule-
book" and "collective perception", and it is this "common perception" that reflects this speech community's history and way of thinking, which equals their
"culture". What exists behind a language is exactly this "culture". Therefore,
"translation" is not just simply the substitution of words.

Furthermore, when substituting word "a" of language "A" into word "b" of
language "B", there exists the question of "equivalence". For example, when
substituting "狗 *gǒu*" with "dog", it is obvious that their phonetic and morphological forms are far from equivalent. So, what then does "equivalence" mean?
The reason why translators have to endure birth pangs when striving for equivalence, is that the translation of language is actually the translation of culture.
This is probably also the reason why the missionaries placed so much importance
on "translated words" during the translation of their most important book – the
Bible. If one intends to spread a foreign culture, then such entanglements have
to be dealt with.

Within cultural interaction studies, the concept of the "translation of culture" has to be always kept in mind.

7. Conclusion

In this article I discussed one aspect within the field of cultural interaction studies, which is the situation of Chinese linguistics and the "peripheral research" approach. Furthermore, I described the relation between "individual" and "general", "special" and "universal", as well as the problem of the "translation of culture". Within the area of "cultural interaction studies" that we try to establish, the research topics that are to be tackled are piling up like a mountain. As for the research area of the author, there are problems such as the formation of concepts (for example the concept of a "nation"), the relation of education to publishing and printing, and how to define these problems within the framework of cultural interaction studies. These issues have to be discussed in future work.

References

Ban, Gu 班固. 111. *Book of Han (Hanshu)* 漢書.

Bernard-Maitre, Henri 斐化行. 1937. *Le Père Matthieu Ricci et la société chinoise de son temps* 利瑪竇司鐸和當代中國社會 [Father Matteo Ricci and the Chinese society of his time]. Beijing: the Commercial Press.

Gu, Qiyuan 顧起元. 1617. *Ke zuo zhui yu* 客座贅語 Vol 6.

Gu, Yewang 顧野王. c. 543. *Yupian* 玉篇.

Huang, Bolu 黃柏祿. 1894. *Zheng jiao feng bao* 正教奉褒. Shanghai: Cimutang.

Huang, Gongshao 黃公紹. c. 1292. Yunhui 韻會.

Lancelot, Claude and Antoine Arnauld (translated by Hidetaka Minamitate). 1972. *Pōru-Rowaiyaru Bunpō ポール・ロワイヤル文法 [Grammaire du Port-Royal]*. Tokyo: Taishukan Publishing.

Liu, Qi 劉淇. 1711. *Zhuzi banlüe* 助字辨略.

Luo Chang-pei 羅常培. 1930. Yesuhuishi zai yinyunxue shang de gongxian 耶穌會士在音韻學上的貢獻 [Contribution to the Chinese Phonology by the Jesuits]. In *Bulletin of the Institute of History and Philology* vol. 1 pt. 3. Nanking: Institute of History and Philology, Academia Sinica.

Ma, Jianzhong 馬建忠. 1898-1900. *Mashi Wentong 馬氏文通*.

Mateer, Calvin Wilson 狄考文. 1892. *A course of Mandarin lessons, based on idiom* 官話類編. Shanghai: The American Presbyterian Mission Press.

Morrison, Robert. 1815. *A Dictionary of the Chinese Language, in Three Parts, Part II*, vol. 1, p. viii. The honorable East India Company's Press.

Mozi 墨子. Xiaoqu 小取.

Miura, Tsutomu 三浦つとむ. 1976. *Nihongo wa dōiu gengo ka 日本語はどういう言語か [What kind of language is Japanese]*. Tokyo: Kodansha.

Mun Mooy and Robert Thom. 1840. *Esop's fables written in Chinese by the learned Mun Mooy Seen-Shang.* Canton: Canton Press Office.

Natsume Sōseki 夏目漱. 1909. *Sanshirō* 三四郎. Tokyo: Shunyōdō Publishing.

Ota, Tatsuo. 1950. Shindai no pekingo ni tsuite 清代の北京語について [On the Beijing dialect of the Qing era]. In *Chūgokugogaku* 中國語學 [Chinese Linguistics] vol. 34, pp. 1-5.

Ota, Tatsuo. 1964. Pekingo no bunpō tokuten 北京語の文法特点 [Special points of the Beijing dialect grammar]. In Hisashige Fukusaburō Sensei/Sakamoto Ichirō *Sensei Kanreki Kinen Chūgoku Kenkyū* 久重福三郎先生・坂本一郎先生還暦記念中国研究 [Chinese Studies to celebrate the sixtieth birthdays of Professors Fukusaburo Hisashige and Ichiro Sakamoto], pp. 37-55.

Ota, Tatsuo. 1965. "Kōrōmu" shintan 《紅楼夢》新探 [A new investigation of of "Dream of the Red Chamber"]. In *The Kobe City University of Foreign Studies Journal* vol. 16 no. 3-4.

Poe, Edgar Allen. 1842. *The Mystery of Marie Rogêt.* New York: William W. Snowden.

Pulleyblank, Edwin G. 1991. *Lexicon of Reconstructed Pronunciation: in Early Middle Chinese, Late Middle Chinese, and Early Mandarin.* Vancouver: UBC press.

Ricci, Matteo 利瑪竇. 1615. *De Christiana expeditione apud Sinas* [On the Christian Mission among the Chinese]. Augsburg.

Semedo, Alvaro. 1655. *The history of that great and renowned monarchy of China. Wherein all the particular provinces are accurately described: as also the dispositions, manners, learning, lawes, militia, government, and religion of the people. Together with the traffick and commodities of that countrey.* London: E. Tyler.

Sima, Qian 司馬遷. c. 94 BCE. *Records of the Grand Historian (Shiji)* 史記.

Suzuki, Akira 鈴木朖. 1824. *Gengoshishuron* 言語四種論 [*Study on Japanese particles*]. Benseisha bunko No. 68. Tokyo: Bensei Publishing.

Tokieda, Motoki 時枝誠記. 1941. *Kokugogaku genron* 國語學原論 [*Theory of Japanese*]. Tokyo: Iwanami Shoten.

Uchida, Keiichi 内田慶市. 2001. *Kindai ni okeru tōzai gengo bunka sesshoku no kenkyū* 近代における東西言語文化接触の研究 [*Cultural contact of West and East in Modern Times*]. Osaka: Kansai University Publishing.

Wade, Thomas. 1867. *語言自邇集 (Yü yen tzǔ êrh chi). A progressive course designed to assist the student of colloquial Chinese, as spoken in the capital and the Metropolitan Department.* Peking: Peking University Press.

Wieger, Léon. 1895. *Rudiments de parler et de style chinois, dialecte de Ho-Kien-Fou* 漢語漢文入門 [*An introduction to written and spoken Chinese*]. Ho Kien Fu: the Catholic Mission Press.

Xunzi 荀子. Zhengming 正名 [Rectification of names].

Zhang, Hua 張華. c. 290. Bowuzhi 博物志.

Yu, Genyuan 於根元. 1981. *Yu yan man yu* 語言漫語. Shanghai: Shanghai Education Publishing House.

Zhang, Yufu 張魚甫. 1980. Qiyi shi zenyang chansheng de 歧義是怎樣產生的 [How ambiguity arises]. *Yuyan de aomiao* 語言的奧妙 *[Secrets of language]*. Beijing: Shaonian Ertong Publishing.

Zheng, Qiao 鄭樵. 1161. Tong zhi lüe 通志略.

Chapter 7

Transposing Linguistic Categories and Terminology: Interactions between Western and Chinese Linguistic Traditions

Mariarosaria Gianninoto
ReSO, Paul Valéry University
Montpellier (France)

Abstract

Since the 17th century, Western missionaries wrote grammars and primers of the Chinese languages as didactic tools for Western learners. Teaching Chinese languages to Western-ers required adapting categories and methodologies that had been devised for Western languages. Although the Western model was predominant in the grammars and primers written by missionaries, diplomats, and academics in the 17th-, 18th- and 19th-centuries, which used Western categories and terminologies to describe the features of the different varieties of Chinese, these works also integrated aspects of the Chinese linguistic tradition by borrowing native categories and methodologies, thereby amalgamating Western and Chinese concepts.

This paper focuses on the classifications of parts of speech and the analysis of empty words, considered as two representative examples of the merging of Chinese and West-ern elements in the development of Chinese grammar studies.

In particular, three works will be analyzed: two grammars of Chinese, the *Notitia linguae sinicae* ([1728] 1831) by J. H. M. de Prémare, and the *Syntaxe nouvelle de la langue chinoise* (1869) by S. Julien (with particular attention to the *Traité chinois des particules et des principaux termes de grammaire*); and a grammar of Latin translated in Chinese, the *Làdīng wénzì* 辣丁文字[1] (1859). Their impact on the history of Chinese grammar studies, on the history of Chinese as a foreign language learning, and on the history of linguistics will be underlined

---

1   In the body of the text, the Hanyu Pinyin transcription is used. The original transcriptions are maintained in the quotations. The traditional forms of Chinese characters are used for quoting all imperial sources (prior to the adoption of the simplified forms). Elsewhere, for contemporary sources, the choice between traditional and simplified forms of the characters is determined by the source itself.

(Robins [1967] 1997: 122; Peyraube 2001: 346; Zou 2005; Wang J. 2009: 344; Pellin 2009; Li 2011: 65; Peverelli 2015: 53).

1. Interactions between Western and Chinese linguistic traditions in Qing (1644-1911) period sources

Chinese linguistic tradition is to be considered as one of the oldest and richest traditions of linguistic studies in the world, particularly developed in the fields of exegesis, lexicology, and phonology. The impressive tradition of Chinese philological studies entered in contact with the Western linguistic tradition between the end of the Ming (1368-1644) and the beginning of the Qing (1644-1911) periods. This resulted in considerable transformations in Chinese linguistic studies.

The Western impact on the history of Chinese linguistic studies since the Ming period has been stressed in Chinese linguistic historiography. In his 'History of Chinese Linguistics' (*Zhōngguó yǔyánxué shǐ* 中國語言學史), one of the main figures of 20th century Chinese linguistics, Wáng Lì 王力, claimed that this influence was 'comprehensive, affecting all aspects of linguistics' (*shì quánmiànde, yǐngxiǎngdào yǔyánxué de gège fāngmiàn* 是全面的，影響到語言學的各個方面, see Wang L. [1981]1996: 202).

In his 'History of Chinese Philology' (*Zhōngguó xiǎoxué shǐ* 中国小学史), Hu Qiguang affirms that the introduction of Western culture at the end of the Ming dynasty resulted in important transformations in linguistic studies, the most important being the elaboration of Romanization systems[2] and the development of grammar studies (Hu 1987: 5).

The first Western grammars of the Chinese languages, compiled since the 17th century by Western missionaries as teaching tools for missionaries working in Asia, represented a key contribution to the study of Chinese grammar.

This was part of the 'long process of describing, on the basis of Western grammatical technology, most of the world's languages' (*'long processus de description, sur la base de la technologie grammaticale occidentale, de la plupart des langues du monde'*, Auroux 1989: 29), a process of 'transferring Western (linguistic) tradition to all other (linguistic) traditions [...], which resulted in a relative homogenization of the speculative features of linguistic knowledge' (*'transfert de la tradition occidentale vers toutes les autres traditions [...] d'où résulte une homogénéisation relative des grands traits spéculatifs du savoir linguistique'*, Auroux 1989: 23).

In this process of transposing paradigms, concepts and terms, the Western model was predominant in the grammars written by missionaries and academic

---

2   The first Latin letter transcription systems were elaborated by Catholic missionaries at the end of the 16th century. On these transcriptions see Raini (2010).

sinologists during the 18th and 19th centuries, as these linguistic concepts and terminology were familiar and clear to the Western learners (Zwartjes 2011: 14).

However, these grammars and primers also progressively integrated aspects of the Chinese linguistic tradition, borrowing native concepts and categories. This resulted in merging elements from both Western and Chinese linguistic traditions.

This aspect has been underlined by several authors: Wang Jianjun (2009: 10) stresses the 'multiple interactions existing between Western and Chinese linguistics' (*Xīfāng yǔyánxué yǔ Zhōngguó yǔyánxué zhī jiān yǒuzhe yī céng hùdòng guānxì* 西方语言学与中国语言学之间有着一层互动关系), while Hu (1987: 10) chooses the metaphor of union and giving birth for describing the rise of "new" disciplines as phonology[3] and grammar studies, considered the results of comparative linguistic studies.

This paper aims to analyze the interaction between Western and Chinese linguistic traditions, focusing on two aspects: the classifications of parts of speech and the description of empty words. These two aspects are strictly connected in linguistic description and can be considered as representative examples of the interplay of Chinese and Western elements in the development of Chinese grammar studies.

Part of speech categorization is not only central in Western linguistic tradition (e.g. Colombat 1988: 10; Auroux 1988a: 79-92; 1988b: 109-112), but it is also an important and controversial issue in the history of Chinese linguistics. Described by Lu (2015) as 'an unavoidable issue in Chinese grammar studies' (*hànyǔ yǔfǎ yánjiū zhōng bùkě huíbì de wèntí* 汉语语法研究中不可回避的问题), the question of parts of speech is considered 'one of the most controversial items' (Peverelli 1986: 53) and 'a central and challenging issue' in Chinese grammar studies (*hànyǔ yǔfǎ yánjiū zhōng de rèdiǎn hé nándiǎn* 汉语语法研究中的热点和难点, Pan & Shao 2005: 367). According to Hu (1987: 332), the classification of the parts of speech is a major result of the comparison of Western and Chinese grammars (*Zhōngxī yǔfǎ bǐjiào yánjiū de yī dà chéngguǒ* 中西语法比较研究的一大成果).

Empty words are usually included in parts of speech divisions and their identification and analysis are strictly connected with part of speech categorization.

Moreover, the analysis of empty words occupies an important place in Chinese philological tradition. The exegesis of empty words appeared early in Chinese linguistic tradition in the form of glosses to ancient texts or as dictionary entries (Zhao 2000).

---

3   *Yǔyīnxué* 語音學, i.e. "modern" phonology, deeply influenced by Western linguistics, as opposed to *yīnyùnxué* 音韻學, field of traditional philology, essentially interested in diachronic studies and focused on characters (see Luo 2015).

This point is also underlined by Harbsmeier (1998: 86-87), who affirms that grammar studies in traditional China took 'the form of explanatory glosses on grammatical particles and - much later - dictionary of grammatical particles'. It is in these dictionaries of grammatical particles that can be found the germinal forms of grammatical categorization (Hu 1987: 14).

It is worth stressing that the terms empty words (*xūzì* 虛字 litt. 'empty characters'), and grammatical particles (*cí* 詞, *yǔzhù* 語助, *zhùyǔ* 助語, *zhùzì* 助字) are often used as synonyms (Wang L. 1996: 202; Meng 2014).[4] However, the term "empty words" covers very different meanings and assumed various values in the history of Chinese linguistics.[5]

These two aspects, the parts of speech categorization and the treatment of empty words, will be described by focusing on three representative works, which had a great importance in the history of Chinese linguistic studies.

The *Notitia linguae sinicae* ('An Examination of the Chinese Language', [1728] 1831) by Joseph-Henri M. de Prémare, one of the first grammars of Chinese, destined to exert a strong influence on both Western and Chinese scholars, is relevant in our perspective for both parts of speech divisions and empty word analysis. The *Làdīng wénzì* 辣丁文字 ('Grammar of the Latin Language', 1859), A. Zottoli's Chinese translation of M. Alvarés' Latin grammar, is important for the development of Chinese linguistic terminology (Pellin 2009) and deserves to be mentioned for its parts of speech division. The *Syntaxe nouvelle de la langue chinoise* ('New Syntax of the Chinese Language', 1869) by S. Julien, a famous French grammar of Chinese, is worth noting for including the abridged French translation of the Qing particle glossary *Jīngzhuàn shìcí* 經傳釋詞 ('Explanations of Particles in the Classics and in the Commentaries', [1798]1819).

Two of the works analyzed are translations, because, as stressed by Lackner et al. (2001: 1), 'migrations of knowledge remain above all instances of translation in the 'narrow', non-metaphorical sense of the word'.

---

4   This is clearly shown by the titles of particle glossaries, where these different terms are adopted. We can quote for instance the three main particle glossaries of the Qing period: the *Xūzìshuō* 虛字說 'Treatise on Empty Words' (completed in 1710, published in 1746) by Yuán Rénlín 袁仁林, the *Zhùzì biànlüè* 助字辯略 'Compendium of Grammatical Particles' (1711) by Liú Qí 劉淇 and the *Jīngzhuàn shìcí* 經傳釋詞 'Explanation of Particles in the Classics and the Commentaries' (1798, published in 1819) by Wáng Yǐnzhī 王引之.

5   The term empty words is used in a broader sense (including adjectives and verbs) in Bì Huázhēn's 畢華珍 (fl. 1807-1848) *Yǎn xù cǎotáng bǐjì* 衍緒草堂筆記 'Notes of the Brush from the Abundant Beginnings Hall' and in Joseph Edkins' (1823-1905) *A Grammar of Colloquial Chinese: As Exhibited in the Shanghai Dialect* (cf. Edkins [1853]1868; Uchida 2017). In modern classifications (e. g. Liu Y. 2009), the empty words (*xūcí* 虛词) are considered as a category inclusive of prepositions, conjunctions, adverbs, particles, interjections.

2. Prémare's *Notitia linguae sinicae*

The *Notitia linguae sinicae* by the French Jesuit J.-H. de Prémare (Chinese name *Mǎruòsè* 馬若瑟, 1666-1736) was completed in 1728 and printed in 1831 in Malacca on the initiative of Protestant missionaries.

The *Notitia* is one of the first grammars of Chinese and can be regarded as the first large scale grammar,[6] in comparison with previous short treatises and primers of the Chinese languages (cf. Li 2011: 61). This work was largely appreciated by subsequent scholars (*e.g.* Abel-Rémusat 1822: ix-x; Abel-Rémusat 1829: 269; Edkins 1868).[7]

One of the main features of this work 'is that it covers both Classical Chinese and the vernacular. Different rules are given for each' (Peyraube 2011: 349).

Another feature that deserves to be underlined is the huge number of illustrative examples (nearly twelve thousand, according to Li 2011: 61). This is a pedagogical device, as Prémare explains it:

It seems impossible to find any better method of teaching Chinese than by examples. Let no one be surprised that so many are presented. The route is made short by adducing examples, which by precepts would be comparatively long and tedious (Bridgman transl. 1847: 33).[8]

As for the parts of speech classification, in the section devoted to vernacular Chinese (*De lingua vulgari et familiari stylo,* 'The Spoken Language and Familiar Style' in Bridgman 1847), Prémare lists some of the parts of speech of the Western tradition under the following chapter titles: *De nominibus* (On nouns), *De pronominibus* (On pronouns), *De verbis* (On verbs) and *De reliquis orationis partibus*

---

6 The *Arte de la lengua chio chiu* (1620) is considered as the earliest existing linguistic treatise on a variety of Chinese (cf. Klöter 2011; Chappell and Peyraube 2014).

7 For instance, Abel-Rémusat (1829: 269) wrote that 'his *Notitia linguae sinicae*, the most remarkable and important of all his works, the best, without any doubt, of all those that Europeans have written so far on these subjects' ['*sa Notitia linguae sinicae, le plus remarquable et le plus important de tous ses ouvrages, le meilleur, sans contredit, de tous ceux que les Européens ont composés jusqu'ici sur ces matières*'].

J. Edkins ([1853]1868) also affirmed that: 'among works on Chinese Grammar, that of Prémare, written a century and a half ago, still stands preeminent. Besides a more extended knowledge he possessed a better appreciation of the peculiar beauties of Chinese style, than any other writer on the subject'.

Prémare's work was also praised by the Russian sinologist Nikita Ja. Bičurin in his *Kitajskaja grammatika* (1835) (see Di Toro 2019).

8 In Prémare's original text, we read: 'Primum est quod linguam sinicam melius docere non possum quam per varia exempla. Igitur nequis miretur quod tot phrasis affero; id enim facio quod iter quod per praecepta longum est, per exempla breve fit' (Prémare 1831: 44).

(On the remaining parts of speech). This last chapter includes a section on adverbs and a section on prepositions (Prémare 1831: 40-47).

The first three categories correspond to the inflected word classes of the Latin tradition, while the last one, 'On the remaining parts of speech' includes some adverbs and prepositions.

In Prémare's grammar, the Western word classes are merged with the Chinese divisions of 'full words' and 'empty words' (in Chinese *shízì* 實字 'full characters' and *xūzì* 虛字 'empty characters', in Latin '*litterae plenae seu solidae*' 'full or substantial letters' and '*litterae vacuae*' 'empty letters', see Prémare, 1831: 39), 'dead words' and 'living words' (*sǐzì* 死字 and *huózì* 活字). The latter two categories correspond to verbs ('*per vivas designantur verba*', 'the verbs are designated as living words') and nouns ('*per mortuas nomina*' 'the nouns [are designated as dead words') respectively (Prémare, 1831: 39).

The distinction between empty words and full words, defined by Harbsmeier (1998: 88) as 'the most fundamental and important grammatical distinction in Classical Chinese', can be traced back to the 13th century. These categories were used in a treatise on poetics, the *Cíyuán* 詞源 'Fundamentals of *Ci* poetry' by Zhāng Yán 張炎 (1248–1320), and were later adopted in Yuán Rénlín's 袁仁林 dictionary of empty words, the *Xūzìshuō* 虛字說 'Treatise on Empty Words' (Yuan [1710] 2004: 11). The distinction between living words and dead words can be found in one of the first dictionaries of grammatical particles, the *Yǔzhù* 語助 'Grammatical Particles' by Lú Yǐwěi 盧以緯, which appeared in 1324 (Pellin 2009: 59).

The adoption of Chinese categories is coherent with Jesuit's "accommodationist" approach to China (Mungello 1985: 13, 15; Klöter 2011: 36). The Jesuits' interest in Chinese culture and their outstanding knowledge of the Chinese philology enabled them to appreciate the results of Chinese philology and to borrow Chinese linguistic categories and methodologies in their works.

This merging of Western and Chinese categories can be regarded as an attempt to take into account the specific features of both Chinese language and Chinese philological tradition.

This effort is pointed out by Prémare who wrote:

I am far from thinking to reduce the Chinese language to a conformity with the technicalities of a foreign tongue. On the contrary it is my ardent desire if possible, to induce the missionaries early to commence the practice of analyzing their thoughts, to divest them entirely of their vernacular idiom, and clothe them in pure Chinese (Bridgman transl. 1847: 178).[9]

The attention paid to empty words is to be understood in this perspective. Li (2011: 64) underlines that one third of Prémare's work is devoted to grammatical particles. More than one hundred particles are analyzed and explained through numerous examples, in the two sections devoted respectively to the particles of vernacular and classical Chinese.[10]

In the first part of the *Notitia*, devoted to the 'Spoken Language and Familiar Style' (Bridgman 1847), we find a chapter devoted to the particles of vernacular Chinese, entitled *De particulis in sermone adhiberi solitis* ('Of the Particles in Chinese' according to Bridgman 1847). Two different ways to describe the Chinese particles are adopted: first we find particles listed by categories, like *De particulis negativis* (Negative particles), *De particulis augmentativis* (Augmentative or intensive particles), *De particulis initialibus* (Initial particles), *De particulis finalibus* (Final particles), then long entries devoted to specific particles.[11]

In the second part of the *Notitia*, devoted to the 'Language of the Books' (Bridgman 1847), we find another long section devoted to the grammatical particles (here, the particles of Classical Chinese). This section, entitled *De sinicae*

---

9   'Absit ut ad nostras linguas sinicam revocare velim; nihil è contra cupio magis quam efficere ut missionarii mature assuescant suas ideas resolvere easque a proprio uniuscujusque idiomate abstractas et nudas sinicis vestibus induant' (Prémare 1831: 153).

10 This detailed analysis of the grammatical particles is praised by 19th century French sinologist J. P. Abel-Rémusat who read Prémare's manuscript grammar before its publication:

   'Father Prémare […] describes in details the use of particles, either in the vernacular or in the erudite language, justifying each assertion with numerous examples; or, to put it better, he brings out the rules from the comparison of texts taken from the best authors, compared and explained with the greatest care'.

   ['*Le P. Prémare* […] *entre en de grands détails sur l'emploi des particules, soit dans la langue vulgaire, soit dans la langue savante, en justifiant chaque assertion par de nombreux exemples ; ou, pour mieux dire, il fait sortir les règles qu'il propose, de la comparaison de textes pris dans les meilleurs auteurs, rapprochés et expliqués avec le plus grand soin*'] (Abel-Rémusat 1822: ix-x).

11 This chapter opens with sections devoted respectively to the 'Negative particles' (describing the particles *méi* 沒, *bù* 不, *xiū* 休, *bié* 別, *mò* 莫, *wú* 無, *wèi* 未, *fēi* 非), 'Augmentative or intensive particles' (*tài* 太, *tè* 忒, *shén* 甚, *jí* 極, *jué* 絕, *zuì* 最, *hǎo* 好, *shífēn* 十分, *shā* 煞 or 殺 and *sǐ* 死), 'Diminuitive particles' (*zhǐ* 只, *zhǐ* 止, *dàn* 但, *xiē* 些), 'Initial particles' (*dōu* 哆, *yā* 呀, *āyā* 啊呀, *wù* 兀 and *wù de* 兀的), 'Final particles' (*ā* 阿, *li* 哩, *ér* 兒, *ěr* 耳). Then we find several entries devoted to specific particles (*yòu* 又, *jiù* 就, *què* 卻, *zhe* 着, *dào* 倒 or *dào* 到, *zhuǎn* 轉, *dòu* 斗, *jiào* 教, *jiāo* 交, *kě* 可, *hái* 還, *zé* 則, *qiě* 且, *le* 了, *guò* 過, *yǔ* 與, *tì* 替, *biàn* 便, *lián* 連, *gèng* 更 ; *fàng* 放, *fāng* 方 and *fáng* 妨, *bān* 般, *bàn* 半, *zài* 再, *cái* 纔).

orationis particulis tractatus ('The Chinese Particles' in Bridgman 1847: 178), includes long entries devoted to specific particles,[12] followed by entries organized by categories, such as *De particulis quae tempus designant* (particles denoting time), *De particulis quae augent sensum* (intensive particles), and *De particulis quae interrogant* (interrogative particles).

Hence, in both parts of the *Notitia* (devoted respectively to vernacular and Classical Chinese), several particles are described in the framework of general categories. This testifies an effort to classify Chinese particles and to analyze them by adopting categories accessible to European learners.

However, in both sections most of the particles are described in specific lemmas, which enumerate the different meanings and usages through quotations. For instance, below are some extracts of the first lemma (*articulus primus*) of the *De sinicae orationis particulis tractatus* ('The Chinese Particles'), devoted to the particle *zhī* 之:

> This particle is used in written composition and is equivalent of *tih*, 的, employed in common talk. It is a mark of genitive and possessive case; e.g. *tá hioh chí taú*, 大學之道, great learning's way. [...]
> *Chí* 之 is often made the object of a verb and stands for 其 *k'hí*, he, she, it. It cannot be indeed called a particle. [...]
> *Chí,* 之 is sometimes used as a verb and signifies, to pass in any direction, to arrive at. [...]
> *Chí,* 之 is very frequently joined with both substantives and adjectives, and that not as a sign of the genitive, but as a particle in postposition. *Jin chí* 人之, man [...] *Hwui chí wei jin yé,* 回之為人也 Hwui was a man who, &c.[13]

---

12 This chapter starts with twenty-two entries devoted to specific particles (*zhī* 之, *zhě* 者, *yě* 也, *yú* 於, *hū* 乎, *zhū* 諸, *yé* 耶, *xié* 邪, *yǔ* 與; *ér* 而, *ěr* 爾, *ěr* 耳, *yān* 焉, *rán* 然, *zé* 則, *qiě* 且, *ruò* 若, *rú* 如, *yǐ* 以, *wèi* 為, *zài* 哉, *nǎi* 乃), followed by four sections organized by categories : 'particles denoting time' (describing *jiāng* 將, *céng* 曾, *yǐ* 已), 'intensive particles' (*yù* 愈, *yì* 益, *mí* 彌, *kuàng* 況, *shén* 矧), 'interrogative particles' (*zāi* 哉, *hé* 何, *qǐ* 豈, *xī* 奚, *è* 惡, *hé* 曷, *hú* 胡, *hé* 盍, *shú* 孰, *shuí* 誰), 'final particles' (*yǐ* 已, *yǐ* 矣, *yún* 云). It is important to stress that the sections devoted to the interrogative, final, initial particles do not include all the Classical Chinese particles susceptible to belong to these categories, because some of them are analyzed more in detail in specific entries. For instance, at the end of the section devoted to the interrogative particles, Prémare explains that 'the particles *hú* 乎, *yé* 耶 or *yé* 邪, *yü* 歟, and *yen* 焉 have already been shown to be interrogative' (Bridgman 1847: 219). Similarly, at the beginning of the section 'Final particles' we read that that: 'the particles *yé* 也, *hú* 乎, *yé* 耶 or *yé* 邪, *yü* 與, *'erh* 耳, *yen* 焉 and *tsái* 哉 have been already sufficiently illustrated' and are thus not described in this section (Bridgman transl. 1847: 219).

13 '*Quod in familiari sermone est* 的 *tǐ, hoc in libris est particula* 之 *tchī : notat genitivi casum ; v.g.* 大學之 道 *tá hiŏ tchī táo magna sapientiae ratio, seu id in quo consistit magna disciplina* [...] *Saepe* 之 *fit regimen verbi et supponit pro* 其 *kh'ǐ, ille, illa, illud. Dices, tunc non est particula.* [...] *Eadem littera* 之 *interdum verbaliter sumitur et significat ad aliquem locum transire, accedere.* [...] 之 *Frequentissime jungitur cum*

(Bridgman transl. 1847: 178 and following)

This lemma opens with a comparison between the relative and genitive marker *zhī* 之, mainly used in Classical Chinese ('*in libris*'), and the relative and genitive marker *de* 的, used in the vernacular ('*in familiari sermone*'). This comparison can also be found in an early Qing particle glossary, the 'Treatise on Empty Words' (*Xūzìshuō* 虛字說).[14] The comparison with the personal and demonstrative pronoun *qí* 其 can also be found in another contemporary glossary of particles, the 'Compendium of Grammatical Particles' (*Zhùzì biànlüè* 助字辨略),[15] where the verbal meaning 'to go' and the prepositional usage 'toward, to' are also listed.[16]

Furthermore, in Prémare's lemma we find quotations from the two canonical texts, 'The Great Learning' (*Dàxué* 大學)[17] and 'The Doctrine of the Mean' (*Zhōngyōng* 中庸)[18].

This lemma is thus a representative example of the importance that Prémare recognizes to the Chinese philological tradition.

Prémare's grammar was destined to exert a deep influence on subsequent studies. According to Peyraube (2001: 346), the *Notitia* 'served as a guide for the *Élémens* [*de la grammaire chinoise*, 1822]' by Abel-Rémusat, who 'distinguishes carefully between Classical or literary Chinese and the vernacular'.

According to Peverelli (2015: 53), Prémare's *Notitia* influenced the *Mǎ shì wéntōng* 馬氏文通 (1898) by Mǎ Jiànzhōng 馬建忠 (1845-1900), 'the first full-fledged explicit grammar of Chinese' due to a Chinese author (Lackner 2001: 357). Peyraube (2001: 351) also affirms that:

---

nominibus tam substantivis quam adviectivis, nec tunc est nota genitivi, sed potius videtur esse articulus postpositus 人之 *gîn tchi, homo,* gall. l'homme [...] 回之為人也 *Hoêi tchī ouêi gîn iè Hoei (discipulus Confucii) homo erat qui, etc.*' (Prémare 1831: 153 and following).

14 In the *Xūzìshuō* 'Treatise on Empty Words' we read that it 'is similar to the particle *de* used in common language' (*yǔ súyǔ de zì xiàng lèi* 與俗語的字相類, see Yuan [1710] 2004: 45).

15 Where we read that '*zhī* is like *qí*' (*zhī yóu qí yě* 之猶其也, see Liu Q. [1711] 2004: 6)

16 In the *Zhùzì biànlüè* 'Compendium of Grammatical Particles' we read that '*zhī* has the meaning of *wǎng* [toward, to]' (*zhī yóu wǎng yì* 之有往義, cf. Liu Q. [1711] 2004: 5) and that '*zhī* means *zhì* [to go, to arrive]' (*Zhī zhì yě* 之至也, cf. Liu Q. [1711] 2004: 7). This verbal meaning was already mentioned in previous dictionaries, such as the *Guǎngyùn* 廣韻 by Chén Péngnián 陳彭年 (961–1017), where we read that *zhī* 'means to go, means toward' (*shì yě, wǎng yě* '適也, 往也', cf. Chinese Text Project).

17 The quotation is: *Dàxué zhī dào* 大學之道, 'What the Great Learning teaches' (Legge, cf. Chinese Text Project).

18 The Chinese quotation is: *Huí zhī wéi rén yě* 回之為人也, 'This was the manner of Hui' (Legge, cf. Chinese Text Project).

This grammar was probably the first Ma ever came into contact with when he was a student at the Jesuit college Saint Ignace in Shanghai, long before he was sent to France between 1875/76 and 1880. We know that it was used as a reference work by the Jesuits teaching at the college.

Peyraube stresses the similarities between the two works, arguing that: 'like Prémare, Ma takes the *zi* (*littera*) as the basic grammatical unit, and like Prémare, he adopts the traditional division into 'full' and 'empty' words to divide them into Western parts of speech' (*ibid.*).

It is also important to underline that the reference to these categories became a 'common feature of many of subsequent works […] discussing Chinese and Chinese grammar in terms of the traditional Chinese distinction between function characters (虚字) and content characters (實字)' (Uchida 2017: 59). This combination of Western and Chinese categories in parts of speech classification was destined to have a strong impact on the history of Chinese linguistics.

For Li (2011), this is 'an important contribution by Prémare to the history of Chinese grammar studies' (*Mǎruòsè duì hànyǔ yǔfǎxué de yī dà gòngxiàn* 马若瑟对汉语语法学的一大贡献), which also 'entered in general Western linguistic terminology' (*jìnrù xīfāng pǔtōng yǔyánxué de shùyǔ fànchóu* 进入西方普通语言学的术语范畴). This influence on the history of general linguistics is also stressed by Wang J. (2009: 344) as well as by Robins ([1967]1997: 122), who argues that the distinction 'between "full words", those capable of standing alone and bearing an individual lexical gloss, and "empty words" or particles, serving grammatical purpose […] passed through Prémare into general linguistic usage'.

Actually, this conceptual opposition existed in Western tradition and corresponded to the categorematic-syncategorematic dichotomy of medieval logics (Di Pace and Pannain 2016: 264).[19] However, these were marginal categories in Western philological tradition, and became the object of a renewed interest thanks to the interactions with other linguistic traditions. In a recent essay attempting to retrace the history and the transmission of these categories, Di Pace and Pannain (2016: 271-272), consider that this 'metalinguistic terminological pair has been at the core of a transcultural process, which was realized mainly through the practice of translation proper to missionary linguistics', adding that these categories, after having been translated and adapted, transited 'toward the European intellectual world in which they settled down and remain functional' (our English translation).

---

19 Di Pace & Pannain (2016: 263) precise that Aristotle's *sýndesmoi* can be considered a first form of categorization of empty words in Western tradition.

This point is also stressed by McDonald (2020: 43), who affirms that: 'This classification was introduced into Western thinking about language by way of a Chinese grammar written by the Jesuit missionary Joseph Henri de Prémare [...] It has been recognized by the modern discipline of linguistics as a useful analytical tool to apply to all languages [...] where it is usually framed as a distinction between lexical (content) and grammatical (function) words.'

This combination of Western and Chinese categories and terminologies is an important aspect of late Qing linguistic studies. It was not limited to the grammars of the Chinese languages, but also characterized the Chinese grammars of European languages.

3. The Grammars of Latin in the late Qing period: the *Làdīng wénzì* 辣丁文字

The late Qing period saw the publication of numerous grammars and primers of Latin, written or translated in Chinese by Western missionaries, who played a crucial role in the development of this field.

The Latin language started being taught in China during the eighteenth century thanks to its importance in both diplomacy and education of seminarians. Latin was a *lingua franca* in the diplomatic relations between China and Russia but it was also a central concern in the formation of the Chinese clergy, proficiency in Latin being a prerequisite to be ordained a priest.[20]

Classes of Latin had been taught for fifteen years in the *Xīyángguǎn* 西洋館 'Western institute', established in 1729, the first institute in which official courses of Latin were taught (Fang 1969: 21).

Several seminaries were founded in China. Some of them became important cultural centers, with schools, libraries and publishing houses, such as the seminaries of Yenchowfu (Yǎnzhōu 兖州) in the Shangdong province and the Zikawei (*Xújiāhuì* 徐家彙) in Shanghai, both relevant for the publication of primers and grammars of Latin (Gianninoto 2014).

The *Làdīng wénzì* 辣丁文字 'Grammar of the Latin Language' can be considered as the most important of these grammars. Published in Shanghai in 1859, it was the Chinese "translation" of an important sixteenth century Latin grammar,[21] *De institutione grammatica libri tres* 'Three grammar books', by the Jesuit Manoel

---

20 The decree issued by Pope Paul V in 1615, authorizing Chinese priests to celebrate Mass in Chinese was not applied in China; the bull of Alexander VII, issued in 1659, authorizing the ordination of priests able to read Latin (without understanding the Latin language) was rarely applied (Metzler 1995: 120-124).

21 As indicated by its Latin title, *Emmanuelis Alvarez institutio grammatica ad Sinenses alumnos accomodata* 'Manoel Álvares' grammar adapted for Chinese students'.

Álvares (1526-1583). Álvares's work, published for the first time in Lisbon in 1572, was a reference grammar of Latin. It had been republished several times during the sixteenth, seventeenth and eighteenth centuries, and it was included in the Jesuit *ratio studiorum* in 1586 (Ponce de Léon 2001: xviii). The author of this Chinese version, largely used as Latin language teaching manual in Chinese seminaries (Fang 1969: 19), was the Italian Jesuit Angelo Zottoli (Chinese name *Cháodélì* 晁德蒞, 1826-1902). Zottoli was the director of the Zikawei library and teacher at the Zikawei's St. Ignace College, where both Mǎ Jiànzhōng 馬建忠 (1844-1900) and his brother Mǎ Xiāngbó 馬相伯 (1840-1939) studied. He was also the author of the *Cursus litteraturae sinicae neo-missionnariis accomodatus* ('Course of Chinese Culture adapted for New Missionaries', 5 Volumes, 1879-1882), a monumental work conceived as an articulated and exhaustive introduction to the Chinese language and culture.

The section introducing parts of speech in Zottoli's *Làdīng wénzì* is an interesting example of interactions between Chinese and Western categories.

In the section introducing the parts of speech in Álvares' work, the Latin word classes are listed, briefly distinguishing between the four inflected classes and the four non-inflected ones. Zottoli follows Alvares' classification and lists words into eight grammatical classes, but he introduces elements of the Chinese philological tradition in this classification, borrowing the Chinese categories of empty words and full words:

> Chinese words can be divided into empty and full words. Full words are also divided into dead and living words. The use of empty words is flexible and their classification is difficult to establish. Latin words can also be divided into empty and full words, and full words into dead and living words. There are two categories of dead words, i.e. noun and pronoun, and two categories of living words, i.e. verb and participle. The empty words are divided into four categories: adverb, preposition, conjunction and interjection. (our English translation)[22]

In the macro-category of empty words Zottoli includes four parts of speech of Western linguistic tradition: *zhuàngcí* 狀辭 'adverbs', *qiáncí* 前辭 'prepositions', *liáncí* 連辭 'conjunctions', and *cùcí* 猝辭 'interjections'.

---

22 The original Chinese text reads as follows: '中華文字有虛實之殊而實字中尤分死字活字虛字中運用極神其類難于枚舉辣丁文字亦有虛實之異而實字中亦分死字活字死字又分二類一曰 名 nomen 一曰指名 pronomen 活字又分兩類一曰言 verbum 一曰通言之名 participium 虛字共分四類即如狀辭 adverbium 前辭 praepositio 連辭 conjunctio 猝辭 interjectio.' (Zottoli, transl. 1859: 6)

Among the 'full words', Zottoli distinguishes between *sǐzì* 死字 'dead words' (including *míng* 名 'nouns' and *zhǐmíng* 指名 'pronouns') and *huózì* 活字 'living words' (consisting of *yán* 言 'verbs' and *tōngyánzhīmíng* 通言之名 'participles').

Hence, elements of the Chinese philological tradition are merged with the Western parts of speech classification, in order to make the Western word classes more accessible to the Chinese students of Latin.

The historian Zōu Zhènhuán 邹振环 (2005: 116) points out Zottoli's influence on Mǎ Xiāngbó's 馬相伯 *Lādīng wéntōng* 拉丁文通, the first grammar of Latin written by a Chinese author. Mǎ Xiāngbó was Zottoli's student at the St. Ignace College and his assistant at the Zikawei library. Peverelli highlights the relationship between the *Lādīng wéntōng* 拉丁文通 'Latin Grammar' and the above-mentioned *Mǎ shì wéntōng* 馬氏文通 'Mr Ma's Grammar',[23] affirming that:

> as early as 1886, when the Ma brothers were teaching Latin to Liang Qichao and Cai Yuanpei [...] they used a manuscript of a combined Chinese and Latin grammar. [...] Ma Xiangbo later published a Latin grammar entitled *Lading wentong*, a title analogous to *Mashi wentong* (Peverelli 2015: 42)

Pellin (2009: 132) goes a step further and points out the influence of Zottoli's 辣丁文字 on the terminology of the *Mǎ shì wéntōng*. Like his brother Mǎ Xiāngbó, Mǎ Jiànzhōng was Zottoli's student at the St Ignace College.

More generally, *Lādīng wénzì* represents an important step in the formation of modern Chinese grammatical terminology, being one of the first grammars written in Chinese. The 18th and 19th century grammars of Chinese were written in Western languages and the grammatical terminology was rarely translated. The grammars of Latin written in or translated into Chinese thus represented the first attempts of forging this new terminology. In particular, several terms coined or chosen by Zottoli in his *Lādīng wénzì* were destined to be adopted by subsequent authors (Pellin 2009: 66).

Hence, Zottoli's contribution went beyond the field of Latin studies, influencing both Latin grammar studies and Chinese grammar studies.

4. Stanislas Julien's *Syntaxe nouvelle* and the *Traité chinois des particules*

During the 19th century the production of Chinese grammars and manuals developed considerably, due to the increase in contacts between Western countries and China after the Opium Wars (1839–42; 1856–60) and thanks to the rising

---

23 The word 'grammar' has been chosen for translating the word *wéntōng* in these two titles. However, the word *wéntōng* can also be translated as 'basic principles for writing clearly and coherently' (Peyraube 2001).

number of foreigners needing to acquire a basic knowledge or a good command of Chinese. The compilation of Chinese teaching materials in Western languages was also promoted by the development of sinological studies in different European countries: the first sinological chair in Europe was established at the *Collège royal* (today *Collège de France*) in 1814, when Jean-Pierre Abel-Rémusat (1788–1832) was appointed Professor of *Langue et littérature chinoises et tartares-mandchoues* ('Chinese and Manchu Tartar Languages and Literatures'). Two decades later the appointment of Samuel Kidd as Professor of Chinese Language and Literature at University College, London, inaugurated British Chinese Studies (McLelland 2015: 113). [24]

Stanislas Julien succeeded his teacher J. P. Abel-Rémusat as professor of Chinese and Manchu Tartar Languages and Literatures at the *Collège Royal* and taught vernacular Chinese (*chinois vulgaire*) at the *École spéciale des langues orientales vivantes* 'Special school of living oriental languages' (now the Institut national des langues et civilisations orientales or I.Na.L.C.O.).

'Unquestionably the most brilliant student of Abel-Rémusat', Julien was one of the main figures of nineteenth century European sinology (Chappell and Peyraube 2014: 211).

Among its pedagogical and linguistic works, we can mention the translation of two Chinese primers,[25] the *Sānzìjīng* 三字經 'Three Characters Classic' in Latin and English,[26] and the *Qiānzìwén* 千字文 'Thousand Character Text' in French.[27]

These translations of Chinese primers show the importance attached to the Chinese philological tradition.

Julien was also the author of some linguistic and didactic works. He published the *Ri-tch'ang-k'eou-t'eou-hoa - Dialogues chinois, à l'usage de l'École spéciale des langues orientales vivantes, publiés avec une traduction et un vocabulaire chinois-français de tous les mots* (日常口頭話- Chinese Dialogues, for the use of the Special School of Modern Oriental Languages, published with a Translation and a Chinese-French

---

24 During the 18th century classes of Chinese in Europe had also been taught at the *Collegio dei Cinesi* in Naples (Castorina 2014) and at the Kjachta's School of Chinese language in Russia (Di Toro 2019).

25 These primers were employed by the missionaries for learning Chinese characters and vocabulary since the late sixteenth century (Brockey 2007).

26 San tseu king *Trium litterarum liber a Wang-Pe-Heou sub finem XIII. saeculi compositus* [The Three Letter Book by Wang-Pe-Heou (Wáng Yīnglín 王應麟 (1223-1296), courtesy name Wáng Bóhòu 王伯厚) compiled at the end of the 13th century], 1864.
San -tsze-king *The three character classic published in Chinese and English by S. Julien*, 1864.

27 Thsien-tseu-wen *Le Livre des mille mots, le plus ancien livre élémentaire des Chinois* [The Thousand Word Text, the Oldest Chinese Primer], 1864.

Dictionary of all words) in 1863,[28] and the two volumes of the *Syntaxe nouvelle de la langue chinoise* (New Syntax of the Chinese Language) between 1869 and 1870.

The Chinese title of this last work *Hànwén zhǐnán* 漢文指南 'The Chinese Language Compass' [29] elucidates its didactic aim:

> The expression *Tchi-nan*, compass, is familiar to the Chinese who use it to designate a didactic book that can be used as a guide for students. (our English translation)[30]

The French full title of the first volume also underlines the main features of this work: the full title of the first volume is *Syntaxe nouvelle de la langue chinoise, fondée sur la position des mots, suivie de deux traités sur les particules et les principaux termes de grammaire, d'une table des idiotismes, de fables, de légendes et d'apologues, traduits mot à mot par M. Stanislas Julien* (New Syntax of the Chinese Language, Based on the Word Position, followed by Two Treatises on Particles and the Main Grammatical Terms, a Table of Idiotisms, Fables, Legends and Apologues, translated word for word by Mr. Stanislas Julien). The role played by word position and by grammatical particles is thus clearly stressed. Julien's *Syntaxe* follows Joshua Marshman's[31] approach and is 'based on word position', as clearly shown by Marshman's famous statement 'the whole of Chinese grammar turns on position', quoted by Julien in the front cover (Marshman 1814: 218; Julien 1869).

The title of the first volume mentions, among the supplements, 'two treatises on particles and the main grammatical terms'. This shows the importance accorded by Julien to the analysis of grammatical particles. The "two treatises" are the *Monographies* (Monographs) and the *Supplément aux monographies* (Supplement to the monographs).

The Monographs consist of short chapters (between 4 and 10 pages for each monograph) devoted to frequent particles of classical Chinese, enumerating their meanings and usages, through illustrative examples.[32]

The 'Supplement to the monographs' is the 'Chinese Treatise on the Particles and the Main Grammatical Terms' (*Traité chinois des particules et des principaux termes*

---

28 The dialogues are drawn from a well-known bilingual Chinese-Manchu textbook, the *Qīngwén qǐméng* 清文啟蒙 ('Manchu Primer', 1730) by Wǔ-gé 舞格.

29 Translated in French by Julien as 'La Boussole de la langue chinoise' (Julien 1869: vii).

30 '*L'expression Tchi-nan, boussole, est familière aux Chinois qui l'emploient pour désigner un ouvrage didactique qui peut servir de guide aux étudiants*' (Julien 1869: vii).

31 The British missionary Joshua Marshman (1768–1837) was the author of the *Elements of Chinese Grammar* 中國言法 (Serampore 1814).

32 For instance « *Monographie de tchi* 之 - *Douze emplois* » [Monograph of tchi 之 - Twelve functions].

de grammaire), *i.e.* Julien's translation and adaptation of Wáng Yǐnzhī's 王引之 (1766-1834) *Jīngzhuàn shìcí* 經傳釋詞 'Explanation of particles in the Classics and Commentaries'. The *Jīngzhuàn shìcí* can be considered as the most detailed and systematic repertory of grammatical particles during the Qing dynasty (Hu 1987: 327) and 'one of the main traditional Chinese sources of the *Mǎ shì wéntōng* 馬氏 文通' (Chappell and Peyraube 2014: 111)

As far as we know, this is the first translation of the *Jīngzhuàn shìcí* in a Western language.

This is an abridged 'translation', and only forty-six of the one hundred and sixty entries of the *Jīngzhuàn shìcí* are translated by Julien. Moreover, in translating these entries, Julien omitted not only several examples and quotations, but also some of the meanings and usages of the grammatical particles. Hence, the *Traité* consists of only sixty-nine pages (pp. 153-231), compared to the more than two hundred pages of the consulted edition of the *Jīngzhuàn shìcí* (ed. 1984).

Furthermore, the two works adopt a different structure: the entries are arranged according to phonetic criteria in the *Jīngzhuàn shìcí*, while the entries of the *Traité* are arranged by radicals and strokes.

In his translation Julien tried to adapt Wang's entries to the Western readership, making frequent comparisons between Western and Chinese categories.

For instance, we quote in the first lines of the Julien's entry for *rán* 然:

> 然 *jen* is used when one depicts something (i.e. as adverbial marker)
> You can find it in the Lun-yu [Lúnyǔ 論語 (Confucius's) *Analects*]: 斐然 elegantly, 喟然 with a sigh, 儼然 quietly, without noise. It's a vulgar (common) meaning. (our English translation)[33]

We read that *rán* is 'used when depicting something': this is a periphrasis for the Chinese expression *zhuàng shì zhī cí* 狀事之詞. Julien translates the Chinese term by this periphrasis, but also adds a term more accessible for European learners, that of 'adverbial marker' (*marque de l'adverbe*).[34] The expression "common meaning" translates *chángyǔ* 常語, which indicates a frequent use of a particle (Peyraube 2000) and which Julien translates as 'ordinary meaning' (*sens ordinaire* ou *signification ordinaire*, Julien 1869: 158, 164), or by the Latin word '*vulgo*' (Julien 1869: 173, 200).

---

33 '然 jen *s'emploie lorsqu'on dépeint une chose (c'est-à-dire comme marque de l'adverbe). On le trouve dans le Lun-yu :* 斐然 *élégamment,* 喟然 *en soupirant,* 儼然 *doucement, sans bruit. C'est une signification vulgaire*' (Julien 1869: 203).

34 We can compare this entry with Prémare's definition: 'adverbial marker, the examples are frequent' ('*nota adverbiorum ; exempla passim occurunt'*, Prémare 1831: 173).

Similarly, in the entry *hóng* 洪, we read that it is an 'initial word'. This is a translation of the Chinese term *fāshēng* 發聲, for which Julien adds the explication 'a sort of exclamation of the beginning of a sentence' (*sorte d'exclamation au commencement d'une phrase*):

洪 *hong,* initial word, sort of exclamation at the beginning of a sentence. Chou-king [*Shūjīng* 書經 'Classic of Documents'], chap. Ta-kao [*Dà gào* 大誥 'The Great Statement'] 洪惟我幼沖人 me, young child [...] Wang adds: in these two passages *hong* is an initial word *fa-ching* 發聲. All the commentators who explained it through *ta* 大 greatly were wrong. This criticism also applies to the Manchu translator who makes *hong* by *ambadame* greatly' (our English translation)[35].

As shown by these examples, the *Traité* provides the European audience with an overview of the genre of particle glossary, at the intersection between lexicography and grammatical studies.

In the *Traité*, we find the transposition of Chinese linguistic concepts and the translation of Chinese linguistic terminology in a European language. Julien uses literal translation and periphrases, but also provided equivalents (categories and concepts known by the European learners) and this resulted in amalgamating Chinese and Western linguistic categories.

5. Concluding remarks
Parts of speech classification and empty word analysis can be considered two emblematic examples of the large process of transposing linguistic terms, concepts and categories that characterized the development of Chinese grammar studies.

Western linguistic categories were largely applied to the Chinese languages. Nevertheless, in order to fully describe Chinese languages, new categories had to be added to Western-inspired grammatical descriptions. This was done by borrowing elements from the native linguistic tradition to classify parts of speech,

---

35 '洪 hong, *mot initial, sorte d'exclamation au commencement d'une phrase. Chou-king, chap. Ta-kao* 洪惟 我幼沖人 *moi, jeune enfant* [...] *Wang ajoute : dans ces deux passages* hong *est un mot initial* fa-ching 發聲. *Tous les commentateurs qui l'ont expliqué par* ta 大 *grandement se sont trompés. Cette critique s'applique aussi à l'interprète mandchou qui rend* hong *par* ambadame *grandement'* (Julien 1869: 199-200).

thereby amalgamating Western and Chinese concepts. Furthermore, Chinese categories were adopted in the description of Western languages in Chinese, in order to make these descriptions more accessible for Chinese learners.

Western works and Western linguistic traditions had a strong impact on the history of Chinese linguistic studies, but the Chinese linguistic tradition was also taken into account, with the translation of linguistic and pedagogical works, like primers and glossaries, and the transposition of the Chinese linguistic terminology in the Western languages.

The three works analyzed in this paper, Prémare's *Notitia linguae sinicae*, Zottoli's (transl.) *Làdīng wénzì*, and Julien's (transl.) *Traité chinois des particules et des principaux termes de grammaire*, can be considered representative examples of the interactions between native philology and Western studies during the Qing period.

These works had a strong impact on the history of foreign language learning (being used as learning tools of Chinese or Latin), on the development of Chinese grammar studies (for their influence on the first full-fledged native grammar of Chinese) and more generally on the history of Chinese and general linguistics (Robins 1997: 122; Wang J. 2009: 344; Li 2011), contributing to the vast process of transposition of linguistic terms and categories that took place in the late Qing period.

References

Primary sources

Abel-Rémusat, Jean-Pierre. 1822. *Élémens de la grammaire chinoise ou principes généraux du Kou-wen, ou style antique, et du Kouan-hoa, c'est-à-dire de la langue commune généralement usitée dans l'empire chinois* [Elements of Chinese Grammar or general principles of Kou-wen, or ancient style, and Kouan-hoa, i.e. the common language generally used in the Chinese Empire], Paris: Imprimerie Royale. [In French]

Abel-Rémusat, Jean-Pierre. 1829. *Nouveaux mélanges Asiatiques ou recueil de morceaux de critique et de mémoires relatifs aux religions, aux sciences, aux coutumes, a l'histoire et a la géographie des nations orientales* [New Selected Writings on Asia or a Collection of Pieces of Criticism and Essays related to the Religions, the Sciences, the Habits and Customs, the History and the Geography of Eastern Nations] vol. 2, Paris: Schubart & Heideloff. [In French]

Bridgman, James G., translator. 1847. *The Notitia linguae sinicae of Premare*. By Joseph-Henri de Prémare. Canton: Printed at the Office of the Chinese Repository.

Edkins, Joseph. 1853. *A Grammar of Colloquial Chinese: as Exhibited in the Shanghai Dialect.* 2nd ed., Shanghai: Presbyterian Mission Press, 1868.

Julien, Stanislas. 1869. *Syntaxe nouvelle de la langue chinoise fondée sur la position des mots. suivie de deux traités sur les particules et les principaux termes de grammaire, d'une table des idiotismes, de fables, de légendes et d'apologues traduits mot à mot* [New Syntax of the Chinese Language,

Based on the Word Position, followed by Two Treatises on Particles and the Main Grammatical Terms, a Table of Idiotisms, Fables, Legends and Apologues, translated word for word] vol. 1. Paris: Maisonneuve. [In French]

Julien, Stanislas. 1870. *Syntaxe nouvelle de la langue chinoise fondée sur la position des mots, confirmée par l'analyse d'un texte ancien, suivie d'un petit dictionnaire du roman Des deux cousines, et de dialogues dramatiques traduits mot à mot* [New Syntax of the Chinese Language, Based on the Word Position, confirmed by the Analysis of an Ancient Text, followed by a Small Dictionary of the Novel 'The Two Cousins', and by Dialogues from Dramas, translated word for word] vol. 2. Paris: Maisonneuve. [In French]

Liu, Qi 劉淇. 1711. *Zhùzì biànlüè* 助字辨略 [Compendium of Grammatical Particles]. Beijing: Zhōnghuá shūjú, 2nd edition, 2004. [In Chinese]

Marshman, Joshua. 1814. *Elements of Chinese Grammar.* Serampore: Mission Press.

Prémare, Joseph-Henri de. 1831. *Notitia Linguae Sinicae* [An Examination of the Chinese Language]. Malacca: Cura Academia Anglo-Sinensis. [In Latin]

Wang, Yinzhi 王引之. 1798. *Jīngzhuàn shìcí* 經傳釋詞 [Explanation of Particles in the Classics and in the Commentaries]. Changsha: Yuèlù shūshè, 1984. [In Chinese]

Yuan, Renlin 袁仁林. 1710. *Xūzìshuō* 虛字說 [Treatise on Empty Words]. Beijing: Zhōnghuá shūjú, 2nd edition, 2004. [In Chinese]

Zottoli, Angelo, translator. 1859. 辣丁文字 *Emmanuelis Alvarez institutio grammatica ad sinenses alumnos accomodata* [Grammar of the Latin Language : Manoel Álvares' grammar adapted for Chinese students]. Shanghai: A. H. de Carvalho. [In Latin]

Secondary Sources

Auroux, Sylvain. 1988a. La grammaire générale et les fondements philosophiques des classements de mots [The General Grammar and the Philosophical Basis of Word Classes]. *Langages*, no. 92: pp. 79-92. [In French]

Auroux, Sylvain. 1988b. Annexe I. Les critères de définition des parties du discours [Annex I. Criteria for Defining the Parts of Speech]. *Languages* [Languages], no. 92: pp. 109-112. [In French]

Auroux, Sylvain. 1989. Introduction [Introduction]. In Sylvain Auroux (ed.), *Histoire des idées linguistiques, Tome I : La naissance des métalangages en Orient et en Occident* [History of Linguistic Ideas, Volume I: The Birth of Metalanguages in the East and the West], pp. 13-37. Liège, Brussels: Mardaga. [In French]

Brockey, Liam Matthew. 2007. *Journey to the East: The Jesuit Mission to China, 1579–1724.* Cambridge, MA: Harvard University Press.

Castorina, Miriam. 2014. I materiali didattici del Collegio dei Cinesi di Napoli: una ricerca preliminare [The Pedagogical Materials of Naples' Chinese College: a Preliminary Study]. In Clara Bulfoni and Silvia Pozzi (eds.), *Atti del XIII Convegno dell'Associazione Italiana Studi Cinesi* [Proceedings of the XIIIth Conference of the Italian Association of Chinese Studies], pp. 145–55. Milan: Franco Angeli. [In Italian]

Chinese Text Project. https://ctext.org/.

Colombat, Bernard. 1988. Présentation : Éléments de réflexion pour une histoire des parties du discours [Presentation: Elements of Reflection for a History of the Parts of the Speech]. *Langages* [Languages], no. 92: pp. 5-10. [In French]

Chappell, Hilary and Alain Peyraube. 2014. The History of Chinese Grammar in Chinese and Western Scholarly Tradition. *Language and History* vol. 57, no. 2: pp. 107-136.

Di Pace, Lucia and Rossella Pannain. 2016. Parole piene/vuote. Traduzione e ricezione di una dicotomia tradizionale cinese nella linguistica occidentale [Full/empty words. Translation and reception of a traditional Chinese dichotomy in Western linguistics]. In Oriana Pascussi and Katherine Russo (eds.), *Translating East and West*. Trento: Tangram. [In Italian]

Di Toro, Anna. 2019. The *Kitajskaja grammatika* (1835) and Bičurin's ideas on the "mechanism" of Chinese between European and Chinese grammatical traditions. *Histoire Épistémologie Langage* [History, Epistemology, Language], vol. 41, no. 1: pp. 57-77.

Fang, Hao 方豪. 1969. Lādīng wén chuánrù Zhōngguó kǎo 拉丁文傳入中國考 [A Survey on the Introduction of Latin in China], *Fāng Háo liùshí zì dìnggǎo* 方豪六十自定稿 [Works by Fāng Háo Selected by the Author at Sixty], pp. 1-38. Taipei: Táiwān xuéshēng shūjú. [In Chinese]

Gianninoto, Mariarosaria. 2014. Zhōngwén biānxiě yìzhe de lādīngwén yǔfǎshū: 19 zhì 20 shìjì chū yǔyánxué yánjiū de zhòngyào lǐngyù 中文编写译著的拉丁文语法书：19 至 20 世纪初语言学研究的重要领域 [The Grammars of Latin written and translated in Chinese: an Important Field of Linguistic Studies in the 19th and early 20th centuries]. *Lādīng yǔyán wénhuà yánjiū* 拉丁语言文化研究 [Research on Latin Language and Culture], no. 2: pp. 29-43. [In Chinese]

Harbsmeier, Christoph. 1998. *Language and Logic. Science and Civilization in China*, vol. VII, no. 1. Cambridge: Cambridge University Press.

Hu, Qiguang 胡奇光. 1987. *Zhōngguó xiǎoxué shǐ* 中国小学史 [History of Chinese Philology]. Shànghǎi: Shànghǎi rénmín chūbǎnshè. [In Chinese]

Klöter, Henning. 2011. *The Language of the Sangleys: A Chinese Vernacular in Missionary Sources of the Seventeenth Century*. Leiden, Boston: Brill.

Lackner, Michael, Iwo Amelung, and Joachim Kurtz. 2001. Introduction. In Michael Lackner, Iwo Amelung, and Joachim Kurtz (eds.), *New Terms for New Ideas: Western Knowledge and Lexical Change in Late Imperial China*, pp. 1-12. Leiden, Boston: Brill.

Lackner, Michael. 2001. Circumnavigating the Unfamiliar: Dao'an (314–385) and Yan Fu (1852–1921) on Western Grammar. In Michael Lackner, Iwo Amelung, and Joachim Kurtz (eds.), New Terms for New Ideas: Western Knowledge and Lexical Change in Late Imperial China, pp. 357–72. Leiden: Brill.

Li, Zhen 李真. 2011. 'Zǎoqí lái Huá Yēsūhuìshì duì hànyǔ guānhuà yǔfǎ de yánjiū yǔ gòngxiàn—yǐ Wèikuāngguó, Mǎruòsè wéi zhōngxīn' 早期来华耶稣会士对汉语官话语法的研究与贡献—以卫匡国、马若瑟为中心 [The Contribution of Early Jesuits to the Study of Mandarin Grammar: Focusing on M. Martini and J. de Prémare], *Wakumon* 或問 vol. 20: pp. 59-67. [In Chinese]

Liu, Yun 刘云. 2009. *Hànyǔ xūcí zhīshì kù de jiànshè* 汉语虚词知识库的建设 [Building a Knowledge Base on Chinese Empty Words], Wuhan: Huázhōng shīfàn dàxué chūbǎnshè. [In Chinese]

Lu, Jianming 陆俭明. 2015 Hànyǔ cílèi de tèdiǎn dàodǐ shì shénme? 汉语词类的特点到底是什么？[What exactly are the characteristics of Chinese word classes?]. *Hànyǔ xuébào* 汉语学报 [Chinese Linguistics], no. 3: pp. 2-7. (Available at: http://www.cssn.cn/yyx/yyx_yyxsdt/201509/t20150921_2410811.shtml) [In Chinese]

Luo, Xiaoliang. 2015. Deux méthodes phonologiques pour une même langue' [Two Phonological Approaches to the Same Language], *Histoire, Épistémologie, Langage* [History, Epistemology, Language] vol. 37, no. 1: pp. 99-122. [In French]

McDonald, Edward. 2020. *Grammar West to East: The Investigation of Linguistic Meaning in European and Chinese Traditions,* New York: Springer.

McLelland, Nicola. 2015. Teach Yourself Chinese — How? The History of Chinese Self-instruction Manuals for English Speakers, 1900–2010. *Journal of the Chinese Language Teachers Association* vol. 50: pp. 109–52.

Meng, Zhaolian 孟昭连. 2014. Lùn "cí"——wényán yǔqì cí fēi kǒuyǔ zàishuō 论 "辞" ——文言语气词非口语再说 [About the 'Ci', A New Theory on the Particles of Classical Chinese], *Nánkāi xuébào* 南开学报 [Journal of Nankai University], no. 5. (Available at: http://www.cssn.cn/yyx/yyx_gdhy/201410/t20141022_1372320_2.shtml) [In Chinese]

Metzler, Josef. 1995. La congregazione per l'evangelizzazione dei popoli (De Propaganda Fide) e le missioni in Cina con particolare rapporto all'operato di Emiliano Palladini [The Congregation for the Evangelization of the Peoples (De Propaganda Fide) and the Missions in China with particular relation to the Activities of Emiliano Palladini]. In Francesco D'Arelli and Adolfo Tamburello (eds.), *La missione cattolica in Cina tra i secoli XVI-XVIII : Emiliano Palladini, Atti del Convegno* [Proceedings of the Conference 'The Catholic Mission in China between the 16th and 18th centuries: Emiliano Palladini'], pp. 107-136. Naples. [In Italian]

Mungello, David E. 1989. *Curious Land: Jesuit Accommodation and the Origins of Sinology.* Honolulu: University of Hawaii Press.

Pan, Wuyun 潘悟云 and Shao Jingmin 邵敬敏. 2005. *Èrshí shìjì zhōngguó shèhuì kēxué: Yǔyánxué juǎn* 二十世纪中国社会科学：语言学卷 [Social Sciences of Twentieth Century China: Linguistics]. Shanghai: Shànghǎi rénmín chūbǎnshè. [In Chinese]

Pellin, Tommaso. 2009. *Lessico grammaticale in Cina (1859–1924)* [The Chinese Grammatical Lexicon, 1859-1924]. Milan: Franco Angeli. [In Italian]

Peyraube, Alain. 2000. Jingzhuan shici. *Corpus de textes linguistiques fondamentaux* [Entry 'Explanations of the Particles in the Classics and the Commentaries', from the Corpus of Fundamental Linguistic Texts]. http://ctlf.ens-lyon.fr/n_fiche.asp?n=480

Peyraube, Alain. 2001. Some reflections on the sources of the *Mashi Wentong*. In Michael Lackner, Iwo Amelung, and Joachim Kurtz (eds.), *New Terms for New Ideas. Western Knowledge and Lexical Change in Late Imperial China*, pp. 341–356. Leiden, Boston: Brill.

Peverelli, Peter. 1986. *The History of Modern Chinese Grammar Studies.* Heidelberg, New York, Dordrecht, London: Springer, 2015.

Ponce de Léon Romeo, Rogélio. 2001. El Álvarez en vernáculo: las exégesis de los De Institutione Grammatica Libri tres en Portugal durante el siglo XVII [The translation of Álvarez in a Vernacular Language: the Exegesis of the De Institutione Grammatica Libri tres in Portugal during the 17th century]. *Línguas e Litteraturas. Revista da Facultade de Letras* [Languages and Literatures. Journal of the Faculty of Humanities], no. 18: pp. 317-338. [In Spanish]

Raini, Emanuele. 2010. *Sistemi di romanizzazione del cinese mandarino nei secoli xvi-xviii* [Romanization Systems of Mandarin Chinese during the XVI and XVII centuries]. Unpublished Doctoral Thesis. Rome: Sapienza-Università di Roma. [In Italian]

Robins, Robert Henry. 1967. *A Short History of Linguistics.* 4th edition. Routledge, 1997.

Uchida, Keiichi. 2017. *A Study of Cultural Interaction and Linguistic Contact: Approaching Chinese from the Periphery.* Göttingen: V&R.

Wang, Jianjun 王建军. 2009. *Zhōng-xīfāng yǔyánxué shǐ zhī bǐjiào* 中西方语言学史之比较 [A Comparison between Chinese and Western Histories of Linguistics]. Héféi: Huángshān shūshè. [In Chinese]

Wang, Li 王力. 1981. *Zhōngguó yǔyánxué shǐ* 中國語言學史. Taipei: Wunan Books, 1996. [In Chinese]

Zhao, Zhenduo 赵振铎. 2000. *Zhōngguó yǔyánxué shǐ* 中国语言学史 [History of Chinese Linguistics]. Hebei: Héběi jiàoyù chūbǎnshè. [In Chinese]

Zou, Zhenhuan 邹振环. 2005. *Mǎ Xiāngbó yǔ Lādīng wéntōng* 马相伯与拉丁文通 [Mǎ Xiāngbó and the 'Grammar of Latin']. *Fùdàn xuébào* 复旦学报 [Fudan University Journal], no. 6: pp. 112-119. [In Chinese]

Zwartjes, Otto. 2011. *Portuguese Missionary Grammars in Asia, Africa and Brazil, 1550–1800.* Amsterdam, Philadelphia: John Benjamins.

Chapter 8

Georg von der Gabelentz
and Chinese and East Asian Linguistics

Barbara Meisterernst
National Tsing Hua University
Email: bmeisterernst@gmail.com

Abstract

Georg von der Gabelentz (1840–1893) and his father Hans Conon von der Gabelentz (1807–1874) were two of the most relevant scholars in the research of Chinese and East Asian Linguistics in Germany in the 19th century. The influence of these two scholars has been comprehensively discussed in the linguistic literature, mostly with regard to the history of general linguistics, and much less so with regard to the Chinese language and Chinese linguistics. In this brief chapter, we will focus on this aspect of Georg von der Gabelentz's research. We will particularly concentrate on the influence Gabelentz had on the development of syntactic concepts such as topicalization in Chinese linguistics, but also on other syntactic issues, and on his ideas with respect to grammaticalization processes. Gabelentz proposed a 'spiral course of language history' (*Spirallauf der Sprachgeschichte*), i.e. a constant change from an analytic to a synthetic, then back again to an analytic language in the grammaticalization of languages. The concentration on cross-linguistic syntactic analysis is one of three different aspects in which Georg von der Gabelentz proved to be truly innovative and influential in general linguistic research. Gabelentz can also be considered as the founder of typological research.

1. Introduction

Georg von der Gabelentz (1840–1893) and his father Hans Conon von der Gabelentz (1807–1874) were two of the most relevant scholars in the research of Chinese and East Asian Linguistics in Germany in the 19th century. Both father and son were not part of the historical linguistics mainstream of the time represented by the Neogrammarians, who focused mainly on the historical phonology of the Indo-European languages. They rather followed a more language typology oriented cross-linguistic approach in the tradition of Wilhelm von Humboldt

(1767-1835) and the 'Psychology of People' (Völkerpsychologische) tradition of Moritz Lazarus (1824-1903) and Heymann Steinthal (1823-1899). Hans Conon von der Gabelentz was one of the first who published a comparative grammar on the Melanesian languages (1861 and 1873); additionally, he published a comparative essay on passive constructions in more than 200 languages modeled after Wilhelm von Humboldt's "On the Dual" (McElvenny 2017).

Georg von der Gabelentz's works concentrated on general linguistic issues and on numerous specific languages with a particular focus on Chinese. In the comprehensive article 'Beitrag zur Geschichte der chinesischen Grammatiken [Contribution to the History of Chinese Grammars]' published in 1878, he critically acclaims existing Chinese grammars and manuals. The article consists of two sections. In the first section, Gabelentz discusses, in total, 18 grammars and manuals of the Chinese language. In the second section, he provides a concise resume of the grammatical features of the Written Chinese language in order to relate the difficulties encountered in writing the grammar of a language entirely different from the Indo-European languages. Following this brief introduction to Chinese grammar, he proposes a new concept of grammar writing, which addresses the problem of typological differences in languages. This concept is divided into two basic systems: 1) an analytic system, analyzing the different parts of speech of a sentence and their relation to each other;[1]; and 2) a synthetic system. Gabelentz himself labels the latter 'Synonymic', a system of synonyms, i.e. the system of the different possibilities a language provides to express an intended meaning. Gabelentz subsequently employs the dual system he proposes in his (1878) article, in his Grammar of the Written Chinese Language (1881), and also in an unpublished draft of the grammar of Sanskrit (McElvenny 2017). It was not only the influence of his research on the Chinese language, but also on Manchu, Japanese, Malayan, and Polynesian languages, which caused Gabelentz to focus on syntactic analysis as particularly relevant in linguistic research (1869, 1875). The concentration on cross-linguistic syntactic analysis is one of three different aspects in which Georg von der Gabelentz proved to be truly innovative and influential in general linguistic research (McElvenny 2017). Before Gabelentz, historical linguists focused on the development of sound systems and on morphological changes in language. Additionally, Gabelentz was the first who coined the term 'typology' in his article 'Hypologie[2] [typologie]: eine neue Aufgabe der

---

1   The basis of Gabelentz's linguistic analysis is the sentence as a syntactic unit.
2   This was the first mention of the term 'typology' in the history of linguistics. Due to his untimely passing, Gabelentz was not able to change the typographic mistake before publication of his seminal article.

Linguistik [Typology: a new task in linguistics]' (1894) based on the cross-linguistic approach of his father and his own cross-linguistic research. Furthermore, he is one of the first people who formulated the principles of grammaticalization in a way which is still relevant today in linguistic research, twenty years before the term grammaticalization was introduced by the French linguist Antoine Meillet (1912) (see McElvenny 2017).

The influence of Hans Conon and Georg von der Gabelentz has been comprehensively discussed in the linguistic literature, mostly with regard to the history of general linguistics, and much less so with regard to the Chinese language and Chinese linguistics. In this brief chapter, we will focus on this aspect of Georg von der Gabelentz's research. We will particularly concentrate on the influence Gabelentz had on the development of syntactic concepts such as topicalization in Chinese linguistics, but also on other syntactic issues, and on his ideas with respect to grammaticalization processes. Gabelentz (1891: 250, translated by McElvenny 2016: 35) proposed a 'spiral course of language history' (*Spirallauf der Sprachgeschichte*), i.e. a constant change from an analytic to a synthetic, then back again to an analytic language in the grammaticalization of languages.[3] According to him, this spiral also accounted for Chinese with Modern Chinese showing a tendency towards agglutination, whereas its ancestor, Ancient Chinese, showed traces of a former agglutinative or even inflectional morphology (McElvenny idem). Nevertheless, he claimed that the isolating character of Chinese was different in being an inherent and unchangeable feature of the Chinese language (Gabelentz 1878: 642), which persisted even though signs of agglutination could be perceived; Gabelentz here disregarded the fact that the Indo-European languages also showed a tendency to develop into more isolating languages, and languages with more analytic structures (Schwegler 1990: 4).

2. Georg von der Gabelentz and the Chinese language

2.1. Brief biographical notes

Georg von der Gabelentz became associate professor for Sinology at Leipzig University in July 1878. His chair was the first official chair for Sinology in Germany and thus implemented the study of Sinology at German universities. Von der Gabelentz came from an aristocratic and intellectual family; his father was already extremely interested in cross-linguistic studies. With the support of other scholars of Oriental studies, Gabelentz Senior established the German Oriental

---

3   The change from synthetic to analytic and back to synthetic in Chinese has become an
    important issue in Chinese historical linguistics, e.g. in Feng (2014), Huang and Roberts (2017),
    Feng and Lin (2019), Meisterernst (2020a), Peyraube (ms.) and more.

Society in 1845 and founded the still existing and influential journal of the German Oriental Society (*Zeitschrift der Deutschen Morgenländischen Gesellschaft*). Due to his father's influence and the comprehensive library Gabelentz Senior had collected, Georg von der Gabelentz was exposed to the study of many different non-European languages already at an early age; he started studying Chinese at the age of seventeen. In his position as an associate professor at Leipzig University, Gabelentz was supposed to teach Chinese, Japanese, Manchu, Malay, Tibetan, and Mongolian grammars and general linguistics. Owing to his open-minded education and the liberal and cosmopolitan atmosphere in his family, Gabelentz learned to appreciate the value and high development of Chinese culture from an early age. This certainly contributed to his view of the Chinese language as non-stative and just as well subjected to change as any other language. This approach to the Chinese language could not have been taken for granted at that time in Europe, and neither can it today. His well based knowledge of Chinese contributed widely to his linguistic theories, first and foremost to his proposal of the basic and relevant function of syntax in languages, but also to his theories on grammaticalization and on linguistic typology. Without his acknowledgment of the superior role of syntax in the Chinese language, his claims on the basic function of syntax in language in general may have been less strong. His approach went beyond the leading comparative approach of the Neogrammarians, who confined their linguistic studies to Indo-European languages.[4] Gabelentz appreciated the rigor of the Neogrammarian comparative approach, but for him cross-linguistic studies, including typologically different languages such as the Tibeto-Burman, Altaic, and Austronesian languages, were the more fruitful approach in order to understand the basis of language production and language change.[5] In his founding paper on linguistic typology (1894) he proposed a meticulous program employing statistical methods for linguistic studies including as many languages, and languages as diverse as possible in order to establish a "truly general" grammar accounting for the features attested in the languages of the

---

4   And it certainly contradicted the conception of the Chinese language as being devoid of any grammatical structure comparable to the supposedly more developed inflectional languages such as Greek and Latin (e.g. in Schlegel 1808, Schleicher 1850, also in Humboldt 1843). This view still prevails to a certain extent particularly in work on Chinese philosophy. This can be seen for instance in Jullien (2009: 191f, cf. Roetz 2011: 63), who claims that Chinese basically does not have any syntax to construct ideas, which according to him explains the differences between the Chinese and the Western cultures and philosophies from a linguistic or philological perspective. For a discussion and a refutation of this still prevailing perspective see also Assandri and Meisterernst (2019).

5   The biographical details presented here are mainly based on the very informative website on the history of Sinological studies at Leipzig University (https://sinologie.gko.uni-leipzig.de/institut/geschichte/hans-georg-conon-von-der-gabelentz.)

world (see also Bisang's introduction to the 2010 reprint of Gabelentz's grammar).

In 1889, Gabelentz changed to a position of full professor for General Linguistics and Chinese Studies at Berlin University (today's Humboldt University). Although Gabelentz, due to his premature death in 1893, never established a school of his own, he conferred doctorates to a number of influential Sinologists and Orientalists. Apart from these direct influences, his influence on Sinological and Oriental Studies is undeniable. His successor in Leipzig was August Conrady, who followed Gabelentz in both his rigorous scientific methods and his open-minded cosmopolitan attitude. Conrady conferred both his doctorate and his qualification as a university professor (habilitation) to Bernhard Karlgren in 1915 and 1918, respectively (Malmquist 2011). Karlgren became the instigator of Chinese historical linguistics and Chinese historical phonology based on the comparative method. Additionally, Karlgren was the first to include dialect studies, loanwords in non-Chinese languages, etc., into the reconstruction of the pronunciation of Old Chinese. Although Karlgren conducted most of his doctoral studies in Paris under Edouard Chavannes and Paul Pelliot, the leading French Sinologists, he decided to be promoted in Sweden by Conrady. Pelliot, who would have been Karlgren's natural choice, was not available as an examiner at that time due to his participation in World War I. Chavannes on the other hand was not specialized in linguistic studies. Following Gabelentz's death, up until the time when Karlgren started his Sinologial studies, there were hardly any Sinologists specializing in linguistic studies of Chinese. This was one of Bernhard Karlgren's main motivations to concentrate on Chinese linguistics early on when he decided on his path, according to which he intended to pursue his studies of Chinese (Malmquist 2011).

2.2 Classification of the Chinese language by Gabelentz
a) Classification of Chinese
Gabelentz (1881) classifies the Chinese language as belonging to the so-called Indochinese Languages; these have been proposed to include Chinese, Tibetan, Burmese, Karen, Southern Himalayas, Assam, and Siamese (Tai). Several classifications were proposed for Indochinese in the 19th century; a very detailed discussion of the history of different linguistic affiliations of Chinese can be seen in Van Driem (2001). According to August Conrady, Gabelentz's successor in Leipzig, Indochinese could be divided into a Western Branch, the Tibeto-Burman languages, and an Eastern Branch, which includes Chinese and Siamese; this corresponds to a certain extent to the Hàn-Zàng distinction (*Hànzàng yǔxì* 漢藏語系), which for some scholars included Daic languages and Hmong-Mien languages (van Driem 2001: 343).

Typologically, Chinese was classified as an isolating language by Gabelentz (1881: §4), as it had been by many other scholars preceding him, e.g. by Wilhelm von Humboldt (McElvenny 2016: 32); grammatical relations are expressed by word order and lexical means alone. In contrast to many other early classifications of Chinese, Gabelentz conceded that Chinese displays possible traces of inflection or agglutination, but he did not classify those vestiges of an older system as defining the typological features of the language. This is a consequence of Gabelentz's version of the Agglutination Theory first proposed by Franz Bopp (1791-1867), according to which all languages participate in a constant change from isolating to agglutinative and inflectional, then back to isolating languages:

> Affixes weaken and disappear entirely over time, but their functions or related functions remain and strive for new expression. These expressions are achieved, according to the mechanisms of isolating languages, by word order or by clarifying words. The latter are, over time, subjected to a new agglutination process, and to their weakening and disappearance (Die Affixe verschleifen sich, verschwinden am Ende spurlos; ihre Functionen aber oder ähnliche bleiben und drängen wieder nach Ausdruck. Diesen Ausdruck erhalten sie, nach der Methode der isolirenden Sprachen, durch Wortstellung oder durch verdeutlichende Wörter. Letztere unterliegen wiederum mit der Zeit dem Agglutinationsprozesse, dem Verschliffe und Schwunde, ...) (Gabelentz 1891: 269).

This process is most evident in the Indochinese languages according to Gabelentz (1891: 270), which show different stages of agglutination and the development from agglutinative to isolating languages. Gabelentz claimed that Chinese is the most important and most 'mature' representative of isolating languages ("So ist sie nicht nur die wichtigste Vertreterin, sondern recht eigentlich die gereifteste Frucht isolierender Sprachbildung." (1960: 5)). Although he concedes that Chinese probably had some kind of affixal morphology in its early stages, he does not support any hypotheses about its not being a monosyllabic language (Gabelentz 2016 (1891): 270, 1881: § 5), in which the lexical stems (Stammwörter) are constituted by one syllable. On the other hand, Gabelentz argued against the at the time widespread assumption that Chinese is a so-called root language (Wurzelsprache) (2016: 311) (Schlegel 1818), the words of which have not undergone any change apart from some phonological changes. In the literature preceding Gabelentz, Chinese had been believed to be the well preserved picture of the oldest human speech possible and had been classified accordingly, despite the fact that other supposedly related languages display agglutination, e.g. reflected in the consonant clusters in Tibetan (e.g. Schlegel 1808). Gabelentz's arguments against Chinese as a root language included references to phonological correspondences of semantically related words in order to demonstrate that different forms could be derived from identical roots; his examples are 大 *dà* 'big' *(daH / dajH)* – 太 *tài (thajH)* 'great'; 田 *tián (den)* 'field, hunt' – 佃 *diàn (denH)*[6] 'hunt', etc.

b) Reconstruction of Old Chinese

Before Karlgren started his research on the phonological reconstruction of older stages of Chinese, Gabelentz had already proposed the necessity of a systematic investigation of the different varieties of Chinese, the Chinese 'dialects', as one of several important sources for the reconstruction of Old Chinese. He particularly mentioned the dialects of Fuzhou, Amoy, Fujian, and Canton. Additionally, he referred to the relevance of the indigenous Chinese philological tradition, i.e. Chinese dictionaries, the rhymes in the *Shijing*, but also to the Classical literature, the analysis of the phonetic parts of the Chinese characters, and the comparison with other Indo-Chinese languages. To this, Gabelentz added the analysis of Sino-Japanese, Sino-Korean, and Sino-Vietnamese, and additionally the transcriptions of the Indian words in Buddhist translations, critically referring to Stanislas Julien's (1861) work on Buddhist Chinese. Gabelentz himself chose not to follow this program, since his foremost interest was the analysis of the syntax of Chinese. However, the program he proposed for the reconstruction of Chinese, has in its completeness not always been followed consequently even in present day research. Although Karlgren and his followers acknowledged the relevance of different varieties of Chinese and the comparison with related Tibeto-Burman languages for the reconstruction of the earlier stages of Chinese, they greatly relied on the written sources of Chinese, such as the rhymes of the *Shijing*, the *Qièyùn* 切韻, the rime tables and the philological Chinese traditions. Despite the relevant work of Edwin G. Pulleyblank in this field, transcriptional data, i.e. transcriptions of Chinese Buddhist texts by non-Chinese scripts, such as Tibetan, Sogdian, and Brahmi[7] have not been exploited to the fullest (Norman and Coblin 1995: 582f).[8] Norman and Coblin also argue for more systematic reconstructions of earlier dialectal stages of Chinese based on the comparative method, instead of relying too much on the transmitted rime dictionaries and tables.

c) Grammatical Structure

Despite the lack of inflectional morphology and the typological characterization of Chinese as an isolating language, Gabelentz insisted on the existence of grammatical structure; this evidently contrasted with the widespread assumption

---

6   Reconstructions and glosses are taken from Baxter and Sagart (2014).

7   For a brief overview see Meisterernst (2019) and references therein.

8   See also Yoshida, this volume.

that isolating languages lack a proper grammar in the sense of the Indo-European languages. Gabelentz relates his proposal very clearly in paragraphs 50 and 51 of his *Chinese Grammar (Chinesische Grammatik*, 1881), which outline part of his research program for Chinese.

§ 50 *Grammatical comprehension*
Chinese has grammar, to suppose that because Chinese does not have inflection means that it does not have grammar is wrong.

§ 51 *The grammar of Chinese* is - apart from its phonology and its writing system – solely **syntax**, and it will be comprehended as such. Comprehended, not merely learned.
("Die chinesische Grammatik ist, abgesehen von der Laut- und Schriftlehre, lediglich **Syntax**, und will als solche begriffen sein. Begriffen, nicht nur angelernt").

Gabelentz first related his ideas on comparative syntactic analysis in an early paper "Ideas on comparative syntax (Ideen zur vergleichenden Syntax)" (1869), based on studies of languages including Indo-European, Finno-Tatarian, Indochinese, and Malayo-Polynesian. Gabelentz's objective in this study was to find the connection between the expression of thoughts based on psychological features of individual peoples with the word order rules of their respective languages, and not to discuss language-genealogical relations (Gabelentz 1869: 377). For his study, he deliberately left out any cases of marked word orders; these include rhetorically marked word orders, or word order variations in questions, imperatives, and relative clauses. On the other hand, he pointed to the diachronic relevance of word order in compounds as reflecting older word order rules. Gabelentz did not include the exploration of cross-linguistic universals into the objectives of his study. However, his proposal of a distinction between a Psychological Subject (topic / theme) and a Psychological Predicate (comment / rheme) in the languages under investigation proposed exactly this, namely, the position of the Psychological Subject (topic) in sentence initial position independent of its grammatical status otherwise as a cross-linguistic universal. Gabelentz's comprehensive analysis of the concept of the Psychological Subject is discussed in section 4 below.

In his *magnum opus* "*Linguistics*" (Die Sprachwissenschaft (1891 (2016)), Gabelentz argued for the superiority of the syntactic approach based on his research on the Chinese language. He proposed that a grammar without morphology (including word formation) is possible, but a grammar without phonology and syntax is not. This kind of grammar is possible and even necessary with isolating languages, which do not have morphological distinctions (anymore). A grammar without syntax is strictly speaking an absurdity ("ein Unding"), because it excludes the part where the language is actually used, i.e. where it enters life (Gabelentz 2016: 89). Grammar has to be concerned with the spoken language; the basis of grammatical analysis is the sentence.[9] The approach, Gabelentz proposed, is universalistic, i.e. it is not confined to one particular language, but has to account for all languages (Gabelentz 2016, 92f (§ 4)). Additionally, Gabelentz strongly argued for a formal representation of syntactic structure; the examples he used to demonstrate this are selected from Chinese. Parts of this discussion are presented in example (1) below (I changed the original transcription to *pinyin*) (Gabelentz 2016: 124).

(1)

Paradigme   **Formula**

I. *Wáng*   *bào*   *mín* A^{subj} $B^{v.act.}$ C^{obj} $= \Phi$ (sentence)
    The king   protects   the people BC $= P$ (predicate)

II. *mín*   *bào* C^{subj} $B^{v.pass}$ $= \Phi$ (sentence)
    The people is protected

III. *mín*   *bào*   *yú wáng* C^{subj} $B^{v.pass}$ *yu* A^{agent} $= \Phi$ (sentence)
    The people is protected by the king. ABC

IV. *Bào*   *mín*   *zhī*   *wáng* $p^{attr.}$ *A (or C)*^{noun} $= \underline{\Phi}^{noun}$
    Protect people pr.rel. king   *n* (noun phrase)

The syntactic rules derived from these examples are:
1. The subject precedes the predicate (I, II, III);
2. The transitive (active) verb precedes its object (I);
3. If an otherwise transitive (active) verb appears at the end of the sentence, it is passive (II);
4. The active sentence can be changed into a passive one when the logical object is transferred into the position preceding the verb, and the logical subject into the position following the verb by means of the preposition *yú* 於 (III);
5. Every predicate can be changed into an adnominal attribute, when it appears preceding the logical subject, with the 'relational' particle (Relativpartikel) (*zhī* 之) between the predicate and the logical subject (IV);

---

9   Although Gabelentz takes the sentence as the basis for his grammar, his major contribution to Chinese linguistics, his Grammar of Written Chinese, is not based on the spoken language or any kind of vernacular variety of Chinese.

This example demonstrates Gabelentz's purely syntactic approach to linguistic analysis inspired by the strict word order of Chinese and the typological characteristics of Chinese as an isolating language. Classical Chinese was a language with an impoverished morphology which probably already had lost its productivity almost entirely (see Schuessler 2007). In such a language, case marking on the noun, or (obvious) morphological distinctions on the verb, which facilitate the classification of particular parts of speech, are not available. Thus, the analysis of speech parts depends entirely on their syntactic position and function. However, Gabelentz clearly demonstrated that a meticulous syntactic analysis allows the classification of the different parts of speech even without any help from morphological distinctions. This was an evident innovation in 19th century linguistics. The great number of historical grammars of the Indo-European languages produced during this period focused on the phonology and morphology of the languages they analyzed, the section on syntax was usually confined to agreement rules and stylistics. The arguments Gabelentz provided for a formal representation of syntactic structure include the advantage of an unmediated approach and the independence from individual languages, thus a formal analysis of syntactic structure as a perfect means of scientific representation.

3. Gabelentz's analytic and synthetic systems and the Grammar of Chinese

3.1 The Analytic and the Synthetic Systems and their influence on later linguistic concepts
The terms 'analytic' and 'synthetic' were introduced into linguistics by one of the brothers Schlegel, probably August Wilhelm von Schlegel (Schwegler 1990: 3), in order to account for differences, e.g. between the ancient and modern Indo-European languages. Lehmann claims that Gabelentz is the first to introduce the concept of an analytic and a synthetic system into General Linguistics, referring to language reception and language production respectively (McElvenny 2017: 5). By contrast, McElvenny points out that at least this terminological distinction was already in use in the earlier Chinese grammars by Jean-Pierre Abel-Rémusat (1822) and Henri Joseph Prémare (1831).[10] Another possible influence on Gabelentz regarding the distinction between an analytic and a synthetic system may have been a Greek Manual (1843) with which Gabelentz might have learned the Greek language. The concept was adopted by the Danish linguist Otto Jespersen,

---

10 I am grateful to Alain Peyraube who pointed my attention to Schwegler (1990) and to the fact that both Lehman and McElvenny did not refer to August Wilhelm von Schlegel as the first to introduce this terminology. Peyrauble also pointed out that Abel Rémusat most likely did not employ this terminology. See also Gianninoto, this volume.

but in later years the terms 'analytic' and 'synthetic' were abandoned. In 20th century linguistics, the respective contrasts would be between 'semasiological' and 'onomasiological', or 'structural' and 'functional' analyses.[11]

a) The Analytic System: language as an organic structure

Based on Wilhelm von Humboldt's 'Language as an Organism', Gabelentz pointed to the organic structure of language: Language had to be understood and described from its organism. Because the organism of Chinese is fundamentally different from the organism of the Indo-European languages, the organization of its grammar has to differ greatly from the one Europeans are used to (Gabelentz 1881).

Humboldt provided the following definition of 'Language as an Organism':

On the one hand, the number of words [of a language] represents the range of the world [of its speakers], and on the other hand, the grammatical structure [of a language] represents its view of the organism of thinking... Without doubt, only grammatically fully developed languages [i.e. the inflectional languages according to Humboldt] are fully appropriate for the development of ideas." (Humboldt 1843: 299).[12]

However, Humboldt acknowledged that Chinese with its Classical literature was an astonishing counterexample to this hypothesis. Within Humboldt's analysis, Classical Chinese appeared as the default isolating language (Humboldt 1843: 303), i.e. a language on the lowest stage of development from isolating to agglutinating and to inflectional. In those languages, grammatical relations can only be expressed by word order and separate words ("abgesonderte Wörter"). In this hierarchy, generally proposed in 19th century linguistic work, the inflectional languages, particularly Classical Greek, constitute the representatives of the highest hierarchical level of development. Classical Chinese, on the other hand, had been compared to the Coptic language, another language with impoverished morphology of a culture which was considered highly developed. The structure of the Coptic language had been characterized as constituting a synthetic system by Silvestre de Sacy (Humboldt 1843: 304):[13] "the grammatical system of the Coptic language is ... an entirely synthetic one, i.e. it is a system, in which the grammatical expressions are separated

---

11 https://www.christianlehmann.eu/ling/gesch_sw/Gabelentz/Gabelentz.html

12 Humboldt, Gesammelte Werke Bd. 3, 1843: 299 "Ueber das Entstehen der grammatischen Formen, und ihren Einfluss auf die Ideenentwicklung" [On the origin of grammatical forms and their influence on the development of ideas].

13 Silvestre des Sacy (1758-1838) was the founder of Modern Arabistics.

from and either precede or follow the words referring to the 'things'."[14] According to Humboldt, the Chinese style is supposed to be vague and incoherent and the language had to change to obtain more clarity, definiteness, and variation. Following Humboldt's theory, linguistic characteristics as those proposed for the Chinese language are used in order to postulate a connection between the typological characteristics of a language and the thinking of its speakers. However, based on Chinese, Humboldt had to concede that different forces are able to lead a people with what he calls an 'inefficient' language to high cultural achievements as in the case of the Chinese and the Egyptians, the speakers of the Coptic language, and that any language has the capacity to be used in the most perfect way (Humboldt 1843: 271).

According to Gabelentz (1881, § 270), the analytic system has to answer the questions: how do we understand the grammar of Chinese? What are the grammatical features of Chinese and what is their meaning? The features have to follow the basic rules of linguistic construction; they have to be comprehended accordingly and they have to be organized according to their organic structure.

These basic rules are the rules of **word order** (§ 271). Relevant for those rules are the beginning and end of a sentence; therefore, we have to start within the limits of a **sentence**. Here, Gabelentz unambiguously identified the sentence as the basis of grammatical analysis, in contrast to the morphological parameters, which had been the foremost part of linguistic analysis in the 19th century, e.g., for the diachronic comparative studies of the Neogrammarians. With his approach, Gabelentz clearly established a synchronic perspective of linguistic studies and proposed standards for linguistic analysis, which became programmatic in the 20th century. The grammatical means of a language to be studied are: 1) word order; 2) auxiliary words (function words), the meanings of which depend on their syntactic position "deren Bedeutung wieder von der Wortstellung abhängig ist" (§ 273).

b) The Synthetic System

The function of the synthetic system is to show which devices a language possesses in order to fulfill its purpose. The grammatical features [of the analytic system] and the devices of a language are both part of the grammar. But they approach language from different perspectives and accordingly they have to be presented in a different manner. Gabelentz called the Synthetic System a grammatical Synonymic System (§ 898). The grammatical synonymic system is rooted

---

14 Note the employment of the term 'synthetic' for a structure which is generally characterized as analytic.

in the innate sense of the language of a people and it finds its confirmation in the language's usage (§ 899). The establishment of a synthetic system by Gabelentz was meant to facilitate the acquisition of the variations and the finer points of the Chinese language for speakers of typologically unrelated languages (Schwegler 1990: 14). In his study of Chinese, Gabelentz proposed that the synthetic system reveals that the Chinese language possesses an astounding flexibility and variation of expression (§ 902). The definition of the analytic and the synthetic systems proposed in Gabelentz evidently differs from the way the terminology was first introduced by Schlegel (1818) and later used by Schleicher. As already mentioned, Gabelentz's use of the terms 'analytic' and 'synthetic' had been abandoned in the 20th century, whereas the original concepts had been revived in Sapir (1921). Recently, the terminology has been employed in Chinese linguistics (e.g. in Feng (2014), Huang and Roberts (2017), Feng and Lin (2019), Meisterernst (2020a), Peyraube (ms.) and more) in order to analyze distinctions between Classical and Modern Chinese, proposing that Classical Chinese is a more synthetic language, whereas Modern Chinese is highly analytic.

In the following section, a few examples of the Synthetic System employed will be presented. Gabelentz demonstrated in this system that in the Chinese language the inflexibility of the **rules of word order** could be redressed by simple linguistic devices. He claimed that inversions provide liveliness and grace to the language without impeding its comprehension.

One part of the synthetic system is, for instance, the syntactic analysis of the rules of ellipsis. Gabelentz proposed the following syntactic rules for ellipsis in Classical Chinese (§ 1123) among others:

I.   Words, which are stressed, are not to be deleted.

II. One is not supposed to cut down on expressions of modality and mood, e.g. final particles, modal auxiliary verbs, etc. This statement of Gabelentz implies that the employment of these function words is mandatory in Classical Chinese in the respective contexts.

III. One is supposed to cut down on lexical words (*Stoffwörter*; these overlap with the *shící* 實詞 in Chinese linguistics, see also chapters 5, 6, and 7 in this volume), which include nouns, proper names, adjectives, numerals, verbs, adverbs. Additionally, pronouns, prepositions, postpositions, conjunctions, and the genitive marker *zhī* 之 can be omitted in particular contexts.

IV. Repetition of the same word is considered a means of emphasis and not bad style.

Here, we will only briefly discuss §. 1125, which is concerned with the deletion of the object pronoun *zhī* 之. Gabelentz introduced the following constraints on the deletion of this pronoun:

1) it can be deleted particularly with negated psych verbs (verbs of wishing, thinking, believing, knowing);
2) it can be deleted preceding sentence final *yán* 焉, which in the analytic system is discussed as a sentence final particle;
3) it can be deleted following deontic negative marker *wù* 勿.

Accordingly, Gabelentz proposed that, apart from some exceptions, Classical Chinese does not allow object pro-drop. In this regard, Classical Chinese is different from Modern Chinese, which allows both subject and object pro-drop (Huang *et al.* 2009: 199, cf. Aldridge 2019). Arguments for why Late Archaic (Classical) Chinese (5th – 2nd c. BCE, LAC) is not an object pro-drop language, whereas Modern Mandarin is, are provided in Aldridge (e.g. 2019).

   An extensive discussion centers particularly around the case of the modal negative marker *wù* (**mut*)[15] 勿, its non-modal correspondent *fú* (**put*) 弗, and their differences from the two negators *wú* (**mo*) 毋 / 無 and *bù* (**pə*) 不. Djamouri (1991) proposes that the negators of the first group are confined to the negation of transitive, active verbs, whereas the negators of the second group rather negate intransitive, stative verbs. Wei (2001), by contrast, argues for the more traditional analysis of these negators as including an inherent third person pronoun. Pulleyblank (1995: 105) proposes that the difference between the two classes of negators is an aspectual one, and that the negators *bù* and *fú* possibly differ in the expression of an ongoing state or action (*bù*) in contrast to potentiality or a change of state (*fú*). The three different cases of a null object pronoun are exemplified below. Example (2) represents a negated psych verb. A brief survey of the Academia Sinica Archaic Chinese corpus reveals 1758 hits of *bù zhī* 不知 'not know', in 280 of those instances it appears without a complement, and there are only 10 instances of *bù zhī zhī* 不知之 altogether. However, it has to be conceded that the null object can be accounted for by the presence of negation and not by the category of verbs. Example (3) represents what Gabelentz analyzes as a case of the null pronoun with 'sentence final' *yán* 焉. The classification of *yán* as a kind of sentence-final particle seemed to have been the common assumption at the time (see Kennedy 1940: 1, who cited Couvreur, Legge, Giles, and other 19th century scholars, but also Karlgren for this function). Today, sentence-final *yán*

---

15 Reconstructions are from Baxter and Sagart (2014).

焉 is generally considered as functionally identical with the preposition *yú* 於 and its pronominal third person complement, e.g. *yú zhī* 於之, as an oblique or as a dative pronoun (Aldridge 2015, Smith 2012). In preverbal position it can function as an adverbial similar to *yúshì* 於是, but it predominantly functions as a *wh*-word in preverbal position either referring to an oblique case or as an adverbial *wh*-word 'how, where, whither' (Smith 2012), in this position read *yān* (Pulleyblank 1995: 81). The first to propose the functional identity of *yán/yān* with *yú*+3PP is the *Mǎshì wéntōng*, published a few years after Gabelentz's grammar (cf. Kennedy 1940: 9). Pulleyblank shows that despite the functional identity of *yán/yān* with *yú zhī*, phonologically it cannot be a fusion of the preposition *yú* and the third person object pronoun *zhī* (Pulleyblank 1995: 80), thus the pronominal element has to be a different one, most likely the demonstrative pronoun *shì* 是 (Smith 2012). Example (4) represents the lack of an object pronoun with the modal negator *wù* 勿 'don't', scoping over a transitive verb. Gabelentz proposes a possible fusion with *zhī* 之.

(2) 汝知之乎？曰：不知。 (Gabelentz 1960: 419, no reference).
    Rǔ   zhī   zhī   hū   yuē   bù   zhī
    You know OBJ SFP say NEG know
    'Do you know it? Answer: I do not know it.'

(3) 民無能名焉 (*Lunyu* 8.19, Gabelentz 1960: 420)
    Mín   wú   néng   míng   yán
    People NEG able name YAN
    'And the people were not able to name him. (Das Volk vermochte **es** nicht zu benennen)'

(4) 子路問事君，子曰，勿欺也 (*Lunyu* 14.22, Gabelentz 1960: 420)
    Zǐ lù   wèn   shì   jūn   zǐ   yuē   wù   qī   yě
    Zi Lu ask server ruler master say NEG$_{mod}$ cheat SFP
    'Zi Lu asked how to serve a ruler. The Master said: do not cheat him, … (Täusche **ihn** nicht, …)

3.2. Some examples for Gabelentz's analytic and synthetic systems

In this section we introduce the case of case in Chinese, which is discussed in both the analytic and the synthetic systems in Gabelentz's grammar. Most early grammars of Chinese introduce a case system copying morphologically marked case systems such as in Latin. For instance, Marshman (Singapore 1814) proposed prepositions as *case* markers:

... but in *prepositive characters* to designate the various cases, the Chinese are by no means deficient; on the contrary they have a sufficient variety to express, not merely the cases generally found in European grammars, but also the Instrumental and the Locative of the Sungskrit.

Prémare (1666-1736) in his *Notitia Linguae Sinicae* (Malacca 1831) proposed a number of particles as markers of case: *de* 的 as genitive marker, the preposition *yú* 於, but also *yǔ* 與, *duì* 對, and other markers as dative case markers, the vocative marker *ā* 阿, and plural marking by adjoined characters expressing number (Prémare and Bridgman 1847: 28f); additionally, he proposed a zero marker for the accusative, which appears in postverbal position. Julien (1869), too, proposed prepositions as case markers, similar to Marshman and other grammars preceding him. Additionally, Julien established correspondences between the function of the Chinese prepositions and the different cases in Latin grammar. This approach had been severely criticized by Gabelentz, according to whom Julien lists "with great pleasure and without discrimination point for point the number of possible French translations of one and the same particle" (Gabelentz 1878: 610, 637).

In contrast to these earlier proposals, which were critically discussed in Gabelentz (1878), Gabelentz's own definition of case (§ 370f in the analytic system) is almost purely syntactic. According to this approach, Gabelentz claimed that case in Chinese is marked by word order and not morphologically. In preverbal position, a distinction has to be made in the grammatical analysis between the subject and an adverbial phrase. The object generally appears in postverbal position, and an object in preverbal position constitutes a special case of preposing ("Anteposition"). Not to be included in a definition of case are nouns in absolute positions, such as in vocatives, in appositions and in coordination, or in the position following a genitive, adjectival, or participial modifier. Consequently, Gabelentz listed the following cases:

a) *subject case*,
b) *predicate case* (NP predicates),
c) *object case*, following a verb or a preposition,
d) *genitive case*, preceding a noun and functioning as its determiner and
e) *adverbial* case, in preverbal position (including adjectival verbs), can be immediately preceding or not.

In addition to these categories, Gabelentz proposed a defective morphological case system for personal pronouns in § 1092f in the synthetic system of his grammar. He claims that this defective case system is manifested only in the first and the third person pronouns; the second person does not display any case distinctions; it is only employed in familiar or derogatory speech.

In his discussion on the first person pronouns *wǒ* 我 and *wú* 吾, Gabelentz proposed nominative and accusative cases for *wǒ*; for the pronoun *wú* he proposed that it had mostly, but not exclusively, genitive case. *Wú* can appear as a subject, when an adverb or an auxiliary word follows. When *wú* seems to function as the subject, Gabelentz claimed that the subject has genitive case. This is not mentioned in the analytic system. The examples in (5) represent the two employments of the respective pronouns *wǒ* and *wú*. In (5a), *wǒ* appears in both subject and object position; in (5b), *wú* appears as the subject of a volitional verb. *Wú* typically appears as the subject of modal verbs. As a first person pronoun it is e.g. more frequent in combination with the pre-modal *dé* 得 as both lexical and auxiliary verb than the pronoun 我 *wǒ* (12 ⇔ 7 in *Zuǒzhuàn*). All the can-wish verbs of LAC, i.e. all the early auxiliary verbs, appear more frequently with *wú* than with *wǒ*.

(5) a. 爾為爾，我為我，雖祖裼裸裎於我側，爾焉能浼我哉？ (*Mengzi* 2.1.9)[16]
   Ér wéi ěr   wǒ wéi wǒ   suī   dàn xí   luǒ   chéng   yú wǒ cè
   You be you I   be   I   although bare nude naked denuded at I side
   ěr   yān néng měi wǒ zāi
   you how can defile I Q
   'You are you and I am I, even if you are naked and denuded at my side, how could you defile me?!'

 b. 吾願與伯父圖之 (*Zuozhuan, Zhuang* 14.2.4, Gabelentz 1960: 411)
   Wú   yuàn   yǔ   bófù   tú   zhī
   I   wish with uncle consider OBJ
   'I wish to consider it with you, uncle.'[17]

For the third person, Gabelentz proposed a distinction between accusative and genitive case; the nominative, i.e. the third person pronominal subject is always zero. The third person object is referred to by *zhī* 之, having object case (accusative case). The third person pronoun *qí* 其 has genitive case. The case differences for the third person are also mentioned in the analytic system.

---

16 Gabelentz (1960: 411). Gabelentz only lists the first part of the sentence. Transcriptions and glosses are added.
17 Gabelentz (1960: 411): 'Ich wünsche es mit meinem Oheim zu überlegen.'

The pronouns of Archaic Chinese have subsequently gained a lot of attention in scholarly literature. Numerous distinctions have been proposed particularly for the first person pronouns. There is general consensus that a case distinction existed for the third person pronouns in Late Archaic Chinese, manifested by the accusative pronoun *zhī* 之 and the genitive pronoun *qí* 其.[18] For a discussion on this distinction see most recently Aldridge (2015, 2019 and references therein). In the earliest extant literature, the oracle bone inscriptions, two morphologically distinct groups of pronouns are attested for the first person: the first group is characterized by the approximant initial *j-* in Middle Chinese; Baxter and Sagart (2014) reconstruct *l- for Old Chinese: *yú* 余 (EMC *jiă*, *la)[19], *yŭ* 予 (EMC *jiă'*, *laʔ) and Pre-Classical *yí* 台 (EMC *jĭ*, *lə), together with *zhèn* 朕 (EMC *drim'*, *lrəmʔ).[20]

This group of pronouns refers almost exclusively to the king (Pulleyblank 1995: 76), and has thus been proposed to have singular reference.[21] The second group is characterized by the nasal initial *ŋ-* in Middle and Old Chinese, referring to the Shang collectively, including *wŏ* 我 (EMC *ŋa'*, *ŋˤajʔ),[22] *wú* 吾 (EMC *ŋɔ*, *ŋˤa), and Pre-Classical *áng* 卬 (EMC *ŋaŋ* *ŋˤaŋ);[23] the pronoun *wú* is not yet attested in the earliest texts, the Oracle Bone Inscriptions. Since this group refers to the Shang collectively, it had sometimes been assumed that it originally had plural reference (see Pulleyblank 1995: 76). In Classical Chinese, this distinction, if it was relevant at a time, vanished; the pronoun *wŏ* though, frequently still refers to a plurality of items. A similar, although less obvious distinction can also be shown for the second person pronouns: *ěr* 爾 (EMC *ɲi'*, *n[ə][r]ʔ) and *ruò* 若 (EMC *ɲiak*, *nak) indicate general number (singular and plural) in Classical Chinese, and *rŭ* 汝, 女 (EMC *ɲiă'*, *naʔ) seems to be confined to the singular (Unger 2019: 15, Zhang 2001: 26-27).[24] Additionally, two second person pronouns confined to the modifying position are attested, *ér* 而 (EMC *ɲi*, *nə) and *năi* 乃 (EMC *nəj'*, * nˤəʔ).

---

18 See also for instance Wang (2004), Zhou (1980), Zhang (2001) and others.

19 Early Middle Chinese (EMC): Pulleyblank 1991, the language of the *Qieyun*, 601 CE. This is different from the grammatical period of EMC, referred to later in the chapter in the syntactic discussions, which starts at around the 2nd c. BCE and goes up to the 6th c. This dating merges the Pre-Medieval and the Early Medieval periods proposed in Peyraube 1996.

20 In Wang (1958, 2004: 302) all first person pronouns of this category are reconstructed with the voiced dental initial *d-*.

21 The reconstructions of Middle Chinese are taken from Pulleyblank (1991).

22 Reconstructions of Archaic Chinese are taken from Baxter and Sagart (2014) unless indicated otherwise.

23 For a comprehensive discussion on personal pronouns see also Chou (1959) among many others.

24 This paper does not intend to join the discussions on personal pronouns in Chinese; the hypotheses represented above concerning the system of personal pronouns are merely intended to show the complex morphological relations when it comes to the pronominal system of Chinese.

Table 1: Pronouns in Archaic Chinese

	no constraint	Constraint	constraint	constraint
1st P/ 1st series	予 *laʔ *yǔ*	余 *la *yú*	朕 *lrəmʔ *zhèn*	台 *lə *yí*
1st P /2nd series	我 *ŋˤajʔ *wǒ*	吾 *ŋˤa *wú*		卬 *ŋˤaŋ *áng*
	no constraint	constraint	possessive	possessive
2nd person	爾 *n[ə][r]ʔ *ěr*	汝 *naʔ *rǔ*	乃 *nˤəʔ *nǎi*	而 *nə *ér*

In this table, 'no constraint' designates pronouns which can appear in subject, object and modifying position. All the other pronouns are subject to some constraints, although the constraints are not necessarily absolute; this means that the constrained pronouns appear either exclusively or predominantly in particular syntactic positions. The two *pingsheng* first person pronouns appear predominantly in subject position; *wú* also regularly appears in modifying position; and they are both banned from an end of phrase position. The constrained first person pronouns predominantly appear in modifying position, but can occasionally appear as subjects and even less occasionally as objects (e.g. Chou 1959, Pulleyblank 1995, Zhang 2001, Aldridge 2019, among others).

The distribution of the first person pronouns *wǒ* and *wú* had been of particular interest in linguistic discussions. Karlgren (1920) proposed an original inflectional distinction for Archaic Chinese for the first and second person pronouns between nominative and genitive case on the one hand, and accusative case on the other: nominative/genitive case was marked by –O, and genitive case was marked by –A (see Graham 1969: 20). In LAC, the accusative case of the –A form started to affect the –O system, which according to Karlgren was still intact in the older LAC literature. Subsequent research tried to account for the differences in the employment of the respective pronouns, trying to avoid the concept of case as being too biased towards the study of Indo-European languages. Dobson for instance employed a concept of sub-, and super-ordination; *wú* is confined to subordinate positions, whereas *wǒ* is not; i.e. *wú* appears as a determiner, a determinant word (Dobson 1959: 27). Kennedy proposed a difference in stress due to the differences in tone in order to account for the syntactic differences between *wǒ* and *wú*; a deflecting tone, i.e. the rising tone, implies completion, a level tone implies incompletion and is thus confined to particular positions. Graham (1969) argued against both Dobson's and Kennedy's analyses and proposed a purely syntactic analysis for the distributional differences of *wǒ* and *wú* both in independent and in dependent positions, i.e. as subject or as possessive (Graham 1969: 46). Acknowledging the fact that the pronominal system of Pre- and Early Archaic Chinese differs considerably from that of Late Archaic Chinese, Graham established two different systems a *Pre-classical* and a *Classical system*, consisting of different sets of pronouns in the respective systems. The pronouns were analyzed according to syntactic distribution (1969: 54). The two systems are still reflected in different Late Archaic texts. According to Graham's analysis, both *wǒ* and *wú* belong to the *Classical System*. Graham noted that pronouns are uncommon 'at the end of the phrase' in the earliest documents (Graham 1969: 56), which is to explain the fact that pronouns in the earliest documents are ending in a level tone –O. As a result of a diachronic development of Chinese which requires more pronouns in phrase-final position, a change to the rising tone is induced. This analysis seems to suggest that the forms which in Middle Chinese have the rising tone, and which in Archaic Chinese had been reconstructed with a glottal stop coda, develop from the level tone variants.

4. Discussion of the Psychological Subject: a major contribution to Chinese linguistics[25]

The identification of topicalization structures is certainly one of the major contributions to Chinese linguistics in Gabelentz's syntactic studies of Chinese. In paragraph § 260 Gabelentz notes:

> It seems to be natural and just as desirable for the Chinese as it is for us to start an utterance with what matters [der Gegenstand, the topic] and to continue gradually so that the entirety of the following members [parts of speech] step by step constitutes a manifestation with regard to / a comment to the preceding members [parts of speech]. The first issue of the utterance – **the Psychological Subject** – does not necessarily constitute the grammatical subject (our nominative), but can also constitute different parts of the sentence, e.g. the time, a location, the grammatical object, a genitive belonging to the latter, etc. These words have to be taken out of the syntactic unit and to be **placed in an absolute position**.[26]

---

25 For a more comprehensive discussion on the psychological subject see also Meisterernst (2020b, in German).

26 § 260, in the original German: "Es scheint naturgemäss und ist jedenfalls dem Chinesen nicht weniger Bedürfniss als uns, mit der Rede bei dem zu beginnen, was ihren Gegenstand bilden soll, und nun in der Reihenfolge fortzufahren, dass von Schritt zu Schritt die Gesammtheit der folgenden Glieder sich zu der Gesammtheit der vorausgegangenen als Aussage über diese verhält. Nächster Gegenstand der Rede – **psychologisches Subjekt** – ist aber nicht immer das grammatische Subjekt (unser Nominativ), sondern es kann auch ein anderer Theil des Satzes sein, z.B. eine Zeit und ein Ort, das grammatische Objekt, ein Genitiv, welcher zu letzterem gehört, u.a.w. Solche Wörter müssen also aus dem syntaktischen Verbande herausgerissen und absolut gestellt werden."

According to Gabelentz, the Psychological Subject is something that most likely can be classified as a basic language universal, a category already existent at the earliest stages of language:

> I believe that we have in this way come to know one of the oldest and so to speak embryonic categories of all human language....If my deduction is correct, then this category must be existent in all language, in however many different ways its effects may manifest themselves" (Gabelentz 1891: 392–393).[27]

According to Gabelentz, this proposal is supported by its reflection in child language acquisition. (Gabelentz 1891: 386–388).

The earliest concepts of the linguistic strategy of topicalization were identified by medieval Arabian grammarians who distinguished the respective parts of speech into *mubtada* 'beginning', and *xabar* 'news' (Krifka 2008). Goldenberg (1988: 67) describes this structure as rhematization of the predicate (*axbir / ixbār*), by which the rest of the sentence becomes the nominalized subject *mubtada*. He defines the construction as a kind of cleft; it has been discussed comprehensively in linguistic studies on Medieval Arabic. In modern western science Weil (1844) discussed similar constructions by introducing the terms *le point de depart* and *enunciation*. The terms *Psychological Subject* and *Psychological Predicate* appeared first in Gabelentz's *Ideen zur komparativen Syntax* [*Ideas on comparative syntax*] (1869: 378f) and in Hermann Paul's *Prinzipien der Sprachgeschichte* [*Principles of the history of language*] (1880, 1975: 124f). Both Gabelentz and Paul based their syntactic concepts on psychological models newly introduced into linguistics (see von Heusinger 2002: 107). Paul explicitly referred to Gabelentz, but differed from the latter in his more abstract conceptions particularly of the psychological predicate. Additionally, he acknowledged the relevance of prosody as an important piece of evidence for the identification of the psychological predicate, whereas Gabelentz exclusively relied on syntactic criteria. Since Paul characterized the function of the psychological predicate as conveying new information (1886: 101), he implicitly distinguished between old and new information, a distinction which became relevant in later linguistic studies. The Prague School subsequently employed the terms *thema* and *rhema*, introduced at almost the same time by Vilém Mathesius (1929) and Ammann (1928, cf. von Heusinger 2002: 112). In Ammann the terms are employed with clear reference to Gabelentz (Ammann 1928: 2, cf. Heusinger 2002, note 7); *thema* presents *old information* and *rhema* presents *new information*

---

27 See McElvenny 2017, who also translated this passage from *Die Sprachwissenschaft*.

(Krifka 2007). The first who introduced the terms *topic* and *comment* to general linguistics was the linguist Hockett (1958):

> The most general characterization of predicative constructions is suggested by the terms 'topic" and "comment' […]: The speaker announces a topic and then says something about it.

Chao Yuen-ren in his *Grammar of Spoken Chinese* (1968) was the first to acknowledge the relevance of the term *topic* for the Chinese language. His definition diverges from the one of Gabelentz in identifying the topic with the subject of the sentence but distinguishing it from the actor:

> Subject and Predicate as Topic and Comment. The grammatical meaning of subject and predicate in a Chinese sentence is topic and comment, rather than actor and action. Actor and action can apply as a particular case of topic and comment, … The subject is literally the subject matter to talk about, and the predicate is what the speaker comments on when a subject is presented to be talked about. (Chao 1968: 69f)

The definition proposed subsequently in Li et al. (1981: 94) concurs more with Gabelentz's definition.

In contrast we consider topic and subject to be two different types of notion.

Table 2: Overview of the different traditional concepts of topic and comment

Representative	Terminology	Grammatical Function of Pychological Subject
Gabelentz	Psychological Subject – Psychological Predicate	$\neq/=$ grammatical subject: subject, object, adverbial phrase
Paul	Psychological Subject – Psychological Predicate	$=/\neq$ grammatical subject; no further definition
Prague School	Theme–Rheme; old–new information	$\neq/=$ grammatical subject
Chao	Topic–comment	$=$ grammatical subject
Li/Thompson	Topic–comment	$\neq/=$ grammatical subject

In the remainder of this section, we provide a brief introduction to the different kinds of topics discussed in Gabelentz under the term Psychological Subject. In all examples, the Psychological Subject, the topic, is characterized by its sentence-peripheral position. Unless in combination with a second topic, the Psychological

Subject always appears in sentence-initial position as the external topic. According to Paul and Whitman (2017), the external topic in Chinese occupies [Spec,TopicP], selecting either another TopicP or TP. Many studies have been devoted to topicalization and focalization structures in Modern Chinese (see e.g. Badan and Del Gobbo 2011, Chou 2013, Paul 2015, Paul and Whitman 2017); topics in Classical Chinese have been discussed less systematically.[28] In general, topics can be either base-generated or dislocated. The Psychological Subjects discussed in Gabelentz all seem to be base-generated topics, though. We will base the concise introduction to the Psychological Subject in Gabelentz on the syntactic categorizations of topics in Modern Chinese by Chou (2013) and Badan and Del Gobbo (2011); these are briefly introduced below, followed by Gabelentz's definition of the syntactic position of the Psychological Subject:

1) Chou (2013) distinguishes three different kinds of topics in Modern Chinese: (1) Dangling/Aboutness Topic; (2) Dislocation Topic; and (3) Hanging Topic. Topics of the first category do not have a "syntactic integration" in the commentary part of the sentence (Chou 2013: 125). Dislocation and Hanging topics on the other hand have a syntactic function in the commentary part of the sentence, represented by either a gap (dislocation topics) or a co-referential pronoun (hanging topics). The co-indexed pronoun occupies the thematic position of the sentence-initial topic. Only topics of the first and the third category are base-generated (idem). Example (6) represents a topicalized object in Modern Chinese, a co-indexed pronoun appears in the regular object position. The structure is identical to the structure in Classical Chinese in ex. (7).

(6)   Zhangsan$_i$,   Lisi   hen   xihuan   ta$_i$
      Zhangsan   Lisi   very   like   him
      'As for Zhangsan, Lisi likes him very much.' (from Chou 2013: 125).

2) Badan and Del Gobbo (2011) propose the following distinction between Hanging Topics (HT) and Left Dislocation (LD) for Modern Chinese:
1. HT cannot be PP, while LD can;[29]
2. HT doesn't need to agree in case with the resumptive element;
3. Since there are no clitics in Chinese, LDs leave a gap, while HTs are resumed by an epithet or a tonic pronoun;

---

28 Object topicalization has been discussed in Aldridge (2019).

29 Paul (2015: 227f) argues against Badan and Del Gobbo's classification of PPs as generally left dislocated topics and in favor of the possibility of base generation for at least some of the topic PPs. She claims that Badan and Del Gobbo's classification only refers to argument PPs and not to adjunct PPs.

4. Only multiple LDs are possible;
5. The relative order is HT > LD.

3) Gabelentz defines the syntactic position of the Psychological Subject in the following way:

> When the regular rules of word order change and a part of speech, which usually does not belong there, moves to the first position, this is called **absolute** [position], i.e. [a position] outside the unit of the sentence. It usually has to be replaced within the unit of the sentence by corresponding third person pronouns (之 *ti*, 其 *k'i*) or by the complementless ["prägnant"] verbal particles (以 *i*, 與 *iü*) (Gabelentz 1960: 432f) …The object pronoun is rarely missing.[30]

The examples discussed below include all syntactic instantiations of the Psychological Subject proposed in Gabelenetz. These are: the object as the Psychological Subject, the subject as the Psychological Subject, a genitive modifier as the Psychological Subject, and an adverbial phrase as the Psychological Subject.

a) The Object as the Psychological Subject/Topic
A topicalized object appears in sentence initial position; it requires the presence of a resumptive pronoun in the original object position, thus it qualifies as a base-generated 'hanging topic'.[31] Aldridge (2018, 2019) shows that objects cannot be topicalized by dislocation in LAC, because an object cannot move over the subject.[32] Aldridge (2018) proposes that the topicalized object in Late Archaic Chinese appears in [Spec,CP]; in this case the subject appears in a lower position in TP where it values non-nominative case. Some evidence for this comes from the fact that if the subject is a first person pronoun, it is represented by the pronoun *wú* 吾, for which a non-nominative (possibly genitive) case has been proposed (see also Gabelentz 1881, Graham 1969, Aldridge 2017).

---

30 "Würde dadurch das allgemeine Stellungsgesetz durchbrochen, rückt also ein Satztheil in die erste Stelle, welcher sonst nicht dahin gehörte, so pflegt man diesen **absolut**, d.h. ausserhalb des Satzverbandes zu stellen und meistens im Satzverband durch entsprechende Pronomina der 3. Person (之 *ti*, 其 *k'i*) oder durch prägnante Verbalpartikeln (以 *i*, 與 *iü*) zu ersetzen (Gabelentz 1960: 432) … Selten wird in solchen Fällen das **Pronomen weggelassen**: (idem: 433f)."

31 In the literature on topicalization there is some disagreement with respect to the exact relation between the topic and the co-indexed pronoun (Frey 2005).

32 Aldridge (2019) argues that this can be accounted for by labeling and the fact that the subject has to be licensed by the case feature in C/T. Accordingly, this position cannot be occupied by the object.

(7) 諸侯之禮，吾未之學也。 (*Meng* 3A2)

Zhūhóu	*zhī*	*lǐ*	*wú*	*wèi*	*zhī*	*xué*	*yě*
Feudal.lord	GEN	ceremony	1PGen	NEG$_{asp}$	3POBJ	learn	SFP

'Regarding the ceremonies of the feudal lords, I have not learned them yet.'
(Das Ceremoniell der Lehnsfürsten habe ich noch nicht erlernt.' (Gabelentz 1960: 433, Aldridge 2018: 11))

b) The Subject as the Psychological Subject

Gabelentz merely notes that the Psychological Subject as the subject can be marked by *yě zhě* 也者. The topic (Psychological Subject) refers back to the subject of the preceding utterance, i.e. it presents old information. The Psychological Subject is not resumed by a pronoun in the regular subject position, but it has a function in the commentary part. According to the above definitions, this kind of topic seems to be analyzable as a 'dislocated topic' or LD topic and not a base-generated topic. According to Chou (2013), base-generated topics in Modern Chinese do not allow a gap in the commentary part, unless the gap appears in an island as in (8b), where it appears as the modifier of the following noun phrase. The same situation, but with an overt resumptive pronoun can be seen in example (9). Further analyses are required to establish the status of topicalized subjects of the kind represented by example (8). Since the marking by the two particles *yě* and *zhě* argues for a position of the subject different from the regular position in [Spec,CP] proposed e.g. in Aldridge (2019), the possibility that it is base-generated and resumed by an empty *pro* in the regular subject position seems to be likely. According to Chafe (1976: 50), base generated topics are typical for Chinese; he labels them 'Chinese Style Topics'.

(8) a. 道也者，不可須臾離也(*Zhongyong* 1,1 (*Liji* 31,1))

Dào	*yě*	*zhě*	*bū*	*kě*	*xūyú*	*lí*	*yě*
Way	NOM	NOM	NEG	possible	while	separate	SFP

'Regarding the WAY, it may not be left even for a little while. (Der Pfad (von dem ich sprach) darf nicht einen Augenblick verlassen werden.)' (Gabelentz 1960: 434)

b. Akiu$_i$ [[e$_i$ baba]   hen   congming]
       Akiu   father   very   smart
       'Akiu$_i$,   [his$_i$] father is smart. (Chou 2013: 125)

c) A genitive modifier as Psychological Subject

In the following example presented in Gabelentz, the topic, the Psychological Subject, is co-referential with the genitive modifier of the object in the commentary part of the sentence. The co-indexed pronoun appears in an island, which provides additional evidence for the analysis of the topic as base-generated (see also Aldridge 2019: 10). According to the Left Branch Condition (Ross 1986: 127, cf. Bošković ms., who discusses the phenomenon with respect to adjectives as 'Left Branch Extraction'), movement from the left-most constituent of an NP is not permitted, i.e. a modifier cannot be moved. The topic can be co-referential with the genitive modifier of a subject and an object DP. The example from Gabelentz in (9a) shows an object DP, the example in (9b) shows a subject DP, the modifier of which is co-indexed with the topic. This example is discussed in Unger (2019) under the label 'exposition of a genitive'.

(9) a. 百畝之田，勿奪其時，數口之家可以無饑矣！ (*Meng* 1A/3, Gabelentz 1960: 433)
Bǎi   mǔ   zhī   tián   wù   duó   qí   shí   shù   kǒu   zhī   jiā
Hundred mu   GEN   field   NEG_mod rob   GEN   time   several mouth GEN   family
kě   yǐ   wú   jī   yǐ
can   YI   not.have starve SFP
'Regarding a field of a hundred *mu*, do not deprive them of their time [for tilling the fields], and then a household of several people is able not to starve.'

b. 魯先大夫臧文仲，其身歿矣，其言立於後世。 (*Guoyu, Jin* 8, Unger 2019: 970)
Lǔ   xiān   dàifū   Zāng   Wén zhòng   qí   shēn   mò   yǐ
Lu   early   official   Zang   Wenzhong   GEN   body   die   SFP
qí   yán   lì   yú   hòu   shì
GEN   word   stand   PREP   later   generation
'Regarding the former official Zhang Wenzhong, his body may have died, but his words will survive the later generations.'

d) temporal, locative, causative, and circumstantial adverbials as the Psychological Subject

In addition to the Psychological Subjects discussed above, Gabelentz included sentence-initial temporal, locative, causative, and circumstantial adverbials into the category of possible Psychological Subjects, i.e. topics. These have been categorized as frame setting adverbials in Chafe (1976, cf. Paul 2015: 208). According to Gabelentz, they mark the initial point of an utterance, frequently referring back to the previous narrative, thus they refer to *old* information. On the other hand, Paul (2015) demonstrates that in Modern Chinese, topics do not necessarily convey old information, and the same seems to account for Late Archaic Chinese.

In this brief discussion, we will confine ourselves only to a small number of examples. We start with temporal adverbials. The regular position for temporal adverbials, DPs, or PPs, in Late Archaic and Early Middle Chinese is the sentence-initial position; they set the frame for the following utterance (Meisterernst 2015). They can be compared to the 'Scene-Setting Adverbials' discussed in Benincà and Poletto (2004) in Romance languages; these occupy a very high position, probably following Hanging Topics, but preceding Left Dislocated Topics. Benincà and Poletto also claim that these topics are confined to root clauses. In LAC, frame (scene) setting topics are unlike hanging topics in that they do not have to be resumed by a co-referential pronoun in the commentary part. The following examples involve what Krifka calls 'contrastive topics'; in (10a), there is no reference to the previous narrative, and in (10b), 'yesterday's affair' shows a clear reference to the previous narrative. They convey old information.

(10) a. 古者民有三疾，今也，或是之亡也。 (*Lunyu* 17,16, Gabelentz 1960: 434)

Gǔ	*zhě*	*mín*	*yǒu*	*sān*	*jí*
Antiquity	TOP	people	have	three	disease

jīn	*yě*	*huò*	*shì*	*zhī*	*wáng*	*yě*
today	SFP/TOP	maybe	this	GEN	not.have	SFP

'In antiquity the people had three diseases, today it probably does not have them anymore. (Vor Alters wohl hatte das Volk drei Gebrechen, jetzt freilich hat es vielleicht diese nicht mehr.)'

b. 昨日之事，子為制，今日之事，我為制。」 (*Lüshi chunqiu* 3,1)

Zuò	*rì*	*zhī*	*shì*	*zǐ*	*wéi*	*zhì*
yesterday	day	GEN	affair	you	do	decision

jīn	*rì*	*zhī*	*shì*	*wǒ*	*wéi*	*zhì*
today	day	GEN	affair	I	do	decision

'Regarding yesterday's affair, you took the decision; regarding today's affair, I will decide.'

In the examples in (11), the frame-setting adverbial is a temporal PP with the preposition *dāng* 當 'at (a time)'. The regular position for PPs with *dāng* is the sentence-initial position (Meisterernst 2015); (11b) is one of the few examples in which the PP is preceded by another syntactic element, in this case the topicalized subject. The regular subject position is not occupied, but we tentatively assume that it is resumed by an empty pronoun; in this case, the topicalized subject had to be analyzed as a Hanging Topic. The position preceding a 'Scene-Setting Adverbial' also argues for the analysis of the topic as a Hanging Topic, as a Dislocated Topic would be expected to follow the adverbial, if what Benincà and

Poletto propose for Romance also accounts for Late Archaic (LAC) and Early Middle Chinese (EMC). Following their classification, Scene-Setting Adverbials in LAC and EMC evidently have to be distinguished from 'Aboutness Topics', these precede both Hanging and Left Dislocated Topics according to Badan and Del Gobbo (2010).

(11) a. 當幽王三年，王之後宮見而愛之。 (*Shiji*: 4; 147)

Dāng	*Yōu*	*wáng*	*sān*	*nián*	*wáng*	*zhī*	*hòu*	*gōng*	*jiàn*	*ér*	*ài*	*zhī*
PREP	You	king	three	year	king	go	back	palace	see	CON	love	3Obj

'In the third year of king You, the king went to the women's quarters, and seeing her fell in love with her.'

b. 費昌當夏桀之時，去夏歸商，為湯御，以敗桀於鳴條. (*Shiji*: 5; 174)

Fèi	*Chāng*	*dāng*	*Xià*	*Jié*	*zhī*	*shí*	*qù*	*Xià*	*guī*		*Shāng*
Fei	Chang	PREP	Xia	Jie	GEN	time	leave	Xia	turn-towards		Shang

wéi	*Tāng*	*yù*		*yǐ*	*bài*	*Jié*	*yú*	*Míngtiáo*
become	Tang	charioteer	YI	defeat	Jie	PREP	Mingtiao	

'Regarding Fei Chang, at the time of Jie he left the Xia and turned to the Shang; he became charioteer of Tang and thus defeated Jie in Mingtiao.'

In the examples in (12) a prepositional phrase with *yú* 於 appears in sentence-peripheral position. *Yú* is the most common relational preposition in LAC, its regular position is postverbal, but it can also appear in preverbal position, i.e. following the subject, frequently in contrastive contexts, and in sentence-initial position, preceding the subject.[33] This is clearly the case in (12b). In (12a), no subject is present, but the PP is followed by *zé* 則, which can function as a marker of topicalization. According to Gabelentz (1960: 434), *zé* appears when the sentence-initial adverbial refers to the condition of the following utterance. The definition accounts for the employment of *zé* as a causal complementizer. In (12a), the PP seems to refer to a contrastive topic, similar to the examples in (11) with contrastive temporal adverbials. In (12b), the topicalized PP is resumed by the co-indexed pronoun *yán* 焉 briefly discussed above. This qualifies the topic as a Hanging Topic, different from a Frame-setting or Aboutness Topic.

---

33 A discussion of the syntax of prepositional phrases with *yú* is not at issue in this brief study. Mei (2015: 323f) briefly discusses *yú* in sentence-initial position as introducing a frame-setting topic and in preverbal position as introducing a focus phrase.

(12) a. <u>自稱曰老夫，於其國</u>則稱名。 (*Liji* 1, 1/21, Gabelentz 1960: 434)

     Zì   *chēng* *yuē* *lǎo* *fū* *yú*   *qí*   *guó*   *zé*   *chēng* *míng*

     Self call say old man PREP POSS country TOP call name

     'Referring to himself he says 'old man'; in his state, he uses his name.'

   b. <u>於齊國之士</u>吾必以仲子為巨擘焉 (*Meng* 3B10, Unger 2019: 700)

     Yú   *Qí*   *guó* *zhī*   *shì*   *wú*   *bì*

     PREP Qi state GEN gentleman 1P certainly

     yǐ *Zhòng* *zǐ* *wéi* *jù* *bò* *yán*

     YI Zhong zi make big thumb PP

     'Among the men of Qi, I would certainly consider Zhong zi the thumb.

An Aboutness Topic does not have a grammatical connection to the commentary part of the sentence similar to frame (scene) setting topics. In LAC and EMC, the position of Aboutness Topics is different from temporal adverbials which are allowed to follow a topicalized subject. This seems to be in agreement with Badan and DelGobbo's proposal that Aboutness Topics in Modern Chinese precede both Hanging Topics and Dislocated Topics, if we assume that subject topics preceding temporal adverbials are Hanging Topics. In (13) the subject follows the topic, and a change of position would involve a change in the semantics. According to Paul (2015: 207), aboutness topics are frequently unconnected with *old* information; this is not the case in the example here.

(13) <u>漢東之國</u>，隨為大 (*Zhuozhuan, Huan 6*)

    Hàn dōng *zhī*   *guó Suí wéi dà*

    Han east GEN state Sui be big

    'Regarding the states east of Han, Sui is the biggest.'

The examples demonstrate that the term Psychological Subject in Gabelentz covers different kinds of topics, which all seem to be base generated. This poses the question, whether topics in LAC and EMC are base-generated as a rule. Aldridge (2019) provides some arguments for constraints of movement, extraction constraints, of objects over the subject. These might be extended to prepositional phrases particularly with *yú*, which can also have argument status. But any further classifications of topics in LAC and EMC require more comprehensive research which is not at issue in this brief chapter.

The following kinds of topics can be identified following Gabelentz's analysis of possible Psychological Subjects:

a) Hanging Topics, which include Object Topics, Genitive Topics, Dative/ Locative topics with *yú*, and most likely also Subject Topics with a covert co-referential pronoun;

b) Frame 'Scene Setting' Topics; these show no connection to the sentence; they can be preceded by a topicalized subject (hanging topic); they have to be distinguished from Aboutness Topics;

c) Aboutness Topics; they also do not show a connection to the sentence. Whether they generally precede all other topics, including Hanging Topics as has been proposed for Modern Mandarin in Badan and Del Gobbo (2010) is subject to future research.

With his analysis of the Psychological Subject, Gabelentz was the first who identified and analyzed the syntactic strategy of topicalization based on a purely syntactic approach. Subsequent linguistic research characterized topicalization structures as most typical for the Chinese language. Gabelentz's proposal of the Psychological Subject – Psychological Predicate Structure, i.e. a topic – comment structure, was certainly one of the most groundbreaking innovations in the analysis of the Chinese language. Insights from the structure of Chinese and the universal relevance of syntactic analysis also greatly influenced Gabelentz's contributions to General Linguistic Studies.

5. Conclusion: The influence of Chinese on Gabelentz's general linguistic approach

The impact of Gabelentz's syntactic research on Chinese on general linguistic approaches should have been manifold, regarding the numerous linguistic hypotheses he proposed mainly based on his study of the Chinese language. However, maybe due to the fact that he did not follow the mainstream of linguistic research of his time, or maybe due to his premature death, he was hardly given any credit for his contributions particularly to Chinese linguistics. His contributions on general linguistics are being acknowledged more and more in recent studies on the history of linguistics (see e.g. McElvenny 2017), though.

First of all, Gabelentz relativized the prevalent evaluation of typologically different languages on the basis of the Chinese language and its history. He proposed that even an isolating language such as Chinese took part in the agglutination cycle and might have had some morphology at an earlier period of time, although he did not doubt that Chinese was the most mature and typical example of an isolating language. Gabelentz's greatest contribution to Chinese linguistics was certainly his proposal of the relevance of the Psychological Subject and the Psychological Predicate, i.e. of topicalization structures in the Chinese language, based on his purely syntactic approach. The relevance of the purely syntactic approach for a language of the Chinese type consequently argued for the prevalence of syntax in linguistic studies in general. This was certainly an important contribution to General Linguistics based on Gabelentz's research on Chinese. Additionally, and again influenced by his study of Chinese, Gabelentz proposed a formulaic language as a tool for cross-linguistic syntactic analysis long before this kind of abstract analysis became more common in linguistic research. In addition to these contributions, the development of a binary system of grammar writing distinguishing an analytic from a syntactic approach can be mentioned; this also had serious implications on future linguistic studies. Another innovation of Gabelentz's linguistic approach is the synchronic perspective on linguistic analysis, which was quite in contrast to the mainstream linguistic endeavors of his time. In addition to these achievements, Gabelentz's relevance for the development of typological studies and studies on grammaticalization have to be acknowledged as an important contribution to the history of linguistics. Gabelentz was also the first who explicitly proposed the origin of the Chinese prepositions from verbs; this is still a subject of lively linguistic debates and one of the bases of present day studies on grammaticalization.

6. References

List of relevant literature by Hans Conon and Georg von der Gabelentz

Gabelentz, Hans Conon von der. 1860/73. *Die Melanesischen Sprachen nach ihrem grammatischen Bau und ihrer Verwandtschaft unter sich, und mit den Malaiisch-Polynesischen Sprachen* [The Melanisian languages according to their grammar; their mutual relations and their relations with the Malayian-Polynesian Languages]. Abhh. d. Kgl. Sächs. Ges. d. Wiss. III u. VII.

Gabelentz, Georg von der. 1869. Ideen zu vergleichenden Syntax [Ideas on Comparative Syntax]. In: *Zeitschrift für Völkerpsychologie und Sprachwissenschaft*, 6: 376-384.

Gabelentz, Georg von der. 1875. Weiteres zur vergleichenden Syntax – Wort- und Satzstellung. *Zeitschrift für Völkerpsychologie und Sprachwissenschaft* 8: 129-165, 300-338.

Gabelentz Georg von der. 1878. Beitrag zur Geschichte der chinesischen Grammatiken [Contribution to the History of Chinese Grammars]. *Zeitschrift der Deutschen Morgenländischen Gesellschaft*, 32: 601-665.

Gabelentz, Georg von der. (1881) 1960; 2010. *Chinesische Grammatik, Mit Ausschluss des Niederen Stiles und der Heutigen Umgangssprache* [Chinese Grammar: Under exclusion of the Low Style and the Contemporary Vernacular Language]. Halle: Niemeyer. Tübingen: Julius Groos Verlag, edited by Walter Bisang with a new introduction.

Chinese Translation: Jiabo Lianzi 甲柏連孜. 2015. *Hanwen jingwei* 漢文經緯, translated by Yao Xiaopin 姚小平. *Haiwai Hanyu yanjiu congshu* 海外漢語研究叢書. Beijing: Waiyu jiaoxue yu yanjiu chubanshe.

Gabelentz, Georg von der. 1891. *Die Sprachwissenschaft. Ihre Aufgaben, Methoden und bisherigen Ergebnisse* [Linguistics: its tasks, methods, and present results]. Leipzig:

Weigel Nachf., 2. Aufl. Edited by Manfred Ringmacher and James McElvenny, 2016. Berlin: Language Science Press.

Gabelentz, Georg von der. 1894. Hypology [Typology] der Sprachen, eine neue Aufgabe der Linguistik [Language Typoloy, a new endeavour in Linguistics]. *Indogermanische Forschungen* 4.

General References

Aldridge, Edith. 2015. Pronominal Object shift in Archaic Chinese. In Theresa Biberauer and George Walkden (eds.). *Syntax over time: lexical, morphological and information-structural interactions*, 350-370. Oxford University Press.

Aldridge, Edith. 2017. Extraction asymmetries in ergative and accusative languages. In Michael Yoshitaka Erlewine (ed.). *Proceedings of GLOW in Asia XI*, 1-20. MIT Working Papers in Linguistics.

Aldridge, Edith. 2018. Inherent case in Archaic Chinese. *Proceedings of the Linguistic Society of America*. https://doi.org/10.3765/plsa.v3i1.4284.

Aldridge, Edith. 2019. Subject/non-subject movement asymmetries in Late Archaic Chinese. *Glossa* 4.1, 115: 1-38.

Ammann, Hermann. 1928. *Die Menschliche Rede II*. Lahr. (Neudruck Darmstadt 1962).

Assandri, Friederike, Meisterernst, Barbara. 2019. Chinese Philosophy, Religions, and Language. In Chu-Ren Huang, Zhuo Jing-Schmidt, Barbara Meisterernst (eds.), *The Routledge Handbook of Chinese Applied Linguistics*, 2019.

Badan, Linda, Del Gobbo Francesca. 2011. On the Syntax of Topic and Focus in Chinese. In Paola Benincà and Nicola Murano (eds.) *Mapping the Left Periphery: The Cartography of Syntactic Structures, Vol. 5*, 63-90. OUP.

Baxter, William, Sagart, Laurent. 2014. Old Chinese reconstructions. http://ocbaxtersagart.lsait.lsa.umich.edu/BaxterSagartOCbyMandarinMC2014-09-20.pdf.

Benincà, Paola, Poletto, Cecilia. Topic, Focus, and V2. In Rizzi, Luigi. *The Structure of CP and IP: The Cartography of Syntactic Structures, Vol.2, Oxford Studies in Comparative Syntax*. OUP.

Bošković, Željko. Ms. Left branch extraction, structure of NP, and scrambling. http://web2.uconn.edu/boskovic/papers/leftbranchscrambling2.pdf, accessed 29.01.2018.

Chafe, Wallace (1976). Givenness, Contrastiveness, Definiteness, Subjects and Topics. In Charles N. Li (ed.), *Subject and topic*, 25–55. New York: Academic Press.

Chao Yuen-ren. *A Grammar of Spoken Chinese*. Berkeley, Los Angeles: University of California Press, 1968.

Chou, Chao-Ting Tim. 2013. Unvalued interpretable features and topic A-movement in Chinese raising modal constructions. *Lingua 123*: 118-147.

Chou Fa-kao 周法高. 1959. *Zhongguo gudai yufa: Chengdai bian* 中國古代語法: 稱代編 [A Historical Grammar of Ancient Chinese, vol. 3]. Taipei: Academia Sinica Institute of History and Philology.

Conrady, August. 1896. *Eine indochinesische Causativ-Denominativ-Bildung und ihr Zusammenhang mit den Tonaccenten. Ein Beitrag zur vergleichenden Grammatik der indochinesischen Sprachen, insonderheit des Tibetischen, Barmanischen, Siamesischen und Chinesischen* [An indochinese causative-denominative construction and its relation to tone accencts …], Leipzig.

Djamouri, Redouane. 1991. Particules de négation dans les inscriptions sur bronze de la dynastie des Zhou [Negation particles in the Zhou Dynasty Bronze Inscriptions]. *Cahiers Linguistics sur l'Asie Orientale* 20,1: 5-76.

Dobson, W.A.C.H. 1959. *Late Archaic Chinese: A Grammatical Study.* Toronto: University of Toronto Press.

Feng, Shengli. 2014. Light verb syntax between English and classical Chinese. In Audrey Li, Andrew Simpson, and Dylan W-T Tsai (eds.), *Chinese syntax in a cross-linguistic perspective*, 229–250. Oxford: Oxford University Press.

Feng Shengli 馮勝利 and Liu Liyuan 劉麗媛. 2019. Hanyu zonghe ↔ fenxi shuangxiang yanbian de yunlü jizhi 漢語綜合 ↔分析雙向演變的韻律機制 [Prosodic mechanisms of the change from synthetic to analytic and vice versa in Chinese]. *Lishi yuyanxue yanjiu* 13: 243-268.

Frey, Werner. 2005. Zur Syntax der linken Peripherie im Deutschen [On the syntax of the left periphery in German]. In Franz Josef d'Avis (ed.), *Deutsche Syntax: Empirie und Theorie* [German Syntax: Empiry and Theory] *(Göteborger Germanistische Forschungen 46),* 147-171. Göteborg: Acta Universitatis Gothoburgensis. 2005.

Gabelentz, Georg von der. *Chinesische Grammatik, Mit Ausschluss des Niederen Stiles und der Heutigen Umgangssprache.* Halle: Niemeyer, (1881) 1960.

Gabelentz, Georg von der. 1869. Ideen zu vergleichenden Syntax. In: *Zeitschrift für Völkerpsychologie und Sprachwissenschaft,* 6: 376-384.

Goldenberg, Gideon. 1988. Subject and predicate in Arab grammatical tradition. *Zeitschrift der deutschen morgenländischen Gesellschaft* [Journal of the German Oriental Society] 138: 39-73.

Graham, A.C. 1969. The Archaic Chinese Pronouns. *Asia Major 15,1:* 17-61.

Hockett, Charles. 1958. *Two models of grammatical description.* Readings in Linguistics. Chicago: University of Chicago Press.

Huang, C.-T. James, Y.-H. Audrey Li, and Yafei Li 2009. *The Syntax of Chinese.* Cambridge: Cambridge Unversity Press.

Huang, James C.-T., Roberts, Ian. 2017. Principles and Parameters of Universal Grammar. In Robert, Ian (ed.), *The Oxford Handbook of Universal Grammar.* OUP 2017.

Humboldt, Wilhelm von. 1843. *Gesammelte Werke Bd.* [Collected Works, vol.] 3, Berlin: Reimer.

Julien, Stanislas. 1861. *Méthode pour déchiffrer et transcrire les noms sanscrits qui se rencontrent dans les livres chinois* [Method for deciphering and transcribing the Sanskrit names found in Chinese texts]. Paris: L'Imprimerie Impériale.

Jullien, Francois. 2009. *Das Universelle, das Einförmige, das Gemeinsame und der Dialog zwischen den Kulturen* [The Universal, the Monotonous, the Common and the Dialogue of Cultures]. Berlin: Merve.

Karlgren, Bernhard. 1920. Le proto-chinois, langue inflexionnelle [Proto-Chinese, an inflectional language]. *Journal Asiatique 11,15*: 205-232.

Kennedy, George A. 1940. A Study of the Particle Yen. *Journal of the American Oriental Society 60, 1:* 1-22.

Krifka, Manfred. 2006. The Origin of Topic/Comment Structure, of Predication, and of Focusation in Asymmetric Bimanual Communication. Nascent Language Conference, Bellagio.

Krifka, Manfred. 2007. Basic notions of information structure. In Caroline Féry and Manfred Krifka (eds.) *Interdisciplinary Studies of Information Structure*, vol. 6. University of Potsdam.

Li, Charles N., Thompson, Sandra A. 1989. *Mandarin Chinese*. Berkeley: University of California Press.

Marshman, J. *The Elements of Chinese Grammar*. Serampore 1814.

Malmquist, N.D.G. 2011. Bernhard Karlgren, *Portrait of a Scholar*. Maryland: Lehigh University Press.

Mathesius, Vilém. 1929. Zur Satzperspektive im modernen Englisch [On the sentence perspective in English]. In *Archiv für das Studium der neueren Sprachen und Literaturen* [Archive for the study of newer languages and literatures]84: 202–210.

McElvenny, James. 2017. Grammar, Typology, and the Humboldtian Tradition in the work of Georg von der Gabelentz. *Language and History 60, 1*: 1-20.

Mei Kuang 梅廣. 2015. *Shanggu Hanyu yufa gangyao* 上古漢語語法綱要 [Outline of the grammar of Classical Chinese]. Taipei: Sanmin.

Meisterernst, Barbara. 2014. Chinesische Grammatiken seit Georg von der Gabelentz [Chinese Grammars since GvG]. In: K. Ezawa, F. Hundsnurscher und A. v. Vogel (eds.), *Beiträge zur Gabelentz-Forschung*, Tübingen: Narr, 2014.

Meisterernst, Barbara. 2015. *Tense and Aspect in Han Period Chinese: A linguistic study of the Shiji. Trends in Modern Linguistics Series* 274. Berlin: De Gruyter.

Meisterernst, Barbara. 2019. Chinese Language and the Silk Road. In Chu-Ren Huang, Zhuo Jing-Schmidt, Barbara Meisterernst (eds.). *The Routledge Handbook on Chinese Applied Linguistics*.

Meisterernst, Barbara. 2020a. A Syntactic Approach to the Grammaticalization of the Modal Markers in Middle Chinese: The Modal DANG 當. *Journal of Historical Syntax 5*, 1: 1-52.

Meisterernst, Barbara. 2020b. Georg von der Gabelentz und das Psychologische Subjekt: Die linguistische Strategie der Topikalisierung [Georg von der Gabelentz and the Psychological Subject: The Linguistic Strategy of Topicalization], In: Klöter, Henning, Li Xuetao (eds), *Von Lindenblättern und verderbten Dialekten: Neue Studien zu dem Sinologen und Sprachwissenschaftler Georg von der Gabelentz (1840–1893)* [Lime leaves and corrupted dialects: New Studies on the Sinologist and Linguist GvG], 139-158. Wiesbaden, Harrassowitz.

Norman, Jerry L. And W. South Coblin. 1995. A New Approach to Chinese Historical Linguistics. *Journal of the American Oriental Society* 115,4: 576-584.

Paul, Hermann. 1880,² 1886. *Prinzipien der Sprachgeschichte* [Principles of Language History]. Halle: Max Niemeyer.

Paul, Waltraud. 2015. *New Perspectives on Chinese Syntax*. Berlin: Mouton De Gruyter.

Paul, Waltraud and Whitman, John. 2017. Topic prominence. In Martin Everaert and Henk van Riemsdijk (eds.), *The Blackwell Companion to Syntax, 2nd Edition*, chapter 117. Mal-den, MA: Blackwell.

Peyraube, Alain. 1996. Recent Issues in Chinese Historical Syntax. In C.-T. James Huang, Yen-hui Audrey Li (eds.), *New Horizons in Chinese Linguistics. Natural Languages and Linguistic Theory 36*, 161-213, Dordrecht: Kluwer.

Peyraube, Alain. ms. Has Chinese changed from a synthetic language into an analytic language? Paris: Centre de Recherches Linguistiques sur l'Asie Orientale.

Prémare, Joseph Henri. 1831. *Notitia linguae sinicae*. Malacca: Academia Anglo-Sinesis.

Prémare, Joseph Henri and J.G. Bridgman. 1847. *The Notitia Linguae Sinicae Of Premare*. Canton.

Pulleyblank, Edwin G. 1995. *Outline of Classical Chinese Grammar*. Vancouver: University of British Columbia Press.

Rémusat, Jean-Pierre Abel. 1822. *Élémens de la grammaire chinoise, ou Principes généraux du Kou-wen ou style antique, et du Kouan-hoa, c'est-à-dire, de la langue commune généralement usitée dans l'empire chinois* [Elements of the Chinese grammar, …]. Paris: Imprimerie royale.

Roetz, Heiner. 2011. Die Chinawissenschaft und die chinesischen Dissidenten. Wer betreibt die Komplizenschaft mit der Macht? [Sinology and the Chinese dissidents. Who is an accessory to power?] *BJOAF* 35: 47-79.

Ross, J. R. 1986. *Infinite syntax*. Norwood: Ablex Publishing.

Sapir, Edward. 1921. *Language: An Introduction to the Study of Speech*. New York: Harcourt, Brace.

Schlegel, August Wilhelm von. 1818. *Observations sur la langue et la littérature provençale* [Observations on the Provençal language and literature]. Paris: Librairie grecque-latine-allemande.

Schlegel, Friedrich von. 1808. *Über die Sprache und Weisheit der Indier* [On the language and wisdom of the Indians]. Heidelberg: Mohr und Zimmer.

Schleicher, August. 1850. *Linguistische Untersuchungen. 2. Teil: Die Sprachen Europas in systematischer Übersicht* [Linguistic Investigations. Part 2: A systematic overview of the languages of Europe]. Bonn: H. B. König.

Schuessler, Axel. 2007. *ABC, Etymological Dictionary of Old Chinese*. Honolulu: University of Hawai'i Press.

Schwegler, Armin. 1990. *Analyticity and Syntheticity: A Diachronic Perspective with Special Reference to Romance*. Berlin: Mouton De Gryuter.

Smith, Adam D. 2012 (ms.). The particle yān 焉, and the phonological reduction of prepositional phrases in Old Chinese. Columbia University.

Unger, Ulrich. 2019. *Grammatik des Klassischen Chinesisch* [Grammar of Classical Chinese], *edited by Reinhard Emmerich*. Heidelberg: CrossAsia e-books. https://crossasia-books.ub.uni-heidelberg.de/xasia/reader/download/506/506-42-86246-2-10-20190822.pdf

Van Driem *Languages of the Himalayas, Vol.1 Handbuch der Orientalistik*. Leiden: Brill 2001.

von Heusinger, Klaus. 2002. Prague Linguistic Circle Papers: Travaux du cercle linguistique de Prague nouvelle série. Volume 4, Eva Hajičová, Petr Sgall, Jiří Hana and Tomáš Hoskovec (eds.), 275–305.

Wang Li 王力. (1958) 2004. *Hànyǔ shǐgǎo* 漢語史搞 [Lectures on the history of Chinese]. Beijing: Zhonghua shuju.

Wei Pei-chuan 魏培泉. 2001. "Fu", "wu" binghe shuo xinzheng "弗", "勿"併合說新證. *Zhongyang yanjiu yuan lishi yuyan yanjiusuo jikan*, 72,1: 121-215.

Discourse, Clarendon Press, Oxford.

Weil, Henri. 1844). *The order of words in the ancient languages compared with that of the modern languages*. Paris.

Zhang, Yujin 張玉金. 2001. *Jiaguwen yufaxue* 甲骨文語法學 [Grammar of the Oracle Bone Inscriptions]. Shanghai: Xuelin chubanshe.

Zhōu Shēngyà 周生亚. 1980. Lùn Shànggǔ Hànyǔ rénchēng dàicí fánfù de yuáyīn 论上古汉语人称代词繁复的原因 [Analysis of the diversity of personal pronouns in Archaic Chinese]. *Zhōngguó Yǔwén* 1980,2: 127-136.

Chapter 9

Chinese in Sogdian script and Sogdian in Chinese characters

Yutaka Yoshida
Graduate School of Letters
Kyoto University, Japan

Abstract

Sogdians were an Iranian speaking people who once lived in what is now Uzbekistan and northern Tajikistan, in particular the area surrounding Samarqand. Sogdians are famous for their trade activities along the Silk Road before the Islamization of Central Asia. Before the Tang period, many Sogdians came to China and some of them settled there. In this paper, I am going to discuss the relationship between the Sogdians and their language on the one hand, and the Chinese and the Chinese language on the other, during the first half of the Tang Dynasty. In particular, problems surrounding one Chinese text transcribed in Sogdian script and Sogdians' personal names transcribed in Chinese characters are surveyed. This paper is concluded by a discussion of two Sogdians whom Xuanzang came across when he left China for India in 629 CE.

1 Introduction: Sogdians and Tang China

For us Japanese, the two most famous Chinese poets are no doubt Du Fu 杜甫 (712~770) and Li Bai 李白 (701~762). We learn some of their poems in our high school days. As you may know, Sogdians were an Iranian speaking people who once lived in what is now Uzbekistan and northern Tajikistan, in particular the area surrounding Samarqand. Sogdians are famous for their trade activities along the Silk Road before the Islamization of Central Asia. Before and during the Tang period, many Sogdians came to China and some of them were naturalized. They were quite popular in Chinese metropolises like Chang'an and Luoyang, and many figurines representing Sogdian traders have been discovered in tombs of this period. Li Bai and Du Fu must have been familiar with Sogdians, who were generally referred to as *hu* 胡 in those days,[1] and in fact one can find Sogdian

---

1   On this point see Moriyasu (2015: 376-406).

elements in their poems. One of the most favorites among the Japanese is Li
Bai's poem about Sogdian girls or *huji* 胡姫 serving wine in bars. One of them is
the following, where the face of a Sogdian girl is compared with a flower.

琴奏龍門之綠桐　玉壺美酒清若空　催弦拂柱與君飲　看朱成碧顏
始紅
胡姫貌如花　當壚笑春風　笑春風　舞羅衣　君今不醉欲安歸

The zither plays "The Green Paulownias at Dragon Gate,"
The lovely wine, in its pot of jade, is as clear as the sky.
As I press against the strings, and brush across the studs, I'll drink with you,
milord;
"Vermilion will seem to be prase-green" when our faces begin to redden.
That Western houri with features like a flower———
She stands by the wine-warmer, and laughs with breath of spring
Laughs with breath of spring, Dance in a dress of gauze!
Will you be going somewhere, milord, *now*, before you are drunk?[2]

The following verses are cited from one Du Fu's poem. It is not popular among
Japanese, but I like it because it contains an actual Sogdian word transcribed in
Chinese characters.

花門騰絕漠　拓羯渡臨洮（『喜聞官軍已臨賊寇二十韻』）
Those from Huamen (=Uighur soldiers) will come soaring from the remote
desert. Chakars have already passed Lintao.[3]

Here *tuojie* 拓羯 is a miscopying of *zhejie* 柘羯 transcribing a Sogdian word *chākar*
meaning "brave warrior".

Du Fu's mention of *chākar* seems to indicate the popularity among the
contemporary Chinese of not only Sogdians and their culture, but also their
language, or at least some of their words. Nevertheless, the miscopying of this
word in the later times shows that what we now call Sogdian culture was nothing
but a subculture only for the contemporary Chinese not worth recording in
refined literature and official histories. One interesting case is a masque entitled
zuihuwang (or *suikoō* in Japanese) 醉胡王 "drunken Sogdian king" which has been
handed down to the present-day Japan. Several masks representing zuihuwang

---

2   Shafer's translation (1963: 21).
3   My tentative translation. Incidentally, the title of the poem would be translated "Twenty
    verses composed when hearing the good news of the imperial army having already
    confronted with the rebel army".

are preserved in Shōsōin in Nara, Japan, and the masque seems to have been very popular in the Nara period (710-784 CE). They all wear typical hats and are compared with *sabao*s 薩寶 depicted on the reliefs surrounding funerary beds of rich Sogdian traders recently unearthed in Northern China. As I once showed,[4] *sabao* is the Chinese transcription of a Sogdian word *sārtpāw* meaning "caravan leader", and accordingly *huwang* is another designation of *sabao* or Sogdian caravan leader. In fact, a piece of brocade showing a Sogdian trader leading a camel was once discovered in Turfan, which bears an inscription *huwang*. This play or masque *zuihuwang* 醉胡王 must have once been very popular in Tang China, possibly in Chang'an, and was imported to Japan during the 8th century. In Japan it has survived to this day, while it has long since been forgotten in China.

2 Sogdians and the Chinese language

When they went to China and settled there, Sogdians must have learned the Chinese language and culture, while preserving their own. One Sogdian manuscript discovered in Dunhuang is intriguing in that it betrays the contact between the two cultures. The manuscript is dubbed as the "Rustam fragment" because it is the Sogdian version of a famous epic about an Iranian hero Rustam. One finds him painted on a wall painting excavated in the ruined city of Panjikent in Tajikistan. On the backside of the manuscript one can read *hu qin wang chuan yi juan* 胡秦王伝一卷 "The legend of the Sogdian Qin Wang, Scroll one". Qin Wang is the preregnal name of the second emperor of the Tang Empire called Taizong 太宗 (r. 627-649), who became a legendary hero in China. Obviously, the Sogdians resident in China, who were familiar with both Chinese and Iranian cultures, compared the Iranian legendary hero with Qin Wang.

Of course, when they first came to China, they were not good speakers of Chinese. One intriguing group of Chinese documents discovered in Turfan records a lawsuit between a Sogdian trader (Cao Lushan 曹禄山) and his brother's (Cao Yanyan 曹炎延) Chinese business partner (Li Qinshao 李勤紹).[5] The documents are dated between 670 CE and 673 CE. In the lawsuit, Cao Lushan says that they have lived in the capital with their family, and that while the business partner is a native Chinese and defends his position in eloquent Chinese, he (*or* his brother?), as a foreigner, cannot understand Chinese. Li Qinshao describes the Sogdians as *xingshenghu* 興生胡 "itinerant Sogdian traders". A few other cases of lawsuits are also documented, where interpreters were employed for Sogdian traders.

---

4   See Yoshida (1989: 168-171).
5   See Arakawa (2005).

Nevertheless, one or two generations later, Sogdian Chinese, as it were, were so naturalized in the Chinese society that some of them became formally registered as Chinese Buddhist monks. One finds some biographies of such second or third generation Sogdian monks among Buddhist historiographies. According to one colophon of a Buddhist Sogdian text, the translation was made in 728 CE in Luoyang and it was supported by one Sogdian named Chatvārātsrān of the An family.

> The Sūtra of the condemnation of intoxicating drink: one chapter. The handiwork of the teacher *Pwtty'n*, son of *Srcmyk*, (has) taken four (sheets of) paper.
> It was in the town of Saragh (Lo-yang), in the 16th year of the divine Son of Heaven Kai-ngywan, in the year of the dragon, the first month, that the upāsaka *Ctβ'r'tsr'n* of the An family relied on the ācārya Jñānacinta and besought him and addressed him from the bottom of his heart, and then the bhikṣu Jñānacinta translated it from Indian into a Sogdian book, for love of all the living beings of the dharmadhātu.[6]

The translation and copying of the text must have been done also by Sogdian monks. In fact, the copyist bears a good Sogdian name *pwtty'n* [Butiyān] (*lit.* "Buddha's boon"). Although the translator is called *ny"ncynt*, i.e. Jñānacinta in Sanskrit, he translated an Indian scripture into Sogdian and his mother tongue must have been Sogdian.

The fact that Sogdians studied Buddhist Chinese texts is proved by a few Dunhuang and Turfan manuscripts. One is a Dunhuang Chinese fragment Nai 奈 15, on the verso of which is written its title in Sogdian. Another one, So 14830 of the Berlin Collection, discovered in Turfan, is most unique in that the Chinese text is phonetically transcribed in Sogdian script and it was only later that the corresponding Chinese characters were added. This can be seen in Figure 1. It has been almost 40 years since I first encountered this manuscript, or rather its photograph. At that time I was still a student of a master's program and, as I remember now, my teacher at Kyoto University, Professor Tatsuo Nishida, advised me to consult Luo Changpei's book (*The Northwestern dialects of Tarng and Five Dynasties,* Shanghai 1933).[7]

Although no date is given in the text itself, it would not be impossible to date the manuscript at least broadly by considering the hand writing, morphology of

---

6   See MacKenzie (1976: 11).

7   My study of the manuscript was later published in Japanese (Yoshida 1994). For the text see also Yoshida (2013). Incidentally, in the present article I cite Middle Chinese forms as reconstructed by B. Karlgren (Karlgren 1957).

the paper, and last but not least the pronunciation of the Chinese characters themselves, if the date of the phonological change in Chinese is known. After some consideration I came to the conclusion that the pronunciation of the characters indicates the date earlier than the Tibetan transcriptions extensively studied by Luo Changpei in his monumental work.[8] Here are some indications: While dentilabialization (e.g. *fu* *b'ịuət 佛 βr [fər]), denasalization (e.g. *mo* *muâ 魔 'np' [əmba], nai *nậi 乃 'nt'y [əndai], *ye* *ngịɐp 業 'nk'yp [əngeb], *wu* *nguo 五 γw [γu], and *er* *ńźi 二 ẓy [ži]),[9] and devoicing of voiced fricatives (e.g. *shi* *ẓiɛ 是 ṡy [ṡi]) are already there, there is no dropping of the velar nasal coda (e.g. *chang* *ḍịang 長 c''nk [čang], *sheng* *ṣɐng 生 ṡ'nk [šaŋ], *jing* *tsịäng 精 tsynk [tsiŋ]). Although two similar sounding rhymes are known to have converged in the Chang'an dialect of the latter half of the 8th century, they seem to remain distinguished in this manuscript (e.g. *qie* *ts'ịei 切 ts'y [tsei] vs *shi* *śịäi 世 ṡy'y [šiei]; cf. Tibetan transcriptions of the two characters *tsh-e'i* vs *sh-e'i*).[10] Of course some dialectal features must also be considered. But, as a whole what we find in this manuscript likely reflects the pronunciation of the capital during the first half of the 8th century when the centralization of the great Tang Empire was at its peak. One may also remember that the activities of the Sogdian traders were also at their peak during this period, when the above mentioned Buddhist Sogdian text was produced. The sharp decline of their activities after the Anlushan Rebellion (755-763 CE) is also to be considered.

Thus, if my dating is correct, So 14830 was written or copied when Li Bai and Du Fu were active. In other words, the pronunciation of the Chinese characters found in this manuscript represents the same as that of their poems. In 2009, one famous Japanese professor of Chinese linguistics, Sh. Oshima, published a popular book from the publisher *Iwanami Shoten* entitled *Tōdai no hito wa kanshi wo dō yondaka* "How did Tang-era people recite their poems?", where he shows for the general readership the way Sinologists have reconstructed the Middle Chinese pronunciation of poems. He went so far as to present the reconstructed pronunciation of several famous poems of the Tang time including those of Li Bai and Du Fu. Moreover, he uploaded the actual reciting of the poems reconstructed by him to YouTube, which in my opinion any serious scholar would or should refrain from doing.

Nevertheless, it is of some interest to compare the Sogdian forms with what Oshima reconstructed. For example, one of the most frequent words, *bu* *puət 不, is transcribed *pr* [pər] in So 14830, whereas Oshima's reconstruction is a real

---

8   For more recent and extensive study see Takata (1988).

9   On the diacritics found in the letters *p*, *k*, and *ẓ* and their phonetic values see below.

10 See Takata (*op. cit.*: 322-325).

monster of a consonant cluster: *fiwət). A similar discrepancy is found with a character *mie* *miät 滅: 'np'yr [əmber] vs *mviat. Another important difference is the devoicing of the older voiced consonants: *shi* *źiẹ 是 *śy* [ši] vs *źiəi. It will be a waste of time to see all the differences. It is a pity, in my mind, that scholars like Oshima totally ignore the contemporary phonetic transcriptions in the Sogdian script, which reflect the real and actual pronunciation of the 8th century, while what he has reconstructed is nothing but a theoretical artifact lacking any reality.

In this connection I would like to draw the competent Sinologists' attention to another two peculiarities encountered in the pronunciations found in So 14830. The first is the transcription of *suo* 所. The three attestations of this character are always spelled *š* without any indication of an accompanying vowel:

er	źhe	bu	wei	źhu	mo	e	gui	suo	neng	kong	bu
ńźi	tśịa	puət	jwịe	tśịwo	muâ	·âk	kjwẹi	sịwo	nəng	k'ịwong	p'uo
二	者	不	爲	諸	魔	惡	鬼	所	能	恐	怖
zy	c'	pr	wy	cw	'np'11	''x	kwy12	š	nnk	kwnk	pw.

It is as if this character was pronounced as an enclitic element depending on the preceding character. The second point is the transcriptions of *jie* *kǎi 界 *ky'y*[13] [kiai] and *geng* *kɐng 更 *xy'nk*[14] [kiaŋ], which show the medial -*y*- unexpected for the two rhymes of Grade II. They seem to be very early as well as sporadic examples attesting the palatalization of the velar initials of Grade II rhymes.

3 Chinese people and the Sogdian language

A few Sogdian words entered into the Chinese lexicon we possess today. Du Fu's poem cited above contains the Sogdian word *chākar*. Sabao 薩寶 for *s'rtp'w* [sārtpāw] is another example, while *chibo* 叱撥 meaning "excellent horse" is known to transcribe a Sogdian word *cyrδp'δ* [čerθpāδ] "quadruped".[15] However, in view of the large number of Sogdians that settled in China, one may certainly expect that Chinese people were much more familiar with the Sogdian language

---

11 With a diacritic to the left of the letter *p* indicating a voiced sound [b] (Yoshida 1994: 359). Similarly, a diacritic placed to the left of the letter *k* represents [g].

12 With a diacritic to the right of the body of the letter *k* indicating the palatalized stop sound [k] as distinct from the corresponding fricative sound [ç] (Yoshida 1994: 346).

13 For the diacritic see note 12.

14 With a diacritic to the right of the letter *x* indicating the velar stop sound [k] as distinct from the corresponding fricative sound [x] (Yoshida 1994: 358).

15 Schafer, *op. cit.*, p. 295, n. 29.

than we imagine today. This is in fact betrayed by the Sogdian-Chinese dictionary that once existed in Japan. A union catalogue of all the books preserved in Japan was compiled by Fujiwara no Sukeyo around 891 CE. The catalogue entitled *Nipponkoku kenzai shomokuroku* 日本国見在書目録 lists 16,790 volumes which were available in Japan in those days. Among the list one finds *Fanhuyu* or *Honkogo* 翻胡語, which comprises as many as seven volumes. Unfortunately, the book was later lost or at least we do not know its present whereabouts. However, since we have the Sanskrit counterparts like *Fanfanyu* 翻梵語, *Fanyuqianziwen* 梵語千字文, and *Fanyuzaming* 梵語雑名 we can imagine what it looked like. For example, an old manuscript of *Fanyuqianziwen* 梵語千字文 is preserved as a rare book in Toyo Bunko, Tokyo, Japan. Incidentally, a Turkish-Chinese word-list of the late 8th century(?) has been discovered by the Japanese scholar D. Matsui of Osaka University.[16]

Another source for the Sogdian words transcribed in Chinese characters is proper names. The first Sogdian name reconstructed from the Chinese transcription was An Lushan 安禄山. It was W. B. Henning who identified *lushan* 禄山 with the Sogdian counterpart of an Old Iranian name transcribed in Greek script as Ρωξανη, the name born by Alexander the Great's Iranian wife.[17] Later, plenty of transcribed names have come to light, not only in the historical sources but also in the Chinese texts discovered in Dunhuang and Turfan, as well as epitaphs unearthed in China proper.

Let us see one or two examples. According to one Dunhuang text (S 367), the area lying near Lop-nor had been deserted but during the Zhenguan 貞観 era (627- 649 CE) one Sogdian leader by the name of Kang Yandian 康艶典, obviously a sārtpāw, came there and restored several oasis towns. One is called Shichengzhen 石城鎮 and he settled there. Another town is called Nuzhicheng 弩支城, also called Xincheng 新城 or New town.[18] Another Dunhuang Chinese text (P(elliot chinois) 2005) records that in 691 CE, Sogdian traders were still there and their leader was named Kang Fudanyan 康拂耽延, whose younger brother is called Kang Dishebo 康地舎撥.[19] It is easy to reconstruct a Sogdian word *nūč* from *nuzhi* 弩支. It is a feminine form of an adjective *nawē* meaning

---

16 See Matsui (2016).

17 W. B. Henning *apud* Pulleyblank (1955: 15, with note 37 on p. 111). Nevertheless, *rwxšn*- has never been attested as a Sogdian proper name among the materials written in Sogdian script, while the Chinese names containing 禄山 or its variant form 阿禄山 are frequently encountered in Chinese texts. Therefore, one may identify (阿)禄山 with *ryw'xšy'n*, which is actually attested, (Yoshida 1998: 39-40). On *ryw'xšy'n* cf. Lurje (2010, no. 1048).

18 See de la Vaissière (2016: 113).

19 See de la Vaissière, ibid.

"new", hence the designation in Chinese Xincheng 新城. The reason why we have the feminine form here seems to be due to the fact that that *knδh* [kaṃθ], a Sogdian word for town, is feminine.

Since Kang 康 is a family name borne by the Sogdians originating from Samarqand, the three Sogdian colonizers' given names are *yandian* 艷典, *fudanyan* 拂耽延, and *dishebo* 地舍撥. As a colophon of one Dunhuang Buddhist Sogdian text attests *'prtmy'n* [əftam-yān] (lit. "first boon"), one can easily identify *fudanyan* 拂耽延 with this name. I once discovered a Sogdian name *δšcy'pt* [δəšci-āpat] among the Sogdian texts preserved in the Japanese Otani collection. This name can be etymologized as coming from *δšcy* "the creator, i.e. Ahuramazda" and *'pt* "observed, protected". A variant form of the same name, *δš'pt*, appears in an Uighur text once published by T. Haneda. Thus, *dishebo* 地舍撥 likely represents this variant form.[20] Most difficult is Yandian 艷典. However, Turfan Chinese documents attest such similar names as Kang Yandian 康炎顛 and Shi Randian 石染典, and the latter can be seen as transcribing *$\check{z}\bar{e}mat$-$y\bar{a}n$ "*lit.* (God) Zhēmat's boon". The simplification or weakening of the consonant cluster *šc* to *š* may induce one to assume a similar weakening of *ž̌-* to *y-*, i.e. *žēmatyān* > *yēmatyān*, which may be transcribed by *yandian* 艷典 and *yandian* 炎顛.[21]

4 Xuanzang and Sogdians

The process of reconstructing original forms from their phonetic transcriptions in Chinese characters can often be very difficult as well as complicated. For example Cao Yanyan 曹炎延 will be reconstructed as **y'my'n* [yāmyān] lit. "God Yama's boon", although no such name has hitherto been attested. However, *y'm'kk*, a hypocoristic name based on such a name, is known (Lurje, *op. cit.*, no. 1488). Accordingly, I refrain from discussing this problem any further in this paper. Before concluding this paper I should rather like to talk about two Sogdians who served Xuanzang on his way to India in 629-630 CE and appear in Xuanzang's biography, generally known as *Cienchuan* 慈恩伝. One is a Sogdian boy called Shi Pantuo 石槃陀, whose name can easily be reconstructed as *βntk* [vandak] lit. "slave (of a god)" (Lurje, *op. cit.*, no. 295). He was hired by Xuanzang as a guide to cross the most challenging desert named Moheyanqi 莫賀延蹟 to reach Yiwu 伊吾 or modern Hami, although he finally declined Xuanzang's request. When one reads the biography, one may be puzzled by his curious behaviour, sometimes very friendly and sometimes hostile, even trying to kill Xuanzang (See Appendix 1).[22] I have always wondered if he was one of the models of Sun Wukong 孫悟空 in *Xiyouji* 西遊記.

---

20 On *'prtmy'n* see Yoshida (1989; 172-173). For *δšcy'pt*, etc. see Yoshida 1991: 242-243).

21 On this problem see Yoshida (2016: 64-67).

22 For the English translation of the biography see Beal (1914).

As one can easily imagine, descendants of the Sogdians who had settled in China would eventually bear Chinese given names. Thus, according to Xuanzang's biography, when he departed Gaochang 高昌, or what is now Turfan, the local king Qu Wentai 麴文泰 ordered one of his officials to guide him to the qaghan of West Tujue together with two carriages loaded with expensive textiles and dried fruits. Apart from them, the king presented Xuanzang with the provisions for 20 years, covering his travel to and from India together with 30 horses and 25 couriers. The guide in question is named Shi Huanxin 史歡信 bearing the title *dianzhong shiyu* 殿中侍御 lit. "court attendant" (see Appendix 2). Shi 史 is also a typical family name of the Sogdians originating from Kish, or what is now Shahr-i sabz, situated some 100 km south of Samarqand. Although the family name Shi could be borne by pure Chinese, it is generally assumed that he was a descendant of a Sogdian family,[23] and the fact that he was appointed as an ambassador agrees very well with this assumption.

According to the biography, after Xuanzang left Turfan, he passed Karashahr and arrived at Kucha, where he spent more than sixty days waiting for spring to come so that he might cross the Tianshan mountains to reach West Tujue 突厥 qaghan's court situated in Semirech'e, Kyrgyzstan. Since in those days Karashahr and Turfan were hostile to each other, Xuanzang stayed only one day in Karashahr (see Appendix 3). As a matter of fact, it would have been a very rare occasion for a delegation from Turfan to visit Karashahr in those days, as the two oasis states were not on good terms. Yet, there is one Turfan Chinese document (72TAM155, see Appendix 4) from approximately the same period, i.e. around 630 CE, that records a very unique dispatch by the local king Qu Wentai of as many as eight carts to Karashahr in the 12th month of a certain year.[24] Curiously, the team of the eight carts was headed by Shi Huantai 史歡太, whose name is very similar to Shi Huanxin 史歡信. He bears the title of *shilang* 侍郎. According to Professor Arakawa, who studied the document extensively, *shilang* 侍郎 is a synonym of *shiyu* 侍御, a title borne by Shi Huanxin 史歡信. Accordingly, I venture to suggest that Shi Huantai 史歡太, who lead the team of eight carts, accompanied Xuanzang in the winter of 629, when he departed from Turfan and went to Karashahr, and that Shi Huantai 史歡太 accompanied him even further to visit the West Tujue qaghan in Semirech'e. Shi Huantai 史歡太 may be the same person as Shi Huanxin 史歡信 of the biography, in which case we must presume a miscopying of his name during the transmission of the text. It may also be possible that Shi Huantai 史歡太 and Shi Huangxin 史歡信 were

---

23 For the Sogdians resident in the Gaochang kingdom see Arakawa (2020).
24 This document was extensively studied by Arakawa (2008).

brothers, whose names shared one character, and Shi Huantai 史歡太 accompanied Xuanzang in his brother's place.

If this daring assumption of mine turns out to be correct, this Turfan Chinese document will be the very unique direct witness of Xuanzang's travel to India so far not recognized as such. I, as a Sogdianist, am very happy that this witness is borne by Sogdians.

5 Concluding remarks

When Xuanzang crossed the desert Moheyanqi 莫賀延磧 and arrived in Yiwu 伊吾 or modern Hami, he was welcomed by *huseng* 胡僧 "Sogdian monk" and *huwang* 胡王 "Sogdian king". As I argued in my paper, the latter term specifically refers to a *sabao* 薩寶, or leader of Sogdian traders. The Dunhuang text (S 367) mentioned above also records one Sogdian leader named Shi Wannian 石萬年, who offered the submission of seven towns belonging to him to the Tang's rule in Spring, 630 CE and was invited to the imperial court later in September of that year. I venture to identify the *huwang* Xuanzang encountered with Shi Wannian. In this way, the Sogdians' popularity among the Tang Chinese or their omnipresence in contemporary Chinese society has so far been masked by an ambiguous and vague character *hu* 胡.

References

Arakawa, Masaharu. 2005. Sogdian merchants and Chinese Han merchants during the Tang Dynasty. In Etienne de la Vaissière and Eric Trombert (eds.), *Les Sogdiens en Chine*: 231-242. Paris:École française d'Extrême-Orient.

Arakawa, Masaharu. 2008. Sogdians and the royal house of Ch'ü in the Kao-ch'ang Kingdom. *Acta Asiatica* vol. 94: 67-93.

Arakawa, Masaharu. 2020. The Kao-ch'ang kingdom's rule of Turfan and its Sogdian colonies in the sixth century. *Acta Asiatica* vol. 119: 43-65.

Beal, Samuel. 1914. *The life of Hiuen-Tsiang, by the shaman Hwui Li; with an introduction containing an account of the works of I-tsing, by Samuel Beal; with a preface L. Cranmer-Byng.* London.

Karlgren, Bernhard. 1957. *Grammata Serica Recensa*. Stockholm.

Lurje, Pavel. 2010. *Personal Names in Sogdian Sources*. Vienna: Verlag der österreichischen Akademie der Wissenschaften.

MacKenzie, David Neil. 1976. *The Buddhist Sogdian texts of the British Library,* Acta Iranica 10. Leiden/Tehran.

Matsui, Dai. 2016. The Bilingual Vocabulary Or. 12380/3948 of the Stein Collection in the British Library. *Tōhōgaku* vol. 132: 87-73.

Moriyasu, Takao. 2015. *Tōzai Uiguru to Chūōyūrashia [East and West Uighur empires and Central Asia]*. Nagoya: University of Nagoya Press.

Pulleyblank, Edwin George. 1955. *The background of the rebellion of An Lu-shan*. London: Oxford University Press.

Shafer, Edward. 1963. The golden peaches of Samarkand. Berkley: University of California Press.

Takata, Tokio. 1988. *A historical study of the Chinese language based on Dunhuang materials. The Hexi 河西 dialect of the ninth and tenth centuries*. Tokyo: Sōbunsha. (in Japanese with an English summary)

Vaissière, Etienne de la. 2016. *Histoire des marchands sogdiens [History of the Sogdian merchants]*. Paris: College de France, Institut des Hautes Etudes Chinoises.

Yoshida, Yutaka. 1989. Sogdian Miscellany II. *Oriento* vol. 31 no. 2: 165-176. (in Japanese)

Yoshida, Yutaka. 1991. Sogdian Miscellany III. In Ronald E. Emmerick and Dieter Weber (eds.) *Corolla Iranica. Papers in honour of Prof. Dr. David Neil MacKenzie on the occasion of his 65th birthday on April 8th, 1991*: 237-242. Frankfurt am Main/Bern/New York/Paris: Peter Lang.

Yoshida, Yutaka. 1994. Chinese in Sogdian script. *The Toho Gakuho [Journal of Oriental studies]* vol. 66: 271-380. Kyoto: Institute for Research in Humanities, Kyoto University. (in Japanese)

Yoshida, Yutaka. 1998. Sino-Iranica. *Bulletin of the Society for Western and Southern Asiatic studies* vol. 48: 33-51. (in Japanese)

Yoshida, Yutaka. 2013. Buddhist texts produced by the Sogdians in China. In Mauro Maggi et al. (eds.), *Buddhism among the Iranian peoples of Central Asia*: 155-179. Vienna: Austrian Academy of Sciences Press.

Yoshida, Yutaka. 2016. Sogdian version of Shijun's epitaph going back to the Beizhou Dynasty and unearthed in Xi'an. In Kiyohiro Iwami (ed.), *Studies of the epitaphs of Chinese Sogdians*: 61-80. Tokyo: Kyuko Shoin. (in Japanese)

Appendix 1 (TT vol.50, 223b07-c06)：石槃陀

更入道場禮請。俄有一胡人來入禮佛。逐法師行二三匝。問其姓名。云姓石字槃陀。此胡即請受戒。乃爲授五戒。胡甚喜辭還。少時齋餅菓更來。法師見其明健貌又恭肅。遂告行意。胡人許諾言。送師過五烽。法師大喜。乃更貿衣資爲買馬而期焉。 ＊＊＊ 與胡人相去可五十餘步。各下褥而眠。少時胡人乃拔刀而起徐向法師。未到十步許又迴。不知何意。疑有異心。

Appendix 2　(TT vol.50, 225b26-c06)：史歡信

日日如此。講訖爲法師度四沙彌。以充給侍。製法服三十具。以西土多寒。又造面衣手衣靴韈等各數事。黃金一百兩銀錢三萬。綾及絹等五百匹。充法師往還二十年所用之資給馬三十匹手力二十五人。遣殿中侍御史歡信送至葉護可汗衙。又作二十四封書。通屈支等二十四國。每一封書附大綾一匹爲信。又以綾絹五百匹果味兩車。獻葉護可汗并書稱。法師者是奴弟。欲求法於婆羅門國。願可汗憐師如憐奴。仍請勅以西諸國。給鄔落馬遞送出境。

Appendix 3 (TT vol.50, 226b28-227a08)：阿耆尼 (Karashahr) and 高昌

漸去遙見王都。阿耆尼王與諸臣來迎延入供養。其國先被高昌寇擾有恨不肯給馬。法師停一宿而過。＊＊＊ 時爲淩山雪路未開不得進發。淹停六十餘日。

Appendix 4: 72 TM 155

【a】

1   (車 得)
    ] □□圀錢陸文。□□保牛，得銀錢拾壹図。[

2   (合 車)
□□牛貳具。次始昌孫圀□田，得銀錢拾圀□，[(文)

3   圀足田，圀圀錢壹人。[[文]   (合 車 牛)
                                ] □□□

4 拾具，乘牛壹頭，得近道價，□□□□往河畔中取悢木。次田□ 【b】 (二?月)
[

5 傳，始昌圀行車牛子名，董安伯牛，得銀錢貳拾陸文。[

6 參文。參軍師祐牛，得銀錢貳拾陸文。劉延明圀□□□□。 (得 銀 錢 拾 參 文)
□□延車
牛

7 壹具，得銀錢參拾究文。張延敘牛，得銀錢貳圀□□。 [玖]   (陸 文。 □□□ 車， 得 銀)
              □□□□，□□
錢拾參文。

8 羅寺道明車牛壹具，得銀錢參拾究文。 [玖] 張伯兒車牛壹具，得銀錢參拾圀 [玖]

9 文。張伯臬牛，得銀錢貳拾陸文。唐懷願車，圀□□□□図。 (銀 錢 拾 參)
田來得牛，
得銀錢貳圀□□。 (陸 文)

10 □海意車，得銀錢拾參文。合車牛捌具，供侍郎史歡太馱，往塢耆，得遠
道價。

【c】

11 □□圀二月廿二日，酒泉令陰世皎宣，門下校郎司空明莝・通事令史辛孟
護貳人傳，高(昌)

12 □[   ] 官車牛伍具，單車壹具乘，合得銀錢究拾壹文。次東宮車 [玖]
牛

13 □□，□□圀伍拾壹文。曰車，壹脚破挲付主，得銀錢拾伍□。 (參 具， 得 銀)   單 車 壹 乘   (文)
[

14 □□軸壹，得銀錢貳文。合得銀錢陸拾圀文，并合車牛□□，□□□□[(捌 具， 單 車 壹 乘?)

Translation of section 【b】

Next, on the [?] day of <u>the twelfth month</u>, So-and-so delivered [a royal directive]: "[There follow] the names of the owners of long-distance carts and oxen in Shih-ch'ang 始昌 [district]. Chin An-po 董安伯 received 26 *wen* in silver coins for [having provided] a cart. The adjutant Shih Yu 師祐 received 26 *wen* in silver coins for [having provided] an ox. Liu Yen-ming 劉延明 received 13 *wen* in silver coins for [having provided] a cart. [? ?-]yen (□□延) received 39 wen in silver coins for [having provided] a set of cart and ox. Chang Yen-hsü 張延敘 received 26 *wen* in silver coins for [having provided] an ox. [? ??] received 13 *wen* in silver coins for [having provided] a cart. Tao-ming 道明, who was a monk of Lo-ssu 羅寺 temple, received 39 *wen* in silver coins for [having provided] a set of cart

and ox. Chang Po-erh 張伯兒 received 39 *wen* in silver coins for [having provided]
a set of cart and ox. Chang Po-ch'ou 張伯臭 received 26 *wen* in silver coins for
[having provided] an ox. T'ang Huai-yüan 唐懷願 received 13 *wen* in silver coins
for [having provided] a cart. T'ien lai-te received 26 *wen* in silver coins for [having
provided] an ox. [?] hai-hsi (口海熹) received 13 *wen* in silver coins for [having
provided] a cart. There are altogether eight sets of cart and ox. These were
provided for [transporting] the baggage (*t'uo* 馱) of the attendant gentleman Shih
Huan-t'ai 史歡太, and having gone to Wu-ch'i (Qarashahr), they received long-
distance fees (yüan-tao chia 遠道價).

Fig. 1

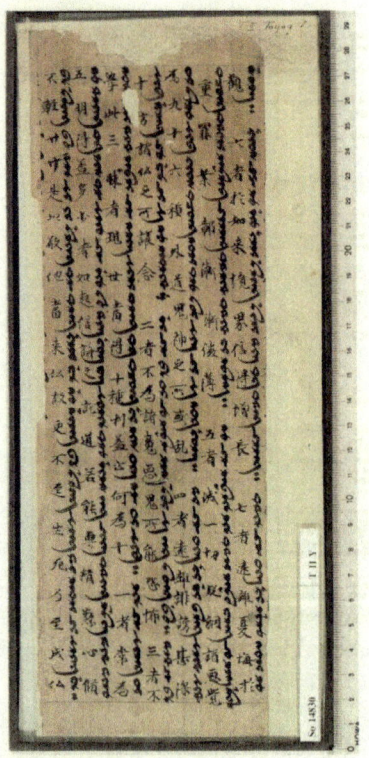

Dipositum der Berlin-Brandenburgischen Akademie der Wissenschaften in der Staats-
bibliothek zu Berlin—Preussischer Kulturbesitz Orientabteilung